中国思想文化术语多语种对外翻译
标准化建设项目成果
CHINESE THINKING AND CULTURE
MULTILINGUAL TERMINOLOGY DATABASE

中华源·河南故事
CHINESE CIVILIZATION
Stories from Henan

汉字
CHINESE CHARACTERS

主编 陈志伟
EDITOR-IN-CHIEF: CHEN ZHIWEI

河南大学出版社
HENAN UNIVERSITY PRESS
·郑州·

图书在版编目（CIP）数据

中华源·河南故事．汉字 / 陈志伟主编．—郑州：河南大学出版社，2019.3（2020.7 重印）

ISBN 978-7-5649-2665-6

Ⅰ．①中… Ⅱ．①陈… Ⅲ．①地方文化－河南－通俗读物 ②汉字－通俗读物 Ⅳ．① G127.61-49 ② H12-49

中国版本图书馆 CIP 数据核字（2019）第 047014 号

责 任 编 辑	屈琳玉
责 任 校 对	时二凤
封 面 设 计	翟淼淼
出 版 发 行	河南大学出版社
	地址：郑州市郑东新区商务外环中华大厦2401号　邮编：450046
	电话：0371-86059701（营销部）　0371-86059753（大众读物分公司）
	网址：hupress.henu.edu.cn
排　　　　版	河南博雅彩印有限公司
印　　　　刷	河南博雅彩印有限公司
版　　　　次	2019年12月第1版　　　印　次　2020年7月第2次印刷
开　　　　本	710 mm×1010 mm　1/16　印　张　18.5
字　　　　数	312千字　　　　　　　　定　价　86.00元

版权所有　侵权必究

本书如有印装质量问题，请与河南大学出版社营销部联系调换

"中华源·河南故事"系列丛书编委会

顾　　问	黄友义　杨　平　范大祺
名誉主任	穆为民　何金平
主　　任	付　静
副 主 任	陈志伟　刁玉华　李向前　李　镇　梁留科　刘金锋
	孔留安　史永庆　许二平　万正峰　杨建伟　杨玮斌
	王建修　王自文　张改平　张松文　赵卫东

主　　编	付　静
执行主编	杨玮斌
编　　委	陈　玮　丁　锐　高　阳　徐恒振

中华源·河南故事·汉字

主　　编	陈志伟
副 主 编	冯克坚　秦建华　梁晓冬（英文）
中文撰稿	李宽生　段艳琴　王双庆　陈瑞华　荣　慧
英文译者	刘国兵　齐建晓　赵护林　吴进善　梁晓冬
英文审校	〔加〕Fay Lin　〔加〕Jordan Ali

The Editorial Committee
Chinese Civilization
Stories from Henan

Consultants	Huang Youyi Yang Ping Fan Daqi
Honorary Directors	Mu Weimin He Jinping
Director	Fu Jing
Deputy Directors	Chen Zhiwei Diao Yuhua Li Xiangqian Li Zhen
	Liang Liuke Liu Jinfeng Kong Liu'an Shi Yongqing
	Xu Erping Wan Zhengfeng Yang Jianwei
	Yang Weibin Wang Jianxiu Wang Ziwen
	Zhang Gaiping Zhang Songwen Zhao Weidong

Chief Editor	Fu Jing
Executive Chief Editor	Yang Weibin
Editors	Chen Wei Ding Rui Gao Yang Xu Hengzhen

Chinese Civilization
Stories from Henan
Chinese Character

Editor-in-Chief	Chen Zhiwei
Associate Editors-in-Chief	Feng Kejian Qin Jianhua Liang Xiaodong (English Text)
Writers	Li Kuansheng Duan Yanqin Wang Shuangqing
	Chen Ruihua Rong Hui
Translators	Liu Guobing Qi Jianxiao Zhao Hulin
	Wu Jinshan Liang Xiaodong
Translation Proofreaders	Fay Lin (Canada) Jordan Ali (Canada)

总 序

中国是世界四大文明古国之一，也是世界上唯一的古代文明传统未曾中断的国家。河南省地处中国中东部，是中华文明和中华民族的重要发祥地，在中国五千年的文明史上，河南作为国家政治、经济、文化的中心就长达三千多年。从某种意义上讲，一部河南史就是半部中国史。这里是中华人文始祖黄帝的故乡，是古丝绸之路的东方起点，是少林功夫和陈氏太极的发源地，这里创建了中国历史上最早的都城，镌刻了中国最古老的文字，诞生了中国最初的商业文明。

伴随着新时代的荣光，河南经济社会发展迅速，人民生活水平显著提升，这是自力更生、艰苦奋斗的历史结果，也是对外开放带来的益处。河南经济社会的发展、人民生活方式的改变都植根于深层次的文化积淀。为了让世界更多地了解河南，让河南更好地走向世界，2018年以来，河南省外事办认真研析了这片古老土地上的历史文化资源和时代风貌，组织各领域权威专家学者，编译了"中华源·河南故事"中外文系列丛书，选取少林功夫、太极拳、中医、汉字、文物、焦裕禄、红旗渠、丝绸之路、古都、农业、手工艺等多个主题，力图以故事的方式向世界展现一个立体、全面、真实的河南。

当今世界，人类文明无论在物质还是精神方面都取得了巨大进步，特别是物质的极大丰富是古代世界完全不能想象的。同时，当代人类也面临着许多突出的难题，比如，贫富差距持续扩大，物欲追求奢华无度，个人主义恶性膨胀，社会诚信不断消减，伦理道德每况愈下，人与自然关系日趋紧张，等等。要解决这些难题，不仅需要运用人类今天发现和发展的智慧和力量,而且需要运用人类历史上积累和储存的智慧和力量。河南历史文化底蕴深厚、包容性强,在今天仍极具现实意义。中原文化蕴含的思想智慧有助于修身养性,推动人类社会进步发展,焦裕禄精神、红旗渠精神所体现的为民爱民、艰苦奋斗的价值取向是构建人类命运共同体的力量源泉。我们期待与读者们一起从河南故事中汲取更多的智慧和力量,共同创造更加美好的未来。

Series Foreword

China is one of the four ancient civilizations in the world, and is also the only country in the world where the ancient civilization has not been interrupted. Located in east-central China, Henan province is an important cradle for the Chinese nation and the Chinese civilization. In the course of the five thousand years of Chinese history, for more than three thousand years it served as the political, economic and cultural center of the country and therefore, as generally accepted, represents half of the history of China. Henan is the native place of Yellow Emperor, the cradle of Chinese culture, the starting point of the ancient Silk Road in the east, and the birthplace of Shaolin Kungfu and Chen-style Taijiquan—typical examples of the world-renowned Chinese martial arts. It was here that the earliest capital city in China was founded, the oldest Chinese characters engraved, and the earliest commerce took shape.

In the new era, Henan has witnessed rapid growth in its economy and remarkable improvement of people's living conditions, owing to the national reform and opening-up policy and unremitting endeavoring of the people. Modern economic achievements and social development as well as the changes of way of life could be traced back to its traditional values and cultural heritages. To enable people from other countries to understand Henan, and let the province integrate more efficiently into the world development, the Foreign Affairs Office of the People's Government of Henan Province, has organized teams of authoritative experts and scholars in relevant fields to compile this *Chinese Civilization: Stories from Henan* in Chinese and other foreign languages since 2018, by crystallizing the excellence of traditions and outstanding features of modern development. The book series include *Shaolin Kungfu, Taijiquan, Traditional Chinese Medicine, Chinese Characters, Cultural Heritage, A Model Official — Jiao Yulu, Man-made River — Hongqiqu Canal, the Silk*

Road, *Ancient Chinese Capitals*, *Handicraft* and *Feeding the People — Agriculture*, etc, attempting to present a panoramic picture of the province.

In today's world, human civilization has made great progress in both material accumulation and cultural and ethical advancement, and the great abundance of materials today, especially, is beyond the imagination of the ancient people. At the same time, however, modern people are also confronted with a lot of problems, such as the widening gap between the rich and the poor, the indulgence in pursuit of luxury and extravagance, the undesirable extension of individualism, the decline of social integrity, and the increasing tension between man and nature. To solve these problems, we need to draw on the wisdom and powers developed today as well as those accumulated in the past. Henan is endowed with a rich historical and cultural heritage characterized by its inclusiveness, and such a heritage remains significant today. The intelligence and wisdom in Henan culture are conducive to self-cultivation and to the promotion of social development. The spirit of serving the people and relentless struggle, as embodied in *Jiao Yulu* and *Hongqiqu Canal*, provides source of strength for building a community with a shared future for mankind. It is our hope that, wisdom and strength from Henan stories, could lead us to a shared brilliant future.

前 言

在世界的东方,有一个幅员辽阔的国家,古老而文明,这个国家叫中国。在中国的大地上,有一个土生土长的民族,勤劳而智慧,这个民族叫汉族。身在天南海北的汉族人,使用着千差万别的方言,陌生而亲切,这些方言有一个共同的名字叫汉语,这些方言都用一种共同的文字来书写,方正而优美,这种文字叫汉字。

汉字起源于中国本土,和古埃及的圣书字、古代两河流域的楔形文字都是独立形成的古老文字,是人类早期文明的重要标志,为人类文明的繁荣与发展做出了不可磨灭的贡献。这些文字起源并不同步,发展轨迹也各不相同,但都经历了数千年的岁月洗礼。中国的汉字从最早的甲骨文,历经多种字体的演变,一脉相承、沿用至今,成为当今世界上使用人数最多的文字。

有人说一个汉字是一幅美丽的画,有人说一个汉字是一首优美的诗。通过对汉字形体的解析,可以帮助人们更加深刻地认知汉字,了解汉字所蕴含的古代文化信息,感受汉字带来的无穷魅力。

如今的汉字,不仅仅是记录汉语的符号系统,更为重要的是,她记载了数千年绵延不绝的中华文化,传承了悠久而辉煌的华夏文明。千百年来,汉字并没有在唱独角戏,而是和世界上许多种文字进行了相互的学习与借鉴,不断增强自身的包容性和创新性。如今的汉字,不仅仅是汉族人使用的文字,也是中国许多民族共同使用的文字;不仅仅是中国人使用的文字,也是许多外国人使用的文字。

源远流长的汉字离不开孕育她的一片沃土,这片沃土就是河南。河南地理位置优越，位于中国腹地，自古便有"中州""中原"之称，又因大部分地区位于黄河以南，所以又称为"河南"。河南历史悠久，文化厚重，是华夏民族的摇篮，是中华文明的重要发祥地。5000年的中华文明史，河南有3000年是全国的政治、经济和文化中心。中国有八大古都，其中洛阳、开封、安阳和郑州都位于河南。

河南是文物大省，也是文字资源大省，地下出土和传世的文字资料数量丰富、种类齐全，上至8000年前舞阳贾湖遗址的甲骨、陶石契刻符号，中有商周时期的甲骨文、金文、陶文、玉石文、古玺文、简牍，下到汉唐及以后的历代碑刻、名人字画、善本古籍，无不应有尽有，其中不乏大量的稀世珍品。

传说中发明文字的仓颉、整理小篆的李斯、撰写《说文解字》的许慎都出生于中原大地。所有学习和研究汉字文化的人，都不能不仰仗河南、取资河南。河南孕育了汉字学、甲骨学，不仅是名副其实的汉字文化圣地，也在逐步实现由文字资源大省向汉字文化学术强省的跨越。

Preface

At the eastern edge of the world, there is an ancient but civilized country with a vast territory called China. On its land, there is a native-born diligent and intelligent nation known as the Han nationality. The Han people speak various dialects which are all called Chinese and written in the same square and graceful Chinese characters.

Like the ancient Egyptian hieroglyphs and cuneiform characters of Mesopotamia, Chinese characters are independent and important symbols developed in ancient China and have made indelible contributions to the development of early human civilization. The origin and transformation of the hieroglyphs, cuneiform, and the Chinese characters are not synchronized, but they all share a history of thousands of years. Chinese characters have evolved from the earliest oracle bone scripts to the most widely used characters in the world across different fonts that can be traced back to the same origin.

Some people say a Chinese character is like a beautiful painting while others say it is like a fine poem .Through analyzing the forms of Chinese characters, we can help people to understand Chinese language more profoundly and better appreciate the cultural information it carries along with its infinite charm.

Today's Chinese characters are not only a literal representation of the Chinese language, but more importantly, they record and inherit the Chinese culture and civilization that have flourished for thousands of years. These characters have not rested on their laurels, but have learned from and been learned by many other characters all over the world, and have thus enhanced their inclusiveness and innovativeness constantly. Today's Chinese characters are used not only by the Han people, but also by many other ethnic groups in China. They are used not only by the Chinese people, but also by many foreigners.

The long-standing and well-established Chinese characters cannot be separated from Henan, the fertile soil that gave birth to them. Henan is located in the hinterland of China and thus has an advantageous geographical position. Henan has been called "Zhong Zhou" and "Zhong Yuan" since ancient times. It is also called "Henan" because it is largely located south of the Yellow River. Henan has a long history and profound culture and has been the cradle of the Chinese people and an important birthplace of Chinese civilization. Throughout the 5,000-year history of China, Henan had stood as the political, economic and cultural center for approximately 3,000 years. China has been home to eight ancient capitals, among which Luoyang, Kaifeng, Anyang and Zhengzhou are all located in Henan.

Henan is a province with a large number of cultural relics and written resources. Written materials that have been unearthed and handed-down are abundant in quantity and complete in variety. Especially notable ones include the carved-symbols and inscriptions on the oracle bones, earthenware and stones at the Jiahu Site of Wuyang dated to as early as 8,000 years ago, jinwen (inscriptions carved on ancient bronze vessels), taowen (inscriptions carved on pottery), yushiwen (inscriptions carved on jade), guxiwen (inscriptions carved on ancient seals) and bamboo slips from the Shang and Zhou dynasties, inscriptions carved on steles, calligraphy and paintings of various celebrities, and rare ancient books from the Han, Tang, and later dynasties, among which there are plenty of rare treasures.

Cang Jie, the legendary inventor of Chinese characters, Li Si, the developer of xiaozhuan (small seal script), and Xu Shen, the author of *Shuowen jiezi* (*The Explanation of Script and Elucidation of Characters*), were all born in the Central Plains. All those who study the culture of Chinese characters must rely on and learn from Henan. Henan has fostered the growth of Chinese character studies and Oracle Bone studies, which not only makes Henan a sacred place of Chinese character culture that truly merits recognition, but also transforms itself from a province with large written resources to a province with fruitful studies in Chinese character culture.

目录　　　　　　　　　　　　　　　　　　Contents

第一章　汉字的源头　　　　　　　　　　　　001
　　一、古代认识　　　　　　　　　　　　　004
　　二、远古符号　　　　　　　　　　　　　010
　　三、甲骨文　　　　　　　　　　　　　　018

Chapter Ⅰ The Source of Chinese Characters　　001
　　Ⅰ. Ancient Views　　　　　　　　　　　005
　　Ⅱ. Ancient Symbols　　　　　　　　　　011
　　Ⅲ. Oracle Bone Scripts　　　　　　　　019

第二章　汉字的演变　　　　　　　　　　　　049
　　一、金文　　　　　　　　　　　　　　　052
　　二、小篆　　　　　　　　　　　　　　　080
　　三、隶书　　　　　　　　　　　　　　　096
　　四、楷书　　　　　　　　　　　　　　　106

Chapter Ⅱ Evolution of Chinese Characters　　049
　　Ⅰ. Bronze Inscription　　　　　　　　053
　　Ⅱ. Small Seal Script　　　　　　　　　081
　　Ⅲ. Clerical Script　　　　　　　　　　097
　　Ⅳ. Regular Script　　　　　　　　　　107

第三章　汉字的构形	115
一、造字方法	118
二、人与人体	124
三、自然万物	142
四、衣食住行	170
五、各类器具	190

Chapter Ⅲ　Configuration of Chinese Characters	115
Ⅰ. Methods of Creating Chinese Characters	119
Ⅱ. Human and Human Body	125
Ⅲ. Nature	143
Ⅳ. Clothing, Food, Housing and Transportation	171
Ⅴ. Various Appliances	191

第四章　汉字的艺术	215
一、书法	218
二、印章	228
三、汉字画	236

Chapter Ⅳ　The Art of Chinese Characters	215
Ⅰ. Calligraphy	219
Ⅱ. Seal	229
Ⅲ. Chinese Character Painting	237

第五章　汉字的交融	239
一、传播	242
二、注音	254
三、外文汉译	260
四、交流平台	266

Chapter V The Blending of Chinese Characters	239
Ⅰ. Dissemination	243
Ⅱ. Phonetic Notation	255
Ⅲ. Loanwords of the Chinese Vocabulary	261
Ⅳ. Communication Platform	267

附录　中国历史年代简表	274
Appendix　A Brief Chronology of Chinese History	274

第一章
汉字的源头

Chapter I

The Source of Chinese Characters

汉字的源头在哪里？汉字是什么时候创造的？关于汉字的起源，正如人的起源一样，古今学者一直在尝试揭开其神秘的面纱。中国古代有多种关于汉字起源的说法，而近代考古表明，汉字的起源和远古时代的刻划符号有着紧密的联系。事实上，100多年前发现的甲骨文，是中国目前发现的最早的成体系的文字，属于严格意义上的汉字。

丁公陶文
Pottery Inscription of Dinggong

Where is the source of Chinese characters? When were Chinese characters created? Scholars of ancient and modern times have been trying to unveil the mystery surrounding the origin of Chinese characters, just like what they have done to the origin of human beings. There are many theories about the origin of Chinese characters in ancient China. Modern archaeology has shown that the origin of Chinese characters is closely related to the carved symbols of ancient times. In fact, the oracle bone scripts discovered more than one hundred years ago are the earliest systematic characters found in China and can be considered Chinese characters in a strict sense.

丁公陶文摹本
A Facsimile Edition of Pottery Inscription of Dinggong

一、古代认识

在中国古代,有多种关于汉字起源的认识和说法,这些认识反映出古人对文字起源过程的初步认识。古人曾将结绳、契刻等远古时代的记事方法看作汉字的起源,也有关于仓颉造字的传说。

1. 结绳

结绳是远古时代的一种记事方法,大事打一个大结,小事打一个小结,相连的事打一个连环结,甚至用各种不同颜色的绳子表示不同的物品、事件等。直到现代,中国少数民族地区仍有结绳记事的遗留。如云南省的纳西族使用结绳方法记日子;傈僳族用结绳方法记账目;哈尼族借债,用同样长的两根绳子打同样的结,各执一半作为凭证。

一户傈僳族人家,在帮助自己兄弟抚养侄儿时使用结绳记事。绳上的结表示代养侄儿时使用的粮食、衣物等的供给数目。用棕绳和麻绳打结作为记忆的帮助,以免日后会错乱和混淆。

结绳记事
Keeping Records by Tying Knots

I. Ancient Views

In ancient China, there were many views and sayings about the origin of Chinese characters that reflected ancient people's basic understanding of the origin of Chinese characters. Ancient Chinese people once regarded a system of tying knots and carving to keep a record as the origin of Chinese characters. There were also legends about Cang Jie's creation of characters.

1. Keeping Records by Tying Knots

Tying knots is a method of keeping records that was used during ancient times. The more important the matter was, the bigger the knot would be, and serial knots would be tied for things linked to each other. People even learned to use ropes of different colors to represent different objects, events, and so on. Even in modern times, in the ethnic minority areas of China, there are still residual signs of record-keeping by tying knots. For example, the Naxi people in Yunnan Province use the knotting method to keep dates, the Lisu people use the knotting method to keep accounts, and the Hani people tie the same knots with two ropes of the same length as mutual agreement and evidence of borrowing money.

A Lisu family recorded the quantity of the food and clothing needed in raising their nephew by tying knots with the palm rope and hemp rope to avoid confusion in the future.

2. 契刻

契刻是在竹木物体上刻画记号，作用主要是记数，后来又发展用来记事，在中国的古籍中有很多对少数民族契刻记事的记载。

哈尼族典当田地时，由买卖双方刻此木刻，各执一半作为凭据。正面的"o"代表100元，"+"代表50元，每一横刻代表10元，每一个洞代表1元。旁边的3个小洞代表3个中间人。

3. 仓颉造字

仓颉造字的传说在中国古代流传最为广泛，也得到了广大读书人的认可。据说，仓颉是黄帝的史官，奉黄帝的命令创造了汉字。黄帝是中国远古时代华夏部落联盟的最高首领，是华夏民族的人文始祖。

仓颉接到命令后，到处观察。天上星宿的分布、地上山川脉络的走向、鸟兽虫鱼的痕迹、草木器具的形状等都在他脑海中留下了深刻的印象。仓颉日思夜想，描摹绘写，为世间万物造出种种不同的符号，并且规定了每个符号所代表的意义，这些符号就逐渐演变成了人们所使用的汉字。

仓颉像
Cang Jie

2. Carving

Ancient Chinese people carved holes in bamboo or wood for accounting and, later on, for recording purposes. In ancient Chinese books, there are many records of ethnic minorities' keeping records by carving.

When Hani people impawned their farmland, the buyer and the seller would carve a piece of wood and each party would hold half of it as evidence of the transaction. Each "o" on the front stands for one hundred yuan, each "+" for fifty yuan, each horizontal line for ten yuan, and each hole for one yuan. The three small holes on the side represent the three middlemen required for this transaction.

3. Cang Jie's Creation of Chinese Characters

The legend of Cang Jie's creation of Chinese characters was best known in ancient China and the legend was widely recognized by intellectuals of the time as well. It is said that Cang Jie was Yellow Emperor's official historian, who created Chinese characters on the command of Yellow Emperor, the supreme leader of the alliance of Chinese tribes in ancient history and the ancestor of the Chinese nation.

After receiving the Emperor's command, Cang Jie started to observe the world around him. He was deeply impressed by the distribution of stars in the sky, the trend of mountains and the course of rivers on the ground, the traces of birds, animals, insects, and fish, and the shapes of the vegetation and utensils. Cang Jie kept thinking day and night, portraying and painting these things until he finally created various symbols for everything in the world. He also defined the meaning of all these symbols, which gradually evolved into Chinese characters used today.

刻木记事
Keeping Records by Carving Holes in Wood

中国古代典籍里也有许多关于仓颉造字的记载，后人甚至将仓颉造字进行神化。记载说仓颉长着四只眼睛，具有异常敏锐的观察力，文字创造之后惊天动地，发生了奇事，白天竟然下起了小米，晚上能够听到鬼的哭声。

结绳与契刻是在文字产生之前，先民们用来处理日常事务的一种方法，世界上很多民族在发展过程中都采用过这些记事方式。而仓颉造字只是关于汉字起源的一个美丽传说，近代考古发掘表明，汉字的起源和远古刻画符号有着紧密的联系。

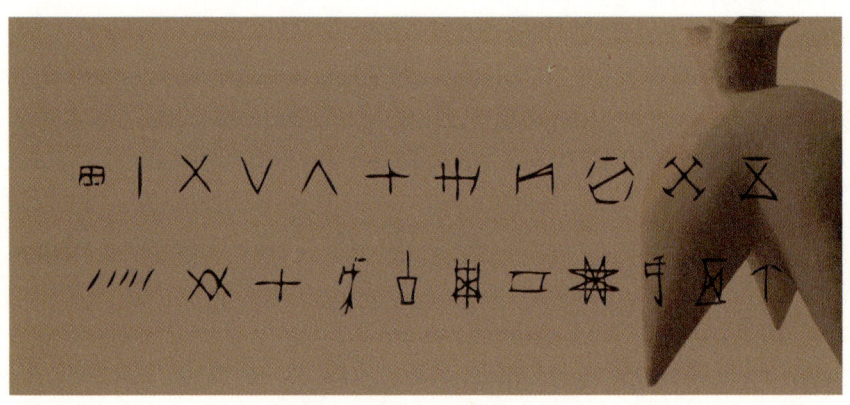

浙江发现的良渚文化刻画符号
Carved Marks of Liangzhu Culture from Zhejiang

There are also many records about Cang Jie's creation of characters in ancient Chinese books. Later generations even deified Cang Jie's creation of characters. It is recorded that Cang Jie had four eyes and thus had unusually keen powers of observation, and that Cang Jie's creation even shocked the ghosts and gods, so much that millet dropped from the sky and ghosts all cried at night.

Tying knots and carving were methods used by our ancestors to deal with daily affairs before characters came into being. Many nations in the world had adopted these methods of recording in the course of their development. Though Cang Jie's creation of characters is only a beautiful legend about the origin of Chinese characters, modern archaeological excavations have shown that the origin of Chinese characters is closely related to the carved symbols of ancient times.

二、远古符号

近代以来,随着田野考古工作的展开,大量与汉字起源有关的资料陆续出土。这些资料主要是指刻划或绘写在史前社会遗物上的各种符号,遗物以陶器居多,也有少量的甲骨、玉器、石器等器物。根据外形上的特点,这些符号大致可以分为两类:一类是象形符号,一类是几何形符号。这些符号遍布中国各地,在许多重要的考古遗址都有发现,它们为解释汉字的起源提供了新的依据。

舞阳贾湖裴李岗文化遗址位于河南省漯河市舞阳县贾湖村,距今约8000多年。舞阳贾湖刻划符号是中国迄今所知年代最早的一种刻划符号,这些符号共十多种,刻划在龟甲、骨器、石器和陶器上。其中有些符号的形状与后来的殷墟甲骨文有一些相似之处,如 ⌀ 这个符号,

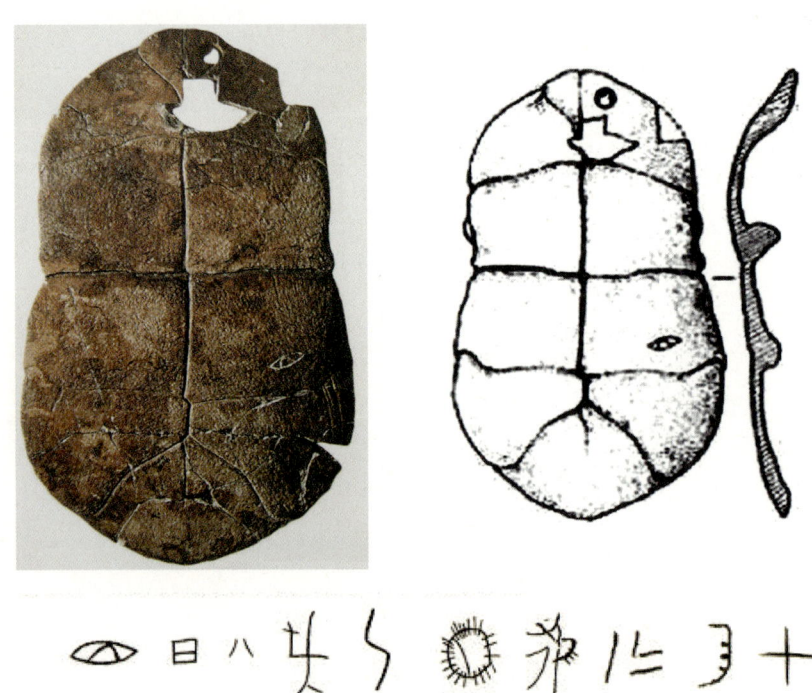

河南舞阳贾湖裴李岗文化刻划符号
Carved Marks from the Jiahu Site of Peiligang Culture, Wuyang, Henan

Ⅱ. Ancient Symbols

Since modern times, with the development of field archaeology, a large number of materials related to the origin of Chinese characters have been unearthed, most of which are various symbols depicted or painted on prehistoric relics. These relics are mainly pottery, but there are a few oracle bones, jade articles, stoneware, and other objects as well. According to the characteristics of their forms, these symbols can be roughly divided into two categories, namely, the pictographic symbol and the geometric symbol. These symbols have been discovered in many important archaeological sites throughout China, providing new bases for explaining the origin of Chinese characters.

The Jiahu Site of Peiligang Culture is located in Jiahu Village, Wuyang County, Luohe City, Henan Province, which is estimated to have existed some 8,000 years ago. The carved symbols of the Peiligang Culture discovered at the Jiahu Site are the earliest known carved symbols in China thus far, which consist of more than ten kinds of symbols carved on tortoiseshell, bone objects, stoneware, and earthenware. Some of these symbols share similarities with the later oracle bone scripts discovered in the Yin Ruins. For example, the symbol ⟨⊙⟩ was

刻在龟腹甲的上面，从外形看，眼眶和眼珠的形象一目了然。殷墟甲骨文的"目"字写作 ▱，表示眼睛的意思，两者看起来似乎有一定的联系。

这些符号与殷墟甲骨文有着惊人的相似：一是刻写工具相同，都是以利器为工具把符号刻在龟甲、骨器上；二是作用相同，殷墟甲骨文主要是用来记载占卜内容的，而贾湖契刻符号也与占卜活动相关。

汉字的形成经历了一个缓慢而长期的发展过程，其源头甚至可追溯至此。这些符号的发现，为中国商代甲骨文的源头探索提供了可靠的证据。

洪山庙仰韶文化遗址位于河南省汝州市洪山庙村，年代距今约5000年。这些符号分别是刻划或彩绘于陶缸的外壁上，如图中1—2是刻划符号，3—6为彩绘符号。在洪山庙遗址中出土的陶缸上，除了这些符号，还发现了大量的浮雕和彩绘图案，其中彩绘图案大都是用黑彩绘出图案，有弧线纹、三角纹、宽带纹、鸟纹等。

河南洪山庙仰韶文化刻绘符号
Carved Symbols of the Yangshao Culture Found at the Hongshanmiao Site, Henan Province

engraved on the ventral shell of the tortoise. In terms of its appearance, the image of the eye socket and the eyeball is clear at a glance. The character 目 (mù, eye) was written as ⟨symbol⟩ in the oracle bone scripts discovered in the Yin Ruins. It seems that there is a certain connection between these two symbols.

The symbols discovered in the Jiahu Site are strikingly similar to the oracle bone scripts discovered in the Yin Ruins. First, they were engraved with the same carving tools, i.e., both of them were engraved on tortoiseshell and bones with sharp tools. Second, they had the same functions. The oracle bone scripts discovered in the Yin Ruins were mainly used to record the predictions of divination and the carved symbols discovered in the Jiahu Site were also related to divination activities.

The formation of Chinese characters has undergone a slow and long-term development, and its origin can be traced back to the symbols discovered in the Jiahu Site. The initial discovery of these symbols provided reliable evidence for the exploration of the origin of Chinese oracle bone scripts in the Shang Dynasty.

The Hongshanmiao Yangshao Cultural Site is located in Hongshanmiao Village, Ruzhou City, Henan Province, which is estimated to have existed some 5,000 years ago. These symbols were engraved or painted on the external layer of pottery jars. For example, picture 1 and 2 are carved symbols and picture 3 to 6 are painted symbols. In addition to these symbols, a large number of reliefs and colored paintings have also been found on the pottery jars unearthed from the Hongshanmiao Site, most of which were painted in black using arching lines, triangular lines, broad band lines, and bird lines.

良渚文化是中国长江下游太湖流域一支重要的古文明，发现于浙江省杭州市余杭区良渚遗址，距今约4500—5300年。其中有些符号仍然属于简单的线性刻画标记的性质，而有些符号则比较规整，在结构和书写特征上都比较接近古汉字的风格。不仅如此，这类符号还多次出现排行连刻的例子，在功能上也非常接近文字的性质。

陶寺文化发现于山西省襄汾县陶寺村南的陶寺遗址，距今约4000余年。陶寺遗址出土了一个扁陶壶，壶的鼓凸面一侧可以见到一个朱书符号，释为现在的"文"字，壶的扁平一侧共有三个符号，这几个符号都是用毛笔之类的工具所写。

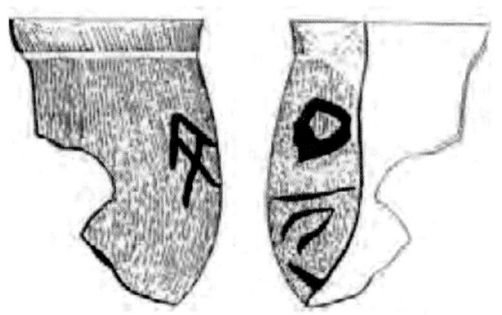

山西襄汾陶寺文化彩绘陶文

Pictorial Marks Painted with Cinnabar Discovered at the Taosi Site in Xiangfen County, Shanxi Province

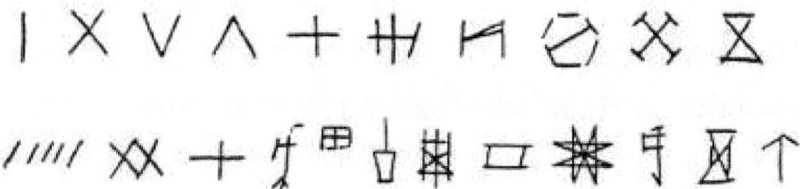

浙江良渚文化刻划符号
Carved Symbols of the Liangzhu Culture of Zhejiang Province

As an important branch of the ancient civilizations in the Taihu Lake Basin downstream of the Yangtze River, Liangzhu Culture was discovered at the Liangzhu Site in Yuhang District, Hangzhou City of Zhejiang Province, which is estimated to have existed some 4,500-5,300 years ago. Some symbols of the Liangzhu Culture were simply carved lines while others were clearly and neatly carved, and thus more closely resembling ancient Chinese characters in terms of structures and writing features. Moreover, some symbols were carved in rows and columns linked together, whose functions were also very similar to those of characters.

Taosi Culture was discovered at the Taosi Site in Xiangfen County of Shanxi Province, which is estimated to have existed about 4,000 years ago. The symbol painted with cinnabar on the convex surface of an oblate pottery pot unearthed at the Taosi Site could be interpreted as 文(wén, word) in modern Chinese characters. There are 3 symbols on the flat side of the pot, which were painted with brush-like tools.

符号 刻于河南省登封市王城岗遗址所出的一件泥质黑陶平底器的残底外部,是烧前刻划上去的。这个符号看起来像一个人的左右两只手在捧着什么东西,而这是古汉字系统中的一个基本构形,有学者把它隶定为"共"字。这一形体出现在一处相当于夏纪年之际的城址之中,虽然例证不多,却是汉字的发明和文明社会到来的一个重要信号。

在中国幅员辽阔的大地上,成熟的夏商文字出现以前,远古先民曾经走过了从结绳记事、契刻、图画符号记事到发明文字的漫长历程。在不同的时空、不同文化背景下的许多富有生命力的符号,都可能逐渐融汇到汉字产生的主流道路上来。中华文字的起源与演进过程并不只有一条单纯的主线,发明文字的人物也远远不止一个仓颉。

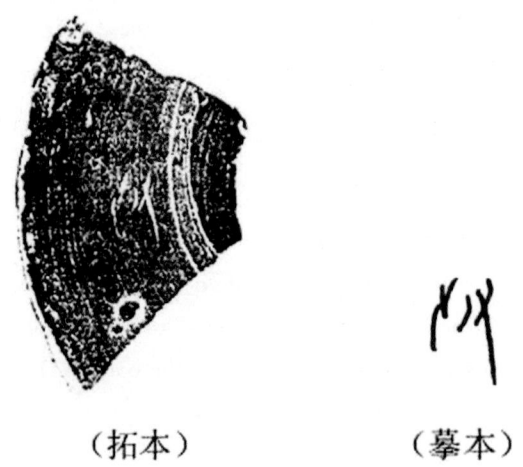

（拓本）　　　　（摹本）

河南登封王城岗龙山文化刻划符号

Carved Symbols of the Longshan Culture Found at Wangchenggang in Dengfeng County, Henan Province

The symbol ⟨symbol⟩ on the outer layer of the fragmented bottom of an earthen black flat pottery pot unearthed at the Wangchenggang Site in Dengfeng City of Henan Province was engraved before the pot was baked. This symbol looks like a person's left and right hands holding something, which is a basic configuration in the ancient Chinese character system, and some scholars have defined it as the character共(gòng, together). Although there are not many examples, this symbol appearing in a city site existing in the Xia Dynasty is still an important sign of the invention of Chinese characters and the arrival of civilized society.

On China's vast land, before the emergence of the mature characters used in Xia and Shang dynasties, our remote ancestors went through a long process of tying knots, carving, painting pictorial symbols, and then inventing characters. Many vivid symbols from different times, places, and cultural backgrounds may gradually merge into the mainstream of Chinese characters. There existed more than one consolidated line of history in the origination and evolution of Chinese characters, and the creation of Chinese characters involved far more than one Cang Jie.

三、甲骨文

甲骨文主要发现于河南省安阳市小屯村,是中国商朝时期的文字,距今已有3000多年的历史。甲骨文是中国目前发现最早的成体系的文字,已经能够完整地记录当时语言所要表达的内容。甲骨文于2017年11月成功入选《世界记忆名录》,这标志着甲骨文的重要文化价值及历史意义已在世界范围内得到高度认可。

1. 甲骨文的发现

清朝末年,河南省北部有一个叫小屯的村庄,这里曾经是商朝晚期的都城所在地。商朝是中国3000多年前的一个王朝,后来被西周所灭,商朝都城也成了一片废墟,很少有人居住。到了清朝,这里的人口逐渐多了起来,耕地范围也不断扩大,一些甲骨的碎片开始从土里被刨出来。村民并不知道这些甲骨片上面刻着的符号便是震惊世界的甲骨文,只是把这些碎片当作一种叫"龙骨"的药材卖到中药铺,然后销往全国各地。

甲骨文之父——王懿荣
Wang Yirong, the Father of Oracle Bone Script

III. Oracle Bone Scripts

Oracle bone scripts were mainly discovered in Xiaotun Village, Anyang City, Henan Province. They were characters used in the Shang Dynasty and had a history of more than 3,000 years. Oracle bone scripts are the earliest systematic characters discovered in China, and they were already capable of recording content expressed by the language of that time. Oracle bone scripts were included in the *Memory of the World Register* in November 2017, indicating that the important cultural value and historical significance of oracle bone scripts have been highly recognized worldwide.

1. The Discovery of Oracle Bone Scripts

In the late Qing Dynasty, there was a village called Xiaotun in the north of Henan Province, which was once the capital of the late Shang Dynasty. The Shang Dynasty existed more than 3,000 years ago in China, until it was destroyed by the Western Zhou Dynasty. Since then, the capital of the Shang Dynasty has been in ruins and rarely inhabited. By the Qing Dynasty, with the steady growth in population and the gradual expansion of cultivated land in this area, some fragments of oracle bones began to be dug out of the ground by the villagers here. Not knowing that the bones and tortoiseshell with inscriptions would become the oracle bones which would shock the world, these villagers sold them as medicinal materials named "dragon bones" to traditional Chinese medicine shops, where they were then sold throughout the country.

1899年，距离安阳500多公里的清朝都城——北京有个人生病了，无意中发现所买的中药"龙骨"上居然有些类似古汉字的刻纹。这个人就是王懿荣，当时担任国子监祭酒（相当于国家最高学府的行政长官），恰好是著名的金石学家，对古文字的研究有着很深的造诣。他马上意识到这些刻纹非比寻常，后经过仔细研究，认定"龙骨"上面所刻的符号便是商朝时期的文字，比当时人们了解的任何文字都古老。然后，他开始大量高价收集甲骨，甲骨也从极其便宜的中药变为具有重大学术价值的珍宝，并在全球范围内引起轰动。甲骨文就在这样偶然的机会中被发现了，王懿荣因此被学术界誉为"甲骨文之父"。

2. 甲骨文的概念

甲骨文是指刻写在龟甲和兽骨上的文字。龟甲大部分是龟腹甲，即乌龟壳的肚子那一块，背甲很少；兽骨主要是指牛的肩胛骨，也有少量的鹿骨、虎骨、犀牛骨等兽骨。龟甲兽骨简称甲骨，刻在上面的文字就是甲骨文。

龟腹甲

Plastron of a Tortoise

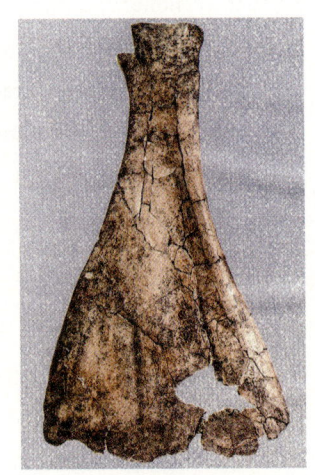

牛肩胛骨

Shoulder Blade of an Ox

In 1899, a man in Beijing, the capital city of the Qing Dynasty which is more than 500 kilometers away from Anyang, became ill. He accidentally found some carved lines resembling ancient Chinese characters on the traditional Chinese medicinal "dragon bones" he bought. This man was Wang Yirong, who was then the officer in charge of the Imperial College (the chief executive of the highest academic institution of the Qing Dynasty). It so happened that Wang was also a famous epigraphist with profound knowledge of ancient Chinese characters. He immediately realized that these carved lines were unusual. After careful study, he affirmed that the symbols carved on the "dragon bones" were characters used by the Shang Dynasty, which were older than any other characters known by people at that time. From then on, he began to collect oracle bones at a high price, and thus the oracle bones were transformed from cheap Chinese medicinal materials to treasures of great academic value that caused a worldwide sensation. Wang Yirong was thus praised as "the father of oracle bone scripts" by academic circles because of his discovery of the oracle bone scripts by chance.

2. The Definition of Oracle Bone Scripts

Oracle bone scripts refer to ancient characters carved on animal bones and tortoiseshell. Most of the shells are plastrons, i.e. the ventral shells, whereas dorsal shells were rarely used; most of the animal bones are the shoulder blades of oxen, but there are also a small number of deer bones, tiger bones, rhino bones and bones of other animals. The tortoiseshell and animal bones are called oracle bones for short, and the characters carved on them are called oracle bone scripts.

鹿头骨

Skull of a Deer

甲骨文这个名称确定之前，人们给它起了好多不同的名字：有的按文字书写方法命名，称它为"契文"，就是用刀刻的文字；有的按甲骨文的用途命名，称它为"卜辞"，就是记录占卜内容的文字；有的按甲骨文的出土地命名，称它为"殷墟文字"，就是出土于安阳殷墟的文字。但这些名字都不能准确、全面地反映甲骨文的本质和特征，最后只有"甲骨文"这个名称得到了学界的一致认可。

3. 甲骨文的用途

用龟来占卜，进而预测事情是吉还是凶，现在已很少有人相信了。但在中国古代，人们却认为它非常灵验。龟在中国先民的心中并不是一般性的动物，而是具有神灵性的动物。商王确信自己逝去祖先的灵魂在上天神灵的周围，当他想与上天神灵和自己祖先的灵魂联系时，就使用龟甲占卜。

通过占卜这种形式，商王可以提出各种问题和良好的愿望。商朝的占卜活动非常频繁，可以说是天天卜，事事卜。甲骨文的用途便是把占卜的时间、参与人员、占卜的事由、卜兆的吉凶等内容记录下来，有的还把后来是否应验的结果刻上去。这些记录占卜内容的甲骨文也叫甲骨卜辞，其中大部分是商王的占卜记录，小部分是跟商王有密切联系的大贵族的占卜记录。商朝人有时也在甲骨上刻一些跟占卜无关的事情，只不过这部分甲骨文所占比例非常低。

Before the name "oracle bone scripts" was adopted, people gave these kinds of characters many different names. Some people called them契文(qì wén, characters carved on oracle bones), according to their writing method, i.e., characters carved with knives; some called them卜辞(bǔ cí, inscriptions for recording divination), according to their functions, i.e., characters to record divination predictions; some called them殷墟文字(yīn xū wén zì, characters discovered at the Yin Ruins), according to the place where they were discovered, i.e., characters discovered at the Yin Ruins in Anyang. However, none of these names can accurately and comprehensively reflect the nature and characteristics of oracle bone scripts. Finally, only the name "oracle bone scripts" was unanimously recognized by the academic community.

3. The Function of Oracle Bone Scripts

Nowadays, few people believe in practicing divination with tortoises to predict the future. But in ancient China, people believed this practice was highly effective. To ancient Chinese people, the tortoise was not a common animal but a divine one. Kings of the Shang Dynasty believed that the souls of their deceased ancestors were with the gods in heaven. When they wanted to contact the gods and the souls of their ancestors in heaven, they would use tortoiseshells for divination.

By means of divination, kings of the Shang Dynasty could raise various questions and make good wishes. The Shang Dynasty practiced divination frequently, to the degree that they would divine every day and for any matter. Oracle bone scripts were then used to record the contents of the divination, such as its time, participants, causes, and good or bad omens. Sometimes the accuracy of the divination results would also be recorded. These oracle bone scripts recording the contents of the divination are also called甲骨卜辞(jiǎ gǔ bǔ cí, oracle bone inscriptions for recording divination). Most of them are records of the divination practiced by the kings of the Shang Dynasty, and a few of them are records of the divination practiced by the great aristocrats closely related to the kings of the Shang Dynasty. People of the Shang Dynasty sometimes also engraved things unrelated to divination on tortoiseshells and animal bones, but this was a relatively uncommon practice and thus the proportion of this kind of oracle bone inscription is very low.

4. 甲骨占卜的过程

商朝的占卜过程是非常庄重、神圣和严肃的，大致可分为三个阶段，即准备、占卜和记录。

在正式占卜之前，贞人（即负责管理占卜事务的人）需要做好各方面的准备，最重要的就是对龟甲和牛肩胛骨进行整治。简单说来，就是选取适合占卜的龟、骨等材料，并对这些材料进行处理。把甲骨的突起部分尽量削平，把粗糙的地方进行打磨处理，使甲骨变得平直、平滑。然后用特定工具在甲骨背面钻出一种较长的、椭圆形的坑和一种较小的圆洞，这叫作钻凿。这样做的目的是使甲骨变得薄一些，在占卜烧灼甲骨时，甲骨正面就容易出现裂纹。最重要的是，钻凿时不能把甲骨给钻透了。

占卜时，贞人把整治好的甲骨拿来，询问所要占卜的事情，同时用燃烧的小木棍对甲骨背面的小坑进行灼烧，灼烧的痕迹就是甲骨背面的黑点。甲骨经过钻凿以后厚薄不匀，烧到一定程度以后它就开裂了，甲骨正面便会出现纵横不同的裂纹，这种裂纹叫作卜兆。然后，根据卜兆的走向来判断吉和凶。例如，商王看了卜兆后就会说，根据这个卜兆，

经钻凿、烧灼的龟腹甲背面
The Back of a Plastron that Has Been Drilled and Burned

4. The Process of Divination with Tortoiseshell and Animal Bones

The process of divination in the Shang Dynasty was very solemn, sacred, and serious, and could be roughly divided into three stages: preparation, divination, and recording.

Before the formal divination, 贞人(zhēn rén, the augur, i.e. the person in charge of divination affairs) had to make various preparations, the most important one being the processing of the tortoiseshell and shoulder blade bones of the oxen. First, they had to select tortoiseshell, bones, and other materials suitable for divination and process these materials beforehand. Any protruding parts of the oracle bones would be trimmed as flat as possible and the rough surfaces would be polished to make the oracle bones straight and smooth. They would then drill long and elliptical holes and small holes on the back of the oracle bones with specific tools. The purpose of drilling was to thin down the bone so that cracks would appear on the front of the oracle bones easily when they were burned in divination. Crucially, the oracle bones could not be penetrated during the drilling process.

While divining, 贞人 would bring the processed oracle bones and ask divination questions. Concurrently, he would burn small holes on the back of the oracle bones with a burning stick. The black spots on the back of the oracle bones in the above picture are burned marks made during this process. The thickness of the oracle bone was uneven after being drilled. Consequently, it would crack after being burned to a certain extent and various vertical and horizontal cracks would appear on its front side. These cracks were called 卜兆(bǔ zhào), from the direction of which good or bad luck could be foretold. For example, after observing the 卜兆, the King of Shang would say that according to this 卜兆, the

下一次打仗一定会胜利,去打猎一定会很安全,今年会有好的收成。

最后,贞人把占卜的相关情况刻写在所占卜的甲骨上,这就完成了占卜的过程。当然,过了一段时间,贞人有可能会再次找到上次占卜的甲骨,并把应验的结果补刻上去。

但是,什么样的卜兆是好的结果,什么样的卜兆是不好的结果,这是一个非常有意思的问题,很多人想知道。因为占卜一般是先裂个竖纹,然后裂个横纹,"占卜"的"卜"字于是就形成了,如丫、⺅、卜、卜。一个竖纹一个横纹,形成了一个夹角。有学者专门做过研究,就是根据卜兆的夹角去研究。看看夹角是锐角或者钝角时和吉凶的对应关系,想找出规律来,结果很遗憾没找出任何规律。

5. 甲骨文的格式

一条完整的甲骨卜辞一般由四个部分组成:具体的占卜时间和人员;询问的事情;所问事情的结果如何,是吉还是凶;最后吉凶的应验情况如何。

但从现有甲骨文看来,很多卜辞往往没有第四部分,这是因为占卜结果需要时间来验证。也就是说,第四部分是过了一段时间后刻上去的,而大多数情况下并没有把应验的情况刻上去。

"癸丑卜,争贞:旬亡囚?王固(占)曰:㞢求,㞢梦。甲寅,允㞢来嬉(艰)。"这是一条完整的卜辞,大意是:癸丑这一天,一位名字叫争的贞人来实施占卜。问的事情是下一旬是否有什么灾祸发生?商王看了卜兆后说,未来十天会有灾祸,而且还会有噩梦。占卜后的第二天甲寅日,果然有灾祸发生。这则卜辞的第四部分肯定是在灾祸发生后刻上去的,只是不知道发生了什么灾祸。

next battle would be a success, the next hunting would be safe, and there would be a good harvest that year.

Finally, 贞人 would inscribe the relevant information about this divination on the oracle bone, which was conducted as the last step of the divination. After some time, 贞人 may find the oracle bone of the previous divination and engrave the result of fulfillment on it.

What kinds of 卜兆 are good? What kinds of 卜兆 are bad? These questions are very interesting and their answers are highly sought. In most cases, while divining, the vertical crack would appear first on the oracle bone, followed by the horizontal. Thus the character 卜(bǔ, foretell), the second character of the phrase 占卜(zhānbǔ, divine) was formed. For example, ㄠ, ㄅ, ㅏ and ㅑ are all the different forms of the character 卜 formed by those cracks. An inclined angle would be formed by the vertical crack and the horizontal crack in the practice of 卜兆. Some scholars have carried out specific research on these inclined angles to find out whether there existed a corresponding relationship between the angles and the degree of luck foretold. Unfortunately, no such rules have yet been found.

5. The Format of Oracle Bone Scripts

A complete oracle bone inscription generally consists of four parts: time of the divination and the people involved, the things to be divined, the result of the divination, and the final result of fulfillment.

However, according to the existing oracle bone scripts, many inscriptions often lack the fourth component because it took time to verify the result of the divination. That is to say, though the result of fulfillment was to be carved on the oracle bone after a period of time, in most cases, they were not.

Here reads a complete oracle bone inscription,"癸丑卜，争贞：旬亡囚？王固（占）曰：业求，业梦。甲寅，允业来婎（艰）", whose main points could be summarized as follows: on the day of 癸丑(guǐ chǒu), a 贞人 named Zheng practiced divination to tell whether there would be any disasters in the next ten days. After observing the 占卜，the King of Shang proclaimed there would be disasters and nightmares in the next ten days. On the day of 甲寅(jiǎ yín), the day directly following the divination, a disaster did occur. The fourth part of this oracle bone inscription was engraved on the oracle bone after the disaster, but it did not tell us what disaster occurred.

实际上，这是一条贞旬卜辞，即询问未来十天的吉凶情况。我们今天一周是七天，一个月是四周。可是在商朝的时候，一个月不是按周而是按旬来划分的，一个月分为三旬，十天就是一旬，所以卜辞里经常会问，下一旬做什么事情会不会顺利，下一旬会不会下雨。直到今天，中国的一个月仍然分为上旬、中旬和下旬。旬也在很多场合使用，如有的刊物就是旬刊，即十天出版一期。

6. 甲骨的片数

根据学者统计，现在一共出土了大概十几万片甲骨，统计数据有一些出入，一般认为大概有13万片。现在，中国社会科学院考古研究所仍然在殷墟保留着安阳工作站，继续着甲骨文的研究与发掘。

这13万片甲骨中只有少数是完整的龟甲和兽骨，大部分都是面积不大的碎片，比如王懿荣收集的甲骨片就全是碎片。为什么呢？因为甲骨经过钻凿、烧灼，又在地下经过3000多年的腐蚀，很多甲骨出土时是村民挖地挖出来的，村民也不懂，有时直接就给敲成了碎片。

除了中国，别的国家也收藏有大量甲骨，其中日本和加拿大最多，各有7000多片，英国有3000多片，美国有1000多片，德国、俄罗斯、法国等国也有一定数量的收藏，甲骨片在世界其他国家的收藏总数约26000多片。

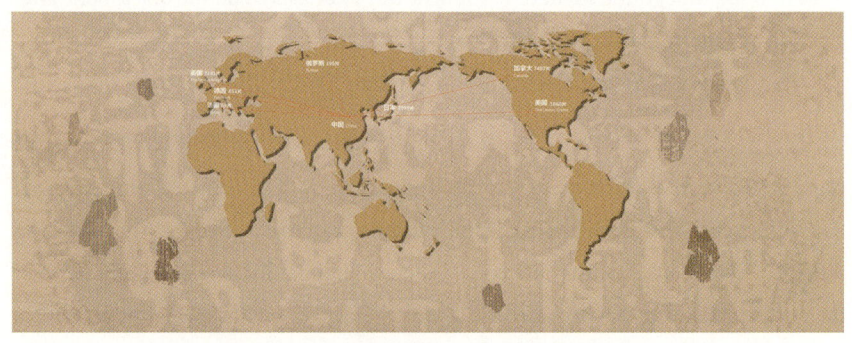

刻辞甲骨在世界主要国家的收藏与分布
Inscribed Oracle Bones Collected by Other Countries in the World

In fact, the above-mentioned oracle bone inscription belonged to a 贞旬卜辞 (zhēn xún bǔ cí), that is, a divination asking about good or bad luck in the next ten days. Nowadays, we have seven days in a week and four weeks in a month. However, in the Shang Dynasty, a month was divided not by week but by 旬 (xún, ten days). A month was divided into 3旬 (xún) and a 旬 had ten days. Therefore, people often asked in the oracle bone scripts whether things would go smoothly or whether it would rain in the next ten days. To this day, in China, a month is still divided into 上旬(shàng xún, the first ten days), 中旬 (zhōng xún, the middle ten days) and 下旬 (xià xún, the last ten days). 旬 is also used on many occasions, for example, some periodicals are 旬刊(xún kān), i.e., they are published once every ten days.

6. The Number of Oracle Bones

According to scholars' statistics, more than 100,000 pieces of oracle bones have now been unearthed. There are some discrepancies in the statistics, and it is generally believed that there are about 130,000 pieces. At present, the Institute of Archaeology of the Chinese Academy of Social Sciences still keeps its Anyang Workstation in the Yin Ruins and continues its research and excavation of oracle bone scripts.

Only a few of the 130,000 pieces of oracle bones are complete tortoiseshell and animal bones; the majority of unearthed bones are small-sized fragments. For example, the oracle bones collected by Wang Yirong are all fragments. The oracle bones had been drilled, burned and corroded underground for more than 3,000 years, and many of the oracle bones were dug up by villagers who, unaware of the bones' history, sometimes broke them into pieces themselves.

Besides China, other countries also have large collections of oracle bones, among which Japan and Canada have the largest collections, with each featuring more than 7,000 pieces. Britain has more than 3,000 pieces and the United States has more than 1,000 pieces. Germany, Russia, France and other countries also have a certain number of collections. The total number of the oracle bones collected in other countries around the world is about 26,000-odd pieces.

甲骨文发现后,可以说是"一片甲骨惊天下"。私人挖掘成风,很多人纷纷来到安阳收购甲骨,许多外国人也参与进来,如加拿大人明义士(James Mellon Menzies)、美国人方法敛(Frank Herring Chalfant)、英国人库寿龄(Samuel Couling)、德国人威尔茨(Wirtz)、日本人林泰辅(Lin Taifu)等。

明义士是第一个到访殷墟的西方学者,他于1914年走进殷墟并开始搜购甲骨,1917年用摹本出版《殷墟卜辞》,开创了著录甲骨不用拓本的新手段,这是西方学者研究甲骨文的第一部著作。

7. 甲骨文的字数

目前整理出来的甲骨文单字约4500个,被学者识读、能与现在使用的汉字相对应的有将近1500字,这些字主要是与人体、自然、农业、战争等有关的常用字,没有被识读出来的字主要是地名、人名、氏族名等,现在已经不再使用。

这1000多个甲骨文,和现在汉字的外形已有很大的差别,但是,只要从形体上稍作分析和解释,丝毫不影响如今的中国人对它们的认识与理解。

明义士
James Mellon Menzies

The discovery of oracle bones amazed the world. Private excavations ran rampant and numerous people came to Anyang to buy oracle bones. Many foreigners were also involved such as James Mellon Menzies from Canada, Frank Herring Chalfant from America, Samuel Couling from Britain, Wirtz from Germany, and Lin Taifu from Japan.

James Mellon Menzies is the first Western scholar to visit the Yin Ruins. He went to the Yin Ruins and began to search for oracle bones in 1914. In 1917, he published *Yinxu buci* (*Yin Ruins Oracle Bone Scripts for Recording Divination*) by copying the oracle bone scripts instead of rubbing, which was a new method of recording the oracle bone scripts at that time. *Yinxu buci* is the earliest work on oracle bone scripts written by a Western scholar.

7. The Number of Characters in Oracle Bone Scripts

At present, about 4,500 characters have been identified from the oracle bone scripts, and about 1,500 of them can be read and related to modern Chinese characters by scholars. The recognized characters are mainly common characters related to the human body, nature, agriculture, war and so on. The unrecognized characters are mainly the names of places, persons, and clans which are no longer used.

These 1,000-odd characters in the oracle bone scripts look rather different from modern Chinese characters. However, as we make analyses and interpretations of their forms, they can be easily recognized and understood by Chinese people today.

8. 甲骨文的内容

甲骨文大部分是记录占卜内容的，人们称之为卜辞，还有少量记事的，人们称之为记事刻辞。甲骨文的内容非常丰富，绝大多数跟祭祀、战争、狩猎有关；当然还有表示天象的，比如月食；还有病患，比如商朝一个很有名的女性人物妇好，她得了病，卜问会不会牙齿痛之类的，就讲她的病患；此外还有天气、收成、生育、俘虏、梦幻等等，涉及商代社会的方方面面，为人们探寻商朝人的生活轨迹提供了详实的资料。

9. 记载车祸的卜骨

这块儿卜骨的内容比较多，其中有一条卜辞记录了商王在田猎活动中发生的一次车祸。癸巳日这一天占卜，询问未来十天是否有灾祸发生。商王占卜说会有灾祸发生。结果第二天甲午日，商王乘车外出打猎，在追逐犀牛的过程中，车轴突然断裂，车翻了，人从车上摔了下来。

从图片中可以清晰地看出，这个"车"字的特殊之处，，两个车轮之间的车轴不是一条直线，而是由两条短的直线组成，有学者研究说这个字是对车轴断裂情况的真实记录。

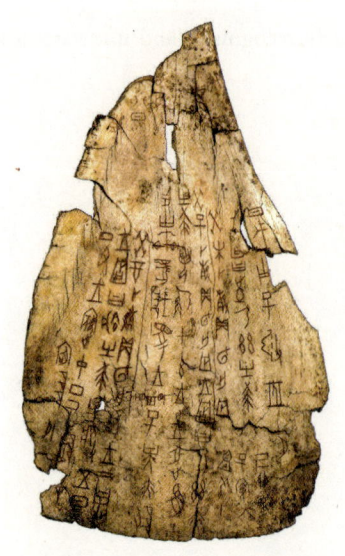

记载车祸的卜骨

An Oracle Bone Recording a Traffic Accident

8. The Contents of Oracle Bone Scripts

Most oracle bone scripts are records of divination, which are called 卜辞(bǔ cí,inscriptions for recording divination). There are also a few inscriptions recording events which are called 记事刻辞 (jì shì kè cí, carved inscriptions for recording events). Oracle bone scripts are rich in content, most of which are related to sacrifice, war, and hunting. Some of them are about astronomical phenomena such as the eclipse of the moon, and some are about illness. For example, a well-known woman named Fu Hao in the Shang Dynasty divined if she would have toothaches and other illnesses. Additionally, there are also inscriptions about weather, harvest, birth, captivity, and dreams, all of which involve various aspects of the Shang society and thus provide detailed information for exploring the Shang people's lives.

9. An Oracle Bone Recording a Traffic Accident

The contents recorded on this piece of oracle bone are quite rich. One piece of its inscriptions has recorded a traffic accident that occurred during a hunting trip led by the King of Shang. The King of Shang divined whether there would be any disasters in the next ten days on the day of 癸巳(guǐ sì), and the result was that there would be disasters. Accordingly, on the afternoon of the next day, the day of 甲午(jiǎ wǔ), the King of Shang went out hunting in a carriage and fell off the carriage in the course of chasing a rhinoceros because the axle suddenly broke and the car overturned.

The special feature of the character "車" (chē, carriage) can be seen clearly from the above picture: the axle between the two wheels is not a straight line, but two short straight lines. Some scholars posit that this character is a record of the fated axle fracture.

第一章 汉字的源头

10. 记载月食的卜骨拓片

这块儿卜骨上的七个甲骨文是："旬壬申夕，月出（有）食。"大意是说：到了壬申这天晚上，发生了月食现象。这是一条珍贵的月食记录，充分说明商朝人已经能够观测关于月食的天象。在别的甲骨文中，也发现了关于日食的记载。

在这条记录中，最后一个字"食"的写法不是很完整，参考别的甲骨文，"食"的写法 ，下面是盛有食物的容器，上面是人张开的口，意思是低头张口吃饭。"月食"就是月亮被吃掉的意思。古代中国民间还不能科学地解释月食现象，认为月食是"天狗吞月"，即天狗要把月亮给吃掉。出现月食情况，人们要通过敲锣打鼓、燃放爆竹等方式来赶走天狗，有的地方到现在仍然留有这种习俗。

记载月食的卜骨拓片
Rubbings of the Oracle Bone Recording the Eclipses of the Moon

10. Rubbings of the Oracle Bone Recording the Eclipses of the Moon

The seven characters on this oracle bone are "旬壬申夕，月㞢（有）食," meaning that there was an eclipse of the moon on the evening of the day of 壬申 (rén shēn). This is a precious record, which fully shows that people of the Shang Dynasty were capable of observing celestial phenomena such as the eclipse of the moon. In other oracle bone scripts, records of solar eclipses have also been discovered.

In this record, the last word 食 (shí, to eat) is not complete. By referring to other oracle bone scripts, we know that 食 should be written as "🍚". The lower part of this character is a container for food, and the upper part is an open mouth, which means to lower the head and open the mouth to eat. 月食 (yuè shí, the eclipse of the moon) means that the moon is being eaten. In ancient China, people could not explain the phenomenon of a lunar eclipse scientifically and they regarded the lunar eclipse as 天狗吞月 (tiān gǒu tūn yuè), that is, the dog from heaven is eating the moon. Whenever a lunar eclipse occurred, people drove away the heavenly dog by beating gongs and drums and setting off firecrackers. Today this custom is still followed in some places of China.

记载生育的卜甲
Oracle Bones Recording a Birth

11. 记载生育的卜甲

这块儿卜甲记载：甲申日这一天占卜，询问妇好分娩是否顺利。商王认为妇好在丁日分娩顺利，在庚日分娩会更好。结果到了第31天的甲寅日，妇好产下一个女婴，商王认为不好。

在古代，男子不仅是家庭的主要劳力，也关系到家族的传承，尤其是王公贵族。中国自古就有重男轻女的思想，所以妇好生下一个女孩被认为是不好。比甲骨文出现稍晚的中国古代第一部诗歌总集《诗经》中也有类似的记载："乃生男子，载寝之床，载衣之裳，载弄之璋。乃生女子，载寝之地，载衣之裼，载弄之瓦。"大意是说，如果生下男孩，就让他睡在床上，穿着衣裳，给他玉璋玩。如果生下女孩，就让她躺在地上，裹着褴褛，玩着陶纺轮。随着社会的进步，重男轻女的思想已逐渐退出主流。

12. 记载田猎的兽骨

这是一条记事刻辞，刻在犀牛骨上。刻辞大意是：壬午这一天，商王在麦地田猎，捕获了犀牛，商王把捕获的犀牛赏赐给大臣宰丰。实际上，这是一块儿骨头的正反面，正面刻有文字，背面刻有图案。从刻辞内容来看，宰丰非常重视商王赏赐这件事情，不仅将此事记录下来，还在骨头上面刻了精美的图案，这在甲骨文中是非常罕见的。

11. Oracle Bones Recording a Birth

The inscriptions on this oracle bone read that a divination was made on the day of 甲申(jiǎ shēn, the 21st day of a month), asking whether Fu Hao would have a smooth delivery. The King of Shang thought that she would have a smooth delivery on the day of 丁(dīng, the 24th day of a month) and it would be even better if the childbirth was on the day of 庚(gēng, the 27th day of a month). However, Fu Hao unluckily gave birth to a girl on the day of 甲寅(jiǎ yín, the 31st day of a month) and the King of Shang was thus unhappy.

In ancient times, men were not only the main labor force of a family, but also related to the inheritance of a family, especially a noble one. During ancient times, Chinese people held the belief of valuing men over women, so it was considered a misfortune for Fu Hao to give birth to a girl. A similar record is found in *Shi Jing (The Book of Songs)*, the first anthology of poetry in ancient China appearing later than the oracle bone scripts: "乃生男子，载寝之床，载衣之裳，载弄之璋。乃生女子，载寝之地，载衣之裼，载弄之瓦." The main idea of this poem is that if a boy was born, his parents would let him sleep in a bed, wear clothes, and play the jade tablet; but if a girl was born, her parents would let her lie on the ground, wear swaddling-clothes, and play the spinning wheel. With the progress of society, the idea of valuing men over women has gradually withdrawn from the mainstream thought of Chinese society.

12. Bones Recording a Hunting

This is an inscription for recording events inscribed on the bone of a rhinoceros. The main idea of this inscription is that on the day of 壬午 (rén wǔ), the King of Shang hunted in the wheat field and captured a rhinoceros. The King gave the captured rhinoceros to the Minister Zai Feng. The left pictures show the two sides of the bone, with words engraved on its front and patterns engraved on its back. Judging from the inscriptions, we can see that Zai Feng attached great importance to the King's reward. He not only recorded it, but also carved exquisite patterns on the bone, which were very rare in the oracle bone scripts.

图片右边黑白部分是犀牛骨的拓片。拓片制作是中国一项古老的传统技艺,是使用宣纸、墨汁等材料将碑刻、器物等文物的形状、文字或图案清晰地拷贝出来的一种技能。有了这块犀牛骨拓片,犀牛骨上的文字、图案就非常清晰地再现在了人们眼前。

从这块犀牛骨上可以看到中国商代文字的排列方式,即自上而下的直行排列法,这种排列法早在商代就已经确立。在甲骨文里,不少原来宽度比较大的字,已经由于直排的需要而改变了字形的方向,〒(马)〒(象)〒(犬)等字,已经头部朝上、尾巴朝下了。商代后期的铜器铭文和兽骨上的记事文字,几乎全都由右向左排行。汉字的这种自上而下、自右而左的排列方式,沿用了3000多年,一直到20世纪50年代中期,才基本上被自左而右、自上而下的横行排列法所取代。但原来的直行排列法也并没有绝迹,现在的书法作品、碑刻、印章、文人书信仍然采取传统的直行排列法。

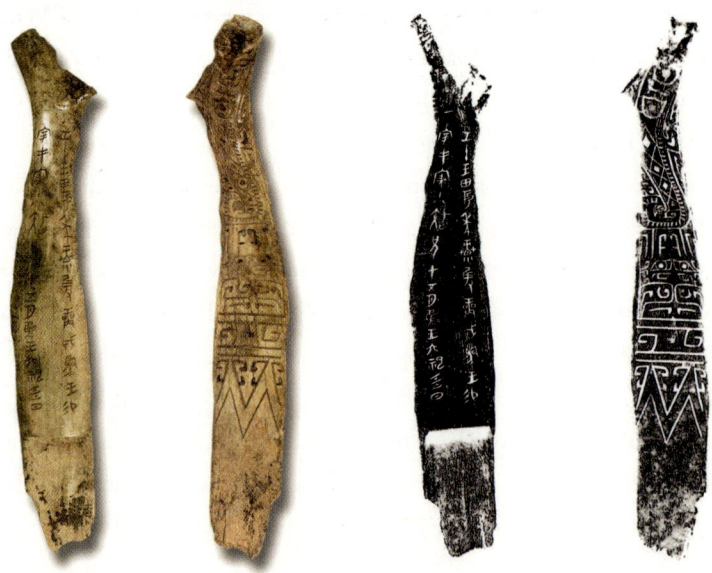

记载田猎的兽骨
Bones Recording a Hunting

The two black-and-white pictures to the right of the inscription in the left pictures are the rubbings of this rhino bone. Rubbing is an ancient traditional skill in China, which uses materials such as rice paper and ink to replicate the shapes, characters, and patterns of inscriptions on tablets, artifacts, and other cultural relics clearly. With these rubbings of the rhinoceros' bone, its characters and patterns can be clearly displayed in front of us.

From this rhino bone, we can see that in the Shang Dynasty, characters were arranged vertically from top to bottom, which proved that the vertical arrangement of characters had been established as early as the Shang Dynasty. In the oracle bone scripts, the writing directions of many wider characters were changed to meet the need of vertical arrangement, for example, characters like 𤕦(horse), 𤉢(elephant), and 𤝿(dog) were written with their heads up and tails down. The inscriptions on bronze vessels and animal bones in the late Shang Dynasty were almost all arranged from right to left. This top-down and right-to-left arrangement of Chinese characters has been used for more than 3,000 years. It was not until the mid-1950s that this vertical arrangement was replaced by the left-to-right and top-down horizontal arrangement. However, the vertical arrangement has not vanished, and it is still used widely in calligraphy works, inscriptions, seals and letters written by the literati.

13. 甲骨文的一次重大发现

1936年6月，安阳殷墟迎来了出土甲骨最多的一次重大发现。发现这些甲骨的甲骨坑编号为YH127，共出土甲骨17096片，其中完整的龟甲300多片，这是殷墟考古至今出土甲骨最多的一次，这坑甲骨震惊了整个考古界。在1996年的第62届国际图联大会上，被专家誉为"世界最早的图书馆""中国最早的档案库"。

当时在发掘时，考虑到野外发掘的不安全性，决定将整坑甲骨搬到室内进行分解。但如何搬运就成了摆在人们面前的一个问题。这坑甲骨不仅体积大，而且重量大，重约6吨。当时没有起重设备，就组织了一支由48个人组成的队伍用杠子抬着慢慢走，发掘地距离火车站不到两公里，却走了整整两天。

在这坑甲骨中，还出土了一片特大的龟甲，长44厘米，宽35厘米。据鉴定，它来自于南方的马来半岛，这也从侧面证明了遥远的南方是殷墟龟甲的一个重要来源地。

YH127甲骨坑发掘现场

The Excavation Site of the YH127 Oracle Bone Pit

13. An Important Discovery of Oracle Bone Scripts

In June 1936, a major discovery yielding the largest number of oracle bones ever unearthed was made in the Yin Ruins of Anyang City. 17,096 pieces of oracle bones were unearthed from the YH127 Oracle Bone Pit, among which more than 300 pieces are complete shells. This is the largest number of oracle bones ever unearthed in the history of archaeological excavations of the Yin Ruins, which shocked archaeological circles not only in China, but abroad. At the 62nd IFLA (The International Federation of Library Associations and Institutions) Congress in 1996, the YH127 Oracle Bone Pit was praised by experts as "the earliest library in the world" and "China's earliest archives".

During the excavation, taking into consideration the precariousness of outdoor conditions, archaeologists decided to move the entire Oracle Bone Pit indoors for disassembly, but the experts were faced with the problem of how to relocate the entire pit. The cube of soil cut from this Oracle Bone Pit was very large and weighed about 6 tons. There was no lifting equipment at that time, so a team of 48 people was organized to carry it with thick sticks. The excavation site was less than two kilometers from the railway station, but it took the carriers two days to get there on foot.

A huge tortoiseshell, 44 centimeters long and 35 centimeters wide, was found in this Oracle Bone Pit. Identification has shown that it came from the Malay Peninsula in the south, proving that the distant south is an important source of tortoiseshells discovered in the Yin Ruins.

14. 甲骨文记载的一位女将军

1976年，在安阳殷墟发现了一座商代王室墓葬，共出土青铜器、玉器、象牙器等文物1928件。这是目前所发现的商代唯一一座保存完整的王族墓葬，经过了3000多年仍然完好无损，不能不说是一个奇迹。后来确定这个墓的主人叫妇好，之所以能够这么肯定，就是因为有甲骨文的佐证。已发现的甲骨片有200多片都曾提到过妇好，甲骨文对妇好的记载使得人们能够比较详细地了解这位传奇的中国第一位女将军。

妇好是商王武丁的妻子，武丁是个很有抱负的君王，在他统治下，商朝国力达到鼎盛。在武丁的赫赫武功中，有着妇好相当一部分的功劳。可以这么说，妇好是中国有文字记载的第一位文武双全的女将军。她曾参与国家大事，主持祭祀，还带兵征伐过羌方、土方等方国，颇具传奇色彩。出土的大量甲骨卜辞表明,在武丁对周边方国、部族的一系列战争中,妇好多次受命代商王征集兵员，也多次担任将军征战沙场。她曾统兵1.3万人进攻羌方，并俘获大批羌人,成为武丁时期在一次征战中率兵最多的将领。

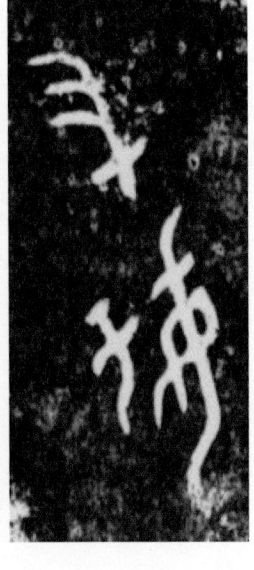

甲骨文和金文"妇（婦）好"对比
Comparison Between 妇（婦）好(Fu Hao) Written in the Oracle Bone Scripts and Bronze Scripts

14. A Female General Recorded in Oracle Bone Scripts

In 1976, a royal tomb of the Shang Dynasty was discovered in the Yin Ruins of Anyang, and 1,928 pieces of bronze, jade, ivory, and other cultural relics were unearthed. It is the only complete royal tomb of the Shang Dynasty that has miraculously remained intact for more than 3,000 years. Later it was verified that the owner of this tomb was Fu Hao, with evidence provided by the oracle bone scripts. Among the unearthed oracle bones, more than 200 pieces mentioned Fu Hao. The oracle bone scripts about Fu Hao have enabled people to know more about this first legendary female general in China.

Fu Hao was the wife of Wu Ding, an aspiring king of the Shang Dynasty. Under Wu Ding's reign, the national strength of the Shang Dynasty reached its peak. During this time, Fu Hao made considerable contributions to Wu Ding's outstanding military accomplishments. It can be said that Fu Hao is the first female general endowed with civil and martial virtues in Chinese written records. She participated in state affairs, presided over sacrifices, and led troops to conquer the State of Qiang and the State of Tu, among others. She was thus quite legendary. A large number of unearthed oracle bones have shown that Fu Hao had been ordered to recruit soldiers on behalf of the King of Shang and to serve as general multiple times in Wu Ding's series of wars against neighboring states and tribes. She once led an army of 13,000 soldiers to attack the State of Qiang and captured a large number of Qiang people, which made her the leader of the largest number of soldiers in a campaign during the reign of Wu Ding.

15. 关于甲骨文的一个误解

由于甲骨文的大量发现，使得很多人对商朝产生了一个误解。很多人以为商朝人日常书写的文字是用刀刻出来的，认为商朝是刀笔文字时代。这只是因为甲骨文材质特殊，碰巧保存下来了。事实上，毛笔是商朝时期最主要的书写工具。

"笔"的繁体字写作"筆"，由"竹"和"聿"两个字构成，甲骨文"聿"写作 ，是"笔"字最初的形体，像一只手拿着一根末端有兽毛的竹管在写字。后来在"聿"的上方加部首"竹"，另造"筆"字，强调"笔"的竹子材质。现在使用的"笔"字其实出现得也比较早，由"竹"和"毛"两个字组成，是个会意字，表示"笔"是以竹管和兽毛为材料制成的。人们虽然已经无法看到用毛笔书写的商代简牍，但是还能在商代后期留下来的甲骨和玉、石、陶等类物品上看到少量毛笔字。

甲骨上的毛笔字有朱书和墨书两种，这说明在商代的时候就已经有了书写用的毛笔和朱砂、墨等文具。

写有毛笔字的卜骨
An Oracle Bone with Characters Written with Writing Brushes

15. A Misunderstanding About Oracle Bone Scripts

As a result of the massive discovery of oracle bone scripts, many people have misconceptions about the Shang Dynasty, believing that the daily writing of the Shang Dynasty was carved out with knives and consequently misnaming the Shang Dynasty as the age of writing with knives. In fact, the most important writing tool during the Shang Dynasty was writing brushes, not knives, but the oracle bone scripts that make up the majority of historical relics from this period were written on special materials and successfully preserved, unlike their painted counterparts.

In traditional Chinese, 笔 (bǐ, pen) is written as 筆, which is composed of two characters, 竹 (zhú, bamboo) and 聿(pen, write). In the oracle bone scripts, 聿 was written as "ᚹ", which is the original form of the character 笔 and looks like a hand holding a bamboo tube with animal hair at its end to write. Later the radical 竹 was put above the character 聿 to create a new character 筆, emphasizing that the pen was made of bamboo. As a matter of fact, the current character笔 also appeared early on. It was formed by two characters:竹 (zhú, bamboo) and毛 (máo, hair), indicating that a pen is made of bamboo tube and animal hair; thus, we can also see that it is an associative character. Although people can no longer see the bamboo slips written with writing brushes in the Shang Dynasty, a small number of characters written with writing brushes can still be seen on oracle bones, jade, stones, pottery and other articles left by the late Shang Dynasty.

There are two kinds of characters on this oracle bone, 朱书(zhū shū,characters written in cinnabar) and 墨书(mò shū,characters written in ink), indicating that stationary like writing brushes, cinnabar and ink had already been used in the Shang Dynasty.

安阳也出土了商朝的一些玉石片,上面有商朝人蘸着朱砂写的红色的毛笔字。种种迹象表明,商王朝是一个用毛笔书写的时代,那时候的日常书写都离不开毛笔。

有红色墨迹的玉石
Jade with Red Ink Marks

Some jade pieces of the Shang Dynasty were also unearthed in Anyang, on which red characters written with cinnabar and writing brushes were discovered. Various signs have shown that the Shang Dynasty was an era of writing with writing brushes, and people's daily writing of that time was inseparable from the writing brush.

第二章

汉字的演变

Chapter II

Evolution of Chinese Characters

第二章 汉字的演变

　　现代汉字是在古代汉字的基础上逐渐发展、演变而来，这个演变过程非常复杂。一般认为，汉字字体演变经历了甲骨文、金文、小篆、隶书、楷书等不同阶段，最后成为现在所使用的方块字。汉字从3000多年前的甲骨文发展到现代汉字，尽管在形体上、读音上或字义上发生了一些变化，但在性质上并没有发生根本性的变化。汉字始终承载着中华民族的文化与文明，凝聚了华夏先民的智慧，是内涵丰富的优秀传统文化的缩影，是华夏文明的活化石。

汉字简化
The Simplification of Chinese Characters

Modern Chinese characters have gradually developed and evolved on the basis of ancient Chinese characters, and this evolution process is very complex. It is generally believed that the evolution of Chinese characters has gone through different stages, starting with the oracle bone scripts and transitioning into jinwen (bronze inscription), xiaozhuan (seal script), lishu (official script) and kaishu (regular script), eventually evolving into the Chinese characters being used today. Although there have been some changes in form, pronunciation or meaning, there has been no fundamental change in the nature of Chinese characters since they have evolved from oracle bone inscription over 3,000 years ago. Modern Chinese language still carries the culture and civilization of the Chinese nation and embodies the wisdom of Chinese ancestors. The characters are the epitome of an excellent traditional culture with rich connotations and stand in as "living fossils" of Chinese civilization.

一、金文

商朝带给人们最震撼的东西，除了甲骨文之外，其实就是青铜器和青铜器上的文字——金文。金文是指商周时期铸、刻在青铜器上的文字的总称。金文的内容主要是关于当时祭祀、赏赐、命令、征战、盟约等事件的记录，以及贵族对先祖功绩的颂扬，侧面反映了当时社会生活的方方面面。

1. 青铜时代

根据劳动生产工具的演进，考古学者将人类社会的发展划分为石器时代、青铜时代和铁器时代。大约4000年前，中国正式进入青铜时代，历经夏、商、西周、春秋时期，前后持续了大约1500年的历史。中国的青铜器制造技术在晚商和西周早期达到高峰，到春秋时逐渐衰微。随着铁器时代的到来，生产力不断提高，青铜器在战国以后逐渐退出历史舞台。

中国青铜时代文化和生产力增长的范围非常广阔，不仅仅在王朝都城，而且已经扩展至黄河流域和长江流域，乃至更南、更北的区域。

实际上，铜器在中国历史上出现得比较早，考古工作者曾经在距今6000多年前的陕西临潼姜寨遗址发现过铜片，还有黄铜管。距今大概4000年前到5000年前之间，铜器就更多了，都是一些小件用具，并不是青铜时代的典型代表。到了夏朝的时候，铜容器才开始出现，而到了商朝，容器的种类日渐丰富多样，器形也更加复杂。

中国的青铜器跟世界其他地方相比都不一样，其他地方的铜器大都是工具、装饰品，偶尔有几个人面像。中国的青铜器用于工具的很少，

Ⅰ. Bronze Inscription

In addition to the oracle bone scripts, another amazing remnant of the Shang Dynasty are the bronze wares and the characters on them—*jinwen* (bronze inscription). *Jinwen* refers to the words cast and engraved on bronze wares during the Shang and Zhou Dynasties (17th century B.C. to 221 B.C.). The bronze scripts are mainly about sacrifices, rewards, orders, battles, treaties, as well as eulogies written by nobles for their ancestors' achievements, reflecting the various aspects of social life at that time.

1. Bronze Age

Based on the evolution of production tools, archaeologists divided the development of human society into the Stone Age, the Bronze Age, and the Iron Age. About 4000 years ago, China formally entered the Bronze Age, going through the Xia, Shang, Western Zhou, and Spring and Autumn Period, which continued for about 1500 years. China's bronze ware making technique reached its peak in the late Shang Dynasty and early Western Zhou Dynasty, and gradually declined in the Spring and Autumn Period. With the advent of the Iron Age, productivity continued to increase, and bronze wares gradually withdrew from the historical arena after the Warring States Period.

The scope of Chinese cultural and productive growth during the Bronze Age is very broad, not only in the capitals, but also in the Yellow River Basin, the Yangtze River Basin, and even the more southern and northern regions.

As a matter of fact, bronze wares appeared very early in Chinese history. Archaeologists once discovered copper sheets and brass tubes at the Jiangzhai Site in Lintong, Shaanxi Province, over 6000 years ago. Between 4000 and 5000 years ago, bronze wares increased in popularity, but most were small tools that were not typical representatives of the Bronze Age. Copper containers began to appear from the Xia Dynasty, and by the Shang Dynasty, types of bronze wares became increasingly diverse and their shapes more complicated.

China's bronze wares are different from those in other parts of the world. Most bronze wares in other regions are tools, decorations, and occasionally several human face-shaped wares. China's bronze wares were rarely used for tools; most were intended to be sacrificial wares and musical instruments. They were often

大多是礼器和乐器，往往被用来作为一种社会符号或者文化符号，融入了政治意愿、精神内涵和宗教信仰，是社会身份、政治地位的象征。

一件青铜器，原料不易获取、工艺复杂，做出来又非常精美，而且坚硬、不易破碎，属于稀缺物品。青铜器上大都有各种漂亮的纹饰，有些纹饰做得很恐怖、很狰狞、很神秘，有的还要再加上铭文。一般人得不到，所以人们非常重视它。

青铜器被埋葬后必然有重见天日的机会，中国历史上很早就有发现青铜器的记载，现世的青铜器历来都被视为瑰宝，甚至被说成是天降祥瑞的征兆。汉武帝年间，曾发现一个青铜鼎，汉武帝为此特意把年号改为"元鼎"，这个年号用了六年。

2. 金文与青铜器

"金文"的"金"不是指黄金，而是指铜。周朝把铜叫作金，所以铜器上的铭文就叫作"金文"或"吉金文字"。商周青铜器以礼器和乐器为主，礼器以鼎为代表，乐器以钟为代表，"钟鼎"可以看作是青铜器的代名词，所以金文也叫"钟鼎文"。

青铜器是以铜为主要原料，并配有一定比例的铅、锡制作而成的器物。考古发现了好几个商代的采矿遗址，或者矿冶遗址。安阳本地曾挖出过商朝时的一大坑铅锭，经认真清理，发现共有297块，重达4.7吨，想一想这可以做多少铜器啊。青铜器刚做出来的时候应该是黄金般的土黄色，看起来金灿灿的，相当漂亮。而青铜器这样的名称只是后人对商周铜器的一种叫法，因为铜器长时间埋在土里，逐渐在表面生成了青绿色的锈，出土时的颜色和刚制作出来时的颜色是不一样的。

used as social symbols or cultural symbols, incorporating political will, spiritual connotation and religious beliefs, and they were symbols of social identity and political status.

Bronze wares were precious goods as they required rare raw materials, complicated craftsmanship and exquisite finishings, and were hard and durable. Most bronze wares featured detailed and beautiful emblazonries, while some were horrendous, ferocious and mysterious, and others still were primarily inscriptions. Ordinary people couldn't obtain bronze wares, so they valued them highly.

Though the bronze wares were buried, they were fated to be unearthed. The discovery of bronze wares has long been recorded in Chinese history. The unearthed bronze wares have always been regarded as treasures, and they are even said to be a sign of auspiciousness from heaven. During the reign of Emperor Wu of the Han Dynasty, a *Qingtong ding* (bronze tripod) was discovered, hence Emperor Wu of the Han Dynasty changed the reigning title to *Yuan Ding*, which lasted six years.

2. Bronze Scripts and Bronze Wares

The word *jin* in *jinwen* (bronze inscription) refers to *tong* (bronze), not *jin* (gold). People in the Zhou Dynasty referred to *tong* (bronze) as *jin* (gold), so the inscription on bronze wares is called *jinwen* (bronze inscription) or *jijin wenzi*. Bronze wares in the Shang and Zhou Dynasties were mainly sacrificial wares and musical instruments. The sacrificial wares are represented by *ding*, and the musical instruments are represented by *zhong*. So *zhong ding* can be regarded as synonymous with bronze wares, and *jinwen* can also be called *zhong ding wen*.

Bronze wares are made of copper as their main raw material with a particular ratio of lead and tin. Archaeological discoveries have been made in several mining sites, or mining and smelting sites in the Shang Dynasty. In Anyang, a large pit of lead pigs of the Shang Dynasty has been dug out. After careful cleaning, 297 pieces were found in the pit, totaling 4.7 tons. When the bronze wares were first made, they were intended to be golden khaki, which looks golden and quite beautiful. The name of bronze wares share a similar history with that of copper wares of the Shang and Zhou Dynasties, as copper wares were buried in the earth for a long time and gradually produced green rust on their surface, and their color when unearthed was different from when they were just made.

中国古代青铜器绝大部分是采用范式铸造方法制作的。范式铸造法工艺流程一般分为五步：

第一步为塑模，用泥土塑造出铜器的基本形状。

第二步为翻范，用事先调和均匀的细质泥土紧紧按贴在泥模表面，拍打后使泥模的外形和纹饰反印在泥片上。

第三步为合范，将翻好的泥片划成数块，取下后烧成陶质，这样的范坚硬不易变形，称为陶范。将陶范拼合形成器物外腔，称为外范。外范制成后，再制作器物的内表面，称为内范，铜器的铭文一般刻在内范上。将内范和外范合成一体，内外范之间的空隙就是铜液留存的地方，两者的间距就是青铜器的厚度。

第四步为浇注，将铜液注入陶范。待铜液凝固后，把内外陶范打碎，取出所铸铜器。

有图案、纹饰的陶范
Pottery Mould with Patterns and Emblazonries

Most ancient Chinese bronze wares were made by the mould casting method. The process of mould casting was generally divided into five steps:

The first step was to mould and use clay to form the basic shape of the bronze ware.

The second step was to adjust the shape, and tightly press and stick fine, pre-mixed clay on the surface of the clay mould. After tapping, the shape and pattern of the mud mould would be reversely printed on the mud sheet.

The third step was to conform to the standard: divide the turned mud sheets into several pieces, remove them, and then burn them into pottery. This kind of mould was hard, not easy to deform, and was called the pottery mould. The pottery mould would be pieced together to form the outer cavity of the bronze ware, called the outside mould. After the outside mould was made, the inner surface of the bronze ware, called the inside mould, would then be made, with the inscription of the bronze ware usually engraved onto this inside face. When the inside and outside moulds were placed together, the gap between the cavities would hold the heated copper liquid, with the spacing determining the thickness of the bronze ware.

The fourth step was to pour the molten copper liquid into the pottery mould. After the copper liquid solidified, the inside and outside pottery moulds would be broken and the cooled bronze ware removed.

好多青铜器是倒过来铸的,比如铜鼎就是倒过来铸的,三条腿朝上。冶炼的铜溶液不能距离陶范太远,因为铜液是很容易冷却的。研究人员做过实验,现代条件下,在一个地方化完铜以后,把坩锅挪过来大概一米左右去浇铸,铜液很快冷却了,就无法浇铸,所以应该就在铸造的旁边化铜,化完铜浇铸,浇铸只要一会儿工夫。上海市有位学者长期研究铜器铸造,他说做一件复杂的铜器,如果一共花了80天时间的话,其实79天都在做陶器,铸造只需要一天。

第五步为打磨和整修。刚铸好的青铜器,表面粗糙,纹饰也不清晰,需要经过打磨整修,才能成为一件精致的铜器。

3. 司母戊鼎——世界青铜器之冠

司母戊鼎于1939年出土于河南省安阳市,高133厘米,重约833公斤,是目前发现的世界上最大最重的青铜器。鼎的主人为商王武丁的妻子,在鼎的内壁一侧铸有铭文"司母戊"三字,结合甲骨文得知,此鼎是商王祖庚或祖甲为祭祀自己的母亲而专门铸造的。

最早的鼎出现于新石器时期,是一种用来蒸煮食物的炊具,那时候的鼎都是陶鼎,后来随着社会生产力的提高,青铜鼎开始出现,并且成为重要的礼器,在商周时期已经成为身份和地位的象征。"鼎"的金文

司母戊鼎
The Simuwu Square Cauldron (Ding)

Many bronze wares were cast in reverse. For example, copper tripods were cast in reverse, with three legs facing up. The smelted copper liquid could not be too far away from the pottery mould as the copper liquid would otherwise cool quickly. Researchers today have conducted an experiment on the technique: under modern conditions, after melting copper in place, the crucible is moved about one meter to be cast. Incredibly, within this short period of time, the molten copper cools down and cannot be cast. Therefore, copper should be melted next to the place of casting, and when it is done, casting will take only a brief while. A scholar in Shanghai who has studied the casting of bronze wares concluded that when making complicated bronze pieces, if the process takes 80 days, 79 days is spent on the making of the pottery mould and only one day on casting it.

The fifth step was to polish and refurbish. The newly-cast bronze ware would have a rough surface and unclear emblazonries. It would be thoroughly polished and refurbished to become a fully complete, delicate bronze ware.

3. The Simuwu Square Cauldron (*Ding*)——the Crown of the World Bronze Ware

The Simuwu Square Cauldron (*Ding*) was unearthed in Anyang, Henan Province in 1939. As the biggest and heaviest bronze cauldron in the world discovered so far, it stands 133cm high and weighs about 833kg. The owner of this bronze cauldron was the wife of King Wuding of the Shang Dynasty. In the inner surface of the cauldron are three characters司母戊(sī mǔ wù). Referring to oracle bone scripts, we have learned that the cauldron was specially made by King Zugeng or Zujia to sacrifice to his mother.

The earliest cauldron appeared in the Neolithic period in the form of a cookware used for cooking food. At that time, the cauldrons were all pottery cauldrons. Later, with the improvement of social productivity, the bronze cauldron began to appear and became an important sacrificial utensil, and consequently a symbol of identity and status in the Shang and Zhou Dynasties (17th century B.C.

写法有很多种，如 ▨、▨、▨、▨，鼎足、鼎身、鼎耳都非常形象，有的字形省略了鼎耳，有的还有简单的纹饰。常见的鼎有三足的圆鼎和四足的方鼎两类，又可分为有盖的和无盖的两种。

鼎是中国青铜文化的代表，历来被视为传国重器，也是国家和权力的象征。商代金文有着鲜明的时代特色，字形较为象形，笔画浑厚，字体大小不一，字数较少，一般只有几个字，到商代晚期才出现少数较长的铭文。有一些铭文的内容可以和甲骨文相互印证。

4. 妇好鸮尊——商朝战神的象征

尊是一种盛酒的容器，鸮就是猫头鹰，妇好是器物的主人。妇好鸮尊以鸮作为原型，挺胸直立，两足粗壮有力，和垂直于地的宽尾巴构成一个平面，给人以沉稳的感觉。鸮在商代被认为是一种神鸟，常被看作是勇武的战神而被赋予避免兵灾的魅力。鸟兽尊是商周青铜器中最具神采与神秘感的一类器物，数量极少，这些鸟兽尊形态各异，除了鸟形外，还有犀形、虎形、象形和牛形，用于不同的祭祀场合。

妇好鸮尊的口下内壁铸有铭文"妇好"二字。商代青铜器中可以多次见到"妇好"的铭文，如▨、▨、▨等，"妇"字为▨，即"帚"，是指一种扫地的工具，有的"妇"字加"女"字旁为▨，即

妇好鸮尊
Fu Hao Xiao Goblet (*Zun*)

to 221 B.C.). There are many kinds of bronze scripts for ding, such as 🝌 , 🝍, 🝎 and 🝏 —the feet, surfaces and ears of the cauldron are very vivid, while some fonts omit its ear, and others have simple emblazonries. The common cauldrons are three-legged round tripods and four-legged square tripods, and they can also be divided into two types, covered and uncovered.

Ding (cauldron) is a representative of Chinese bronze culture. It has always been regarded as a national treasure and a symbol of power and the state. The bronze scripts from the Shang Dynasty carry distinct characteristics of the times. Their fonts are more pictographic, the strokes are thicker, the font size is different, and the number of words is few, with generally only a few words. Only in the late Shang Dynasty did a few long inscriptions appear. Some of these inscriptions can be verified alongside oracle bone scripts.

4. Fu Hao (One of King Wuding's Consorts) Xiao Goblet (*Zun*) — a Symbol of God of War in the Shang Dynasty

Zun (goblet) is a kind of container for wine, *xiao* is owl, and Fu Hao was the owner of the utensil. Fu Hao Xiao Goblet takes the shape of an owl, stands upright, has strong legs, and forms a plane with a wide tail perpendicular to the ground, giving people a calm gaze. In the Shang Dynasty, *xiao* was considered a kind of heavenly bird, and was often regarded as a brave war god endowing protection against military disasters. Bird-beast goblets (*zun*) are the most fascinating and mysterious bronze wares in the Shang and Zhou Dynasties. They are very rare, and have different forms, including the shapes of rhinoceroses, tigers, elephants, oxen, and birds; they are all used in different sacrificial occasions.

The inner surface of the Fu Hao Xiao Goblet was cast with the inscription "Fu Hao" (妇好). On the bronze wares of the Shang Dynasty, the inscription of "Fu Hao" can be seen many times, such as 🝐, 🝑, 🝒. The Chinese character 妇 was written as 🝓, that was 帚, which referred to a tool for sweeping the ground, and

"妇"的繁体字"婦",表示女子在家做扫地等家务。"好"字为一名或两名女子在照顾一个婴儿,"子"字金文写作 ,像一名幼儿两脚被裹在襁褓里,露出圆圆的脑袋,挥动着两臂,"女"字金文写作 ,像一个头戴发簪的女子,双手交叉在胸前,娴静地屈膝跪坐。

5. 利簋——商周更迭大战的唯一物证

利簋,又名武王征商簋,是迄今所见最早的西周青铜器,1976年在陕西省临潼县零口乡西周窖藏出土。

簋是古代的盛食具,类似现代的碗。在北京市有一条以"簋"命名的餐饮一条街——簋街,这条街是中华美食集中展示的一个绝好场所,位于东城区东直门内,簋街一侧的桥头专门做了一个"簋"的大铜塑像。

利簋腹内底铸铭文4行32字。利簋的铭文虽然很简略,却记录了一次重大历史事件,即武王伐商的"牧野大战",并记载了周武王于甲子日灭商的准确时间,为商周断代提供了不可代替的实物标本,具有非常重要的史料价值。

利簋

Li Vessel (*Gui*)

some others added the Chinese character component 女, written as 㛪, becoming the traditional Chinese character 婦, which referred to a woman doing housework at home. The Chinese character 好 meant one or two women who were taking care of a baby. The Chinese character 子 was written as 𡥜 in bronze inscription, like a child with two feet wrapped in a swaddle, revealing a round head and waving both arms. The Chinese character 女 was written as 𠨰 in bronze inscription, like a woman with a hair pin, crossing her hands on her chest and sitting down on her knees quietly.

5. Li Vessel (*Gui*) — The Only Physical Evidence of the War of Dynastic Changes from the Shang Dynasty to the Zhou Dynasty

Li Vessel (*gui*), also known as the Wuwang Zhengshang Vessel, is the earliest Western Zhou bronze ware discovered thus far. It was unearthed in the village of Lingkou Township, Lintong County, Shaanxi Province in 1976.

Gui (vessel) is an ancient food utensil, similar to a modern bowl. In Beijing, there is a food and beverage street named Gui Street which is an excellent place for various kinds of Chinese food to be displayed in close proximity to each other. It is located in Dongzhimen, Dongcheng District, and a large bronze statue of *gui* was specially made at the bridgehead on the side of the Gui Street.

The inscriptions on the inner and bottom surface of the Li Vessel (*gui*) are 4 lines, including 32 Chinese characters. Although the Li Vessel's inscription is very simple, it records a major historical event, namely the "Muye Battle," which is about King Wu's troops conquering Shang's troops. It records the exact time when King Wu destroyed the Shang Dynasty on the first day of the Zhou Dynasty, providing irreplaceable records of the Shang Dynasty being replaced by the Zhou Dynasty, and thus carries very important historical value.

在利簋出土之前，关于牧野之战具体日期的争论从未停止，历代学者根据有关记载推算出的日期有数十种。利簋的作器者名"利"，他追随武王参加战争，胜利后得到的赏赐是铜，他用这些铜铸造了利簋以记功并用来祭奠祖先。可以说，利簋的铭文证实了《尚书》等文献记载的史实，是有关武王征商的唯一文物遗存。

这篇铭文右上角第一个字，也是通篇铭文中一个极其特殊的字，即![字]，认真看就会发现，这实际上是两个字"武王"，右边是"武"，左边是"王"，这种现象叫作合文，在甲骨文中比较常见。![字]是周武王在周代金文中的专用名字，在大盂鼎铭文中也曾出现，写作![字]，只不过在此字下又有一个"王"字，大盂鼎铭文中也出现了周武王父亲周文王的称呼，"文王"的写法也是合文，写作![字]，右边为"文"，左边为"王"。

6. 裘卫盉——一份土地买卖的契约

盉是古代的盛酒器，是古人调和酒、水的器具，用来调和酒味的浓淡。

裘卫盉盖内有铭文132个字，主要记载了周恭王三年，一个名叫矩伯的贵族分两次向裘卫索取了觐见周王的物品，即价值八十朋的玉质礼器和价值二十朋的皮裘礼服，矩伯分两次付给了裘卫等值的农用土地作为索取礼品的代价。裘卫把这件事情报告了执政大臣，得到了大臣的认可，并且进行了授田仪式，从而确认了转移土地归属的合法手续。

裘卫盉铭文把贝作为商品交换的媒介记载了下来，贝不仅具有货

Before Li Vessel was unearthed, the debate on the specific date of the Battle of Muye was still ongoing, and scholars of different generations calculated dozens of dates based on the relevant records. The name of the creator of Li Vessel was 利(lì). He followed King Wu to participate in the war. After the victory, he was rewarded with copper, and he used this copper to cast Li Vessel to record the victory and to pay homage to his ancestors. Li Vessel's inscription confirms the historical facts recorded in *Shang Shu* (*The Book of Documents*) and other documents, and it is the only cultural relic retelling King Wu's conquest of the Shang Dynasty.

The first Chinese character in the upper right corner of this inscription is a very special Chinese character in the inscription, that is ▨. When you look carefully, you will find that it is actually two Chinese characters武王 (King Wu), the right being武(Wǔ), and the left王(King). This phenomenon is called the combination of characters, which is more common in the oracle bone scripts. ▨ is the special name of King Wu in bronze scripts during the Zhou Dynasty. It has also appeared in the inscriptions of Dayu Vessel, written as ▨ , but there is another Chinese character 王under this Chinese character. King Wu's father King Wen also appeared in the inscription of Dayu Vessel, also as a combination of characters, written as ▨, with文(Wén) on the right and王(King) on the left.

6. Qiu Wei Container (*He*) — A Contract for the Sale of Land

He is an ancient wine container, an instrument used by ancestors to blend wine and water, so as to make the wine taste good.

There are 132 Chinese characters inscribed in Qiu Wei Container's cover, which mainly records that in the third year of King Gong's reign, a nobleman named Ju Bo asked Qiu Wei twice for articles to present himself before King Gong, specifically jade sacrificial vessels worth 80 peng (ancient monetary unit, one peng equals to ten shell money) and fur formal attires worth 20 peng. Ju Bo paid Qiu Wei equivalent agricultural land twofold as a price for the gifts. Qiu Wei reported this matter to the ruling minister, received his approval, and conducted a field distribution ceremony to confirm the legal procedures for transferring the land.

The inscription of Qiu Wei Container records the shell as a medium for commodity exchange. The shell not only had monetary function, but also had

裘卫盉
Qiu Wei Container (*He*)

币职能，而且也有具体的衡量和计算商品价值的尺度，这在金文中并不多见。

说到"朋"字，人们马上会想到"朋友"，甚至联想到孔子在《论语》中说的话："有朋自远方来，不亦乐乎？"在裘卫盉铭文中，"朋"是写作▆，"二十朋"是写作▆，是"廿"和"朋"的合文，"廿"是二十的意思。▆看起来和"朋友"一点关系都没有，也不像是由两个"月"字组成的字。实际上，这个字在甲骨文中也非常常见，写作▆，像两串玉石系在同一根绳子上，形成更大的一挂玉串。在商代已开始用作货币单位，以五贝为一系，两系为一朋。这个字经过长时间的演变，最后成为现在的"朋"字。

7. 虢季子白盘——曾被当作马槽的国宝

虢季子白盘于清朝道光年间出土，和大盂鼎、毛公鼎、散氏盘并称为"晚清四大国宝"。虢季子白盘形制奇特，长度将近140厘米，有人说像是一个大浴缸。

Chapter II Evolution of Chinese Characters

裘卫盉铭文拓片——一份土地买卖的契约
Rubbings of the Qiu Wei Container (He)
— A Contract for the Sale of Land

specific measures for measuring and calculating the value of goods, which was rare in bronze scripts.

When it comes to the Chinese character 朋, people will immediately think of 朋友 (friend) and even think of what Confucius said in *The Analects*, "Isn't it a delight to have friends coming from afar?" In the inscription of Qiu Wei Container, the Chinese character 朋 was written as ▦, 二十朋 was written as ▦, which was the combination of 廿 and 朋, and 廿 meant twenty. ▦ doesn't seem to have any relationship with "friends," nor does it seem like a character combined with two 月. In fact, this Chinese character is also very common in the oracle bone scripts, written as ▦, like two strings of jade on the same rope, forming a larger string of jade. In the Shang Dynasty, it emerged as a currency unit, with five shells as one string and two strings as one peng. This Chinese character evolved over a long period of time and eventually became the current 朋.

7. Ji Zibai Bowl of Guo (Pan)—A National Treasure Used as the Manger

Ji Zibai Bowl of Guo (pan) was unearthed during the Daoguang Period of the Qing Dynasty, and it was included among the "Four National Treasures of the Late Qing Dynasty" with Dayu Cauldron (ding), Duke Mao Cauldron (ding) and San Family Bowl (pan). Ji Zibai Bowl (pan) is strangely shaped and nearly 140 centimeters long. Some people say it resembles a large bathtub.

虢季子白盘
Ji Zibai Bowl of the Guo State (*Pan*)

　　这个盘出土后有一段时间曾被当做马槽用来喂马。据说有一天夜半时分，万籁俱寂，清朝有一位姓刘的将领正在临时指挥中心秉烛读书，忽然听到院中有金属撞击的声音，以为有刺客潜入。众人里里外外搜遍，没有发现刺客的踪影，后仔细聆听，发现声音是从马厩里传出的，是马笼头上的铁环撞击马槽发出的叮当之声。

　　"槽"字的偏旁是"木"字，说明马槽一般为木头所制，铁环撞击马槽不会发出如此清脆的金属声音。刘将军心生疑问，当即命令士兵用灯笼照看，发现马槽原来是一件金属制品，后来将马槽洗刷干净才看清楚是一个铜盘。铜盘内底铸有铭文，字体工整优美。刘将军并非普通的武夫，读过很多古书，认为这种文字是商周时期的古文字。他觉得此物年代久远，必是国宝，设法叫士兵运走保存起来。

　　虢季子白盘铭文共111字，讲述西周时期的一个诸侯国虢国的子白奉命抗击来犯的敌人，斩杀敌人500余人，俘虏50人。周王为子白设宴庆功，并赏赐马匹弓箭等物品，虢季子白因而作盘以为纪念。

　　这篇铭文最后一句是金文中非常常见的吉祥语"子子孙孙万年无疆"，有的金文写法稍有不同，是"子子孙孙永宝用"，含义差别不大，都是希望此器能够永世流传，后世子孙也一如既往地铭记和珍爱祖先的功德与荣耀。"子子孙孙"这四个字在金文中的写法很是特别，大

This bowl had been used as a manger for feeding horses for quite a while after it was unearthed. It is said that one day in the middle of the night, when all was quiet, a general surnamed Liu in the Qing Dynasty was reading by candlestick in the temporary command center. Suddenly, he heard a sound of metal colliding in the courtyard, and thought that an assassin had infiltrated the base. Troops searched inside and out, but could not find any traces of an assassin. Then, they listened carefully, and found that the sound was from the stables—the iron ring on the headstall was hitting the manger.

The Chinese character component of 槽(cáo，manger) is 木(mù, wood), which means that a manger is usually made of wood. But an iron ring should not make such a crisp metal sound when hitting the manger. General Liu was suspicious, and immediately ordered soldiers to inspect the manger with lanterns. As his suspicions confirmed, Liu found that the manger was actually a metal product, and then washed it clean before he could see that it was actually a copper plate. Inscriptions were cast in the inner, bottom surface of the copper plate, and their fonts were neat and beautiful. General Liu was not an ordinary warrior. He had read many ancient books and believed that this kind of writing was the ancient writing of the Shang and Zhou Dynasties. He realized this manger was made a long time ago and must be a national treasure. He managed to get the soldiers to transport and save it.

The inscription on the Ji Zibai Bowl (Pan) has a total of 111 Chinese characters. It tells that Ji Zibai of Guo State, a vassal state during the Western Zhou Dynasty, was ordered to fight the invading enemy, and he killed more than 500 people and captured 50. The king of Zhou Dynasty gave a banquet in honor of Ji Zibai and rewarded him with horses, bows and arrows, and other items. Ji Zibai made this bowl as a memorial.

The last sentence of this inscription was a very common auspicious phrase in bronze scripts: 子子孙孙万年无疆(zǐ zǐ sūn sūn wàn nián wú jiāng，offspring will multiply for ever). Some of the writings were slightly different, such as 子子孙孙永宝用(zǐ zǐ sūn sūn yǒng bǎo yòng，offspring will cherish it for ever), and their meanings were slightly different. All inscriptions hoped this bowl would last forever, and the descendants will always remember and cherish the merits and glory of their ancestors. The writing of Chinese characters 子子孙孙 was

都写成 ，即在"子"的右下角和"孙"的下面加了两短横。这和前面所说的"合文" 字是两个概念，因为这两短横不是文字，只是指示性符号，叫做"重文号"，表示一个字连续出现两次。直到现在，人们在非正式的书写场合仍然用两短横来表示这样重复出现的字，只不过有的用两点或者符号"々"来表示。尤其是当一个字笔画非常多的时候，人们更乐意使用这个符号。这种符号的出现，也反映了古人的智慧，青铜器制作不易，铸造铭文更加复杂，人们这么做的可能是为了省时省力吧。

8. 宋公栾簠——战国时代的嫁妆

宋公栾簠出土于河南省信阳市。簠是祭祀和宴飨时盛放黍、稷、稻、粱等饭食的器具。簠的基本形制为长方形，盖和器身形状相同，大小一样，上下对称，合在一起是一件器物，分开可以当做两个器皿。

春秋战国时期，诸侯国之间连年征战，有时为了对付敌人而通过婚姻关系结盟，并由此产生了一个成语"秦晋之好"。春秋时秦、晋两国不止一代互相婚嫁，代表的是一种政治上的联姻，是国家之间的联合，

宋公栾簠
Duke Luan of Song Vessel (Fu)

very special in bronze scripts, and they were written as ▨ ▨in large numbers, just adding two short horizontals in the lower right corner of the 子 and under the 孙. This case is a different concept from "combinations of characters" (▨) mentioned above, because these two short horizontals are not Chinese characters, but only indicative symbols, called重文号(chóng wén hào), indicating that a Chinese character appears twice in succession. Until now, people still use two short horizontals to express such repeated Chinese characters in informal writing situations, but some use two dots or the symbol " 々." Especially when there is a Chinese character with a lot of strokes, people are more apt to use this symbol. The appearance of such symbols also reflects the wisdom of past ancestors. Bronze wares were difficult to make, and casting inscriptions were complicated. People likely resorted to this strategy to save valuable time and effort.

8. Duke Luan of Song Vessel (*Fu*) —The Dowry of the Warring States Period

Duke Luan of Song Vessel (*Fu*) was unearthed in Xinyang, Henan Province. *Fu* was a food container at the time of sacrifice and feasting. The basic shape of the *Fu* is rectangular. Its cover and body have the same shape, the same size, and longitudinal symmetry. When *Fu*'s cover and body are put together, they become a utensil, but when separated, they can be used as two vessels.

During the Spring and Autumn Period and the Warring States Period, vassal states fought for years, and they sometimes formed alliances through marriage in order to deal with a common enemy; thus an idiom came into being: "the amity between Qin and Jin (sealed by a marriage alliance between the two royal families)." In the Spring and Autumn Period, multiple generations of the Qin State and the Jin State married each other, representing a political marriage, a

后来渐渐将男女之间的婚姻也称作"秦晋之好"。

宋公栾簠便是春秋时宋国和吴国联姻的一件实物凭证，簠的器和盖有着相同的铭文共20字："有殷天乙唐（湯）孙，宋公欒作其妹句吴夫人季子滕簠。"宋国原是商朝王室微子启的封国，就是现在的河南省商丘市。宋公栾簠是宋公为其妹季子嫁给吴王夫差所做用于陪嫁的嫁妆，为研究春秋晚期宋、吴两国的关系提供了珍贵的实物资料。

铭文中宋公自称是殷的后裔，而没有说是商的后裔。商王盘庚于公元前14世纪将都城迁到殷，殷作为商朝都城一直到公元前11世纪商朝灭亡，所以商也叫殷，有时连称殷商。商朝灭亡后，都城成为废墟，这也是殷墟的由来。

9. 鄂君启节——古代的通关文牒

鄂君启节于1957年出土于安徽省寿县，外形像剖开的竹子，有车节和舟节两种，是楚王发给鄂城的最高长官鄂君启的水陆两路运输货物的通行凭证。启是鄂君的名字，节是古时由帝王或政府颁发的用于水陆交通的凭证，类似现在的通行证。早期的竹节是用剖开的竹子所做，后来虽然用青铜铸造，但仍然做成竹节的形状。

鄂君启节铭文详细记载了楚王对启进行水陆运输的种种规定，如车船数目、通行路线、装运货物和关税征收等。

union between countries, and later the marriages between men and women were gradually called "the amity between Qin and Jin" as well.

Duke Luan of Song Vessel (*Fu*) is one physical remainder of the marriage between Song State and Wu State in the Spring and Autumn Period. Its body and cover have the same 20-word inscriptions: "有殷天乙唐（湯）孫，宋公欒作其妹句吳夫人季子媵簠." The Song State once was a vassal state of Wei Ziqi who was a member of the royal family in the Shang Dynasty, which is now Shangqiu City in Henan Province. Duke Luan of Song Vessel (Fu) was among the dowries Duke Luan of Song prepared for the marriage of his sister Ji Zi and King Fu Chai of Wu, and it provided valuable material for studying the relationship between the Song State and the Wu State in the late Spring and Autumn Period.

In the inscription, Duke Luan claimed to be a descendant of Yin, but did not say that he was a descendant of Shang. He omitted this lineage because King Pan Geng of the Shang Dynasty moved his capital to Yin in the 14th century BC; accordingly, Yin stood as the capital of the Shang Dynasty until the end of the Shang Dynasty in the 11th century BC. Thus, Shang was also called Yin, and sometimes they were called Yin Shang . After the Shang Dynasty perished, the capital became ruins, and this is the origin of the Yin Ruins.

9. Lord Qi of State E Tallies (*Jie*) —Ancient Customs Clearance

Lord Qi of State E Tallies (*Jie*) was unearthed in Shouxian County, Anhui Province in 1957. Resembling a split bamboo, tallies had two kinds: one for vehicles and the other for boats. It granted permission from King Huai of Chu for Lord Qi, the supreme governor of the State E, to transport goods by land and water. Qi is the name of the lord of the State E. A tally is a certificate issued by the emperor or the government for water and land transportation in ancient times, similar to a modern-day traffic permit. The early bamboo joints were made of split bamboo. Later, although they were cast by bronze, they were still cast into the shape of bamboo joints.

The inscription on the Lord Qi of State E Tallies (*Jie*) gives a detailed record of the king of Chu's requirements about Lord Qi's water and land transportation, including the number of vehicles and boats, the routes, the items as well as taxes.

鄂君启节
Lord Qi of State E Tallies (*Jie*)

　　鄂君启节用了中国青铜时代的一项特殊的精细工艺——金银错工艺。简单来说，金银错就是在器物上布置金银图案纹饰，主要有镶嵌和涂画两种方法。青铜器上的铭文最早是铸造的，后来又有錾刻上去的，但是，无论是铸的，还是錾刻的，铭文与铜器的本色没有区别。金银错工艺兴起后，人们在铜器上用黄金错成铭文，这样，铭文就熠熠生辉，人们一见到青铜器，金光闪动的铭文就抢先进入眼睛，尤其是青铜器经过地下千年埋藏，表面已变成颜色很深的铜绿色，而金银错铭文的光辉丝毫不减，就好像夏夜深蓝色天空闪烁的星星，异常美观。

10. 越王勾践剑——王者之剑

　　越王勾践剑于1965年出土于湖北省江陵县，通长55.7厘米，靠近手柄处有鸟虫书铭文8字"越王勾踐自乍用劍"。此剑保存完好，历经2000多年，仍然光泽悦目、锋利无比。

　　剑的主人越王勾践在中国是家喻户晓，成语"卧薪尝胆"就是关于他的事迹。薪指柴草，成语大意是睡觉睡在柴草上，吃饭睡觉前都尝一

Lord Qi of State E Tallies (*Jie*) used an especially fine crafting method in the Chinese Bronze Age—Jinyincuo craft. Jinyincuo refers to decorating the utensil with gold and silver patterns, mainly by the method of inlaying and painting. The inscription on the bronze wares was first cast, and later engraved, but regardless of method, the natural color of inscriptions and bronze wares was maintained. After the rise of the Jinyincuo craft, people painted gold inscriptions on the bronze wares. In this way, the inscriptions would be sparkling. When people see bronze wares, those gleaming inscriptions would be the first to catch the eye. In particular, after being buried underground for thousands of years, the surface of bronze wares has turned into a deep copper-green color, but the brilliance of the inscriptions made by Jinyincuo craft has not diminished at all. The inscriptions were just like the stars twinkling in the dark blue sky on summer nights, extremely beautiful.

10. The Sword of King Gou Jian of Yue—Sword of Kings

The Sword of King Gou Jian of Yue was unearthed in Jiangling County, Hubei Province in 1965. It has a length of 55.7 cm and an 8-character inscription close to the handle, 越王勾踐自乍用劍 (yuè wáng gōu jiàn zì zhà yòng jiàn , King Gou Jian of Yue's sword). This sword is well preserved, and has maintained its shean and sharpness for more than 2000 years.

The master of the sword, King Gou Jian of Yue, is widely known in China. The idiom 卧薪尝胆(wò xīn cháng dǎn, enduring present hardships to revive) is about his deeds. The Chinese character 薪 refers to firewood. The idiom refers

尝苦胆。原来指中国春秋时期的越王勾践励精图治以图复国的事迹，后用来形容人刻苦自励、发奋图强，最终能够苦尽甘来。

剑上的铭文和别的金文有较大区别，可以说是金文的一种艺术性变体，在字体的上下两端加饰有鸟形或虫形图案纹饰，表现出浓厚的装饰意味，有人称之为鸟虫书，主要流行于南方的楚、蔡、吴、越等诸侯国。

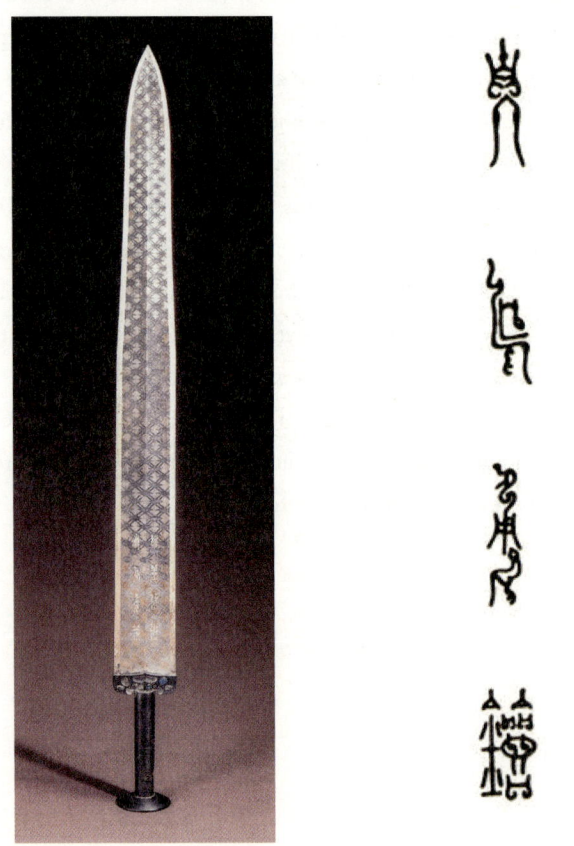

越王勾践剑
The Sword of King Gou Jian of Yue

to sleeping on firewood and tasting the gall bladder before eating and sleeping in order to strengthen one's resolution to wipe out a national humiliation or to attain an ambition. Originally, this idiom was inspired by the story of King Gou Jian of Yue in the Spring and Autumn Period who made great efforts to revitalize his country. From then on, it has been used to describe someone who finally acquires success through hard work and firm resolve.

The inscription on the sword was quite different from other bronze scripts of its time, as it featured a distinct artistic variation. Bird or insect patterns were engraved on the upper and lower ends of the inscription, displaying a strong decorative meaning. Some people called them bird-and-insect script which was mainly popular in the southern vassal states, such as Chu, Cai, Wu and Yue.

先看 ![字], 这是"王"字, 三横没有大的变化, 一竖变得婉转曲折, 字的上面有一对儿对称的蛇形线条装饰。再看 ![字], 这是"用"字, 中间的"用"字非常清晰, 一目了然, "用"字的上下分别是两个鸟形的装饰, 鸟的形象简洁明了。通过这两个字可以看出, 这种添加的装饰没有一点实用性, 主要是为了美观, 甚至为了增加器物主人的权威。

认真对比金文和甲骨文就会发现, 两者有着显著的不同。毛笔是商代主要的书写工具, 所以金文在制作过程中基本上保持了毛笔字的样子。金文布局严整规矩, 字体结构整齐, 笔画圆润精美、清晰流畅。而甲骨文就不同了, 在坚硬的甲骨上刻字, 非常费时费力。刻字的人为了提高效率, 不得不改变毛笔字的笔法, 主要是改圆形为方形, 改填实为勾廓, 改粗笔为细笔。所以甲骨文布局参差错综, 字体大小不一, 笔画较细, 方笔较多。

	天	日	父	子
甲骨文 Oracle Bone Script				
金文 Bronze Inscription				

甲骨文与金文对比举例
Comparison of Bronze Scripts and Oracle Bone Scripts

Firstly, 𐆉 is the Chinese character 王. The three horizontal strokes don't have great variation and the vertical stroke becomes mildly tortuous. The top of this Chinese character features a pair of symmetrical snakelike lines for decoration. Secondly, 𐆊 is the Chinese character 用. Easily recognizable by its middle, the character is also decorated with two simple bird patterns on the top and bottom. Though these characters are beautiful, they also demonstrate that the added decoration has no practical value; it was mainly for the sake of beauty, or to enhance the authority of the owner of the utensil.

A careful comparison of bronze scripts and oracle bone scripts reveals that there is a significant difference between them. The writing brush was the main writing instrument in the Shang Dynasty, so bronze inscriptions essentially take on the forms of brush-written characters in engraving. The layout of bronze inscription was strict and regular, the font structure was neat, and the strokes were round and exquisite, clear and smooth. On the contrary, lettering on the hard oracle bones was very time-consuming and laborious. In order to improve efficiency, people had to change the brushwork of calligraphy, mainly by changing circles to squares, infilling strokes to outlining them, and replacing thick pens with fine pens. Therefore, the layout of oracle bone scripts was irregular and intricate, the font size was different, and the strokes were finer and squarer.

二、小篆

中国自古以来就是一个疆域辽阔的国家，在如此大的疆域之中，存在着许多种不同的语言，或者说方言，彼此之间的差异很大，不必说顺利沟通，有时候甚至完全听不懂。但无论说什么语言，却一直共用同一种文字——汉字，这和秦朝建立统一的国家并在全国推行小篆有着莫大的关系，秦朝建立了以小篆为代表的单一文字系统。

春秋战国时期，中国出现了长达500多年的诸侯割据局面，社会发生了剧烈变化。这对汉字的发展也产生了巨大的影响，同一个汉字各诸侯国出现了多种不同写法的情况，字形的地域差异现象非常严重，远远超出了前后各个时代。秦王嬴政于公元前221年消灭其他诸侯国，建立了统一的国家，国号为秦，并在全国开展了多项统一措施。文字方面，把原来秦国通行的文字规范成小篆，然后在全国推行。

春秋战国时期，诸侯国之间的征伐连绵不断，由最初的100多个变为后来的"战国七雄"，即齐、楚、燕、韩、赵、魏、秦。这七个诸侯国实际上已发展成为相对独立的国家，文字也逐渐形成了晋、楚、齐、燕、秦五大文字体系。春秋时期的晋国后来分裂为韩、赵、魏三国，这三国的文字比较接近，所以统称为晋系文字。

秦、楚、晋、齐、燕文字对比

Comparison of Qin, Chu, Jin, Qi and Yan Characters

Ⅱ. Small Seal Script

China has been a vast country since ancient times. In such a large territory, there exist many different languages or dialects. They are very different from each other. Therefore, sometimes people cannot understand each other at all,not to mention smooth communication. However, no matter what language is spoken, it always shares the same characters—Chinese characters, which are closely related to the establishment of the Qin Dynasty (a unified state) and the implementation of small seal script throughout the country. The Qin Dynasty established a single writing system represented by small seal script.

During the Spring and Autumn Period and the Warring States Period, China had a ruling system of vassal separatist regimes that lasted for over 500 years, during which society underwent dramatic changes. This also had a large impact on the development of Chinese characters. For a single character, there could be many different forms of writing in the different vassal states. The geographical difference between character patterns was far more drastic in this period than in the dynasties that ruled before and after the vassal states. In 221 B.C., Emperor Ying Zheng of the Qin Dynasty ruled out other vassal states, established a unified country, the name of which was Qin, and carried out numerous unified measures throughout the country. In terms of characters, the original characters of the Qin State were standardized into small seal script, which was then implemented throughout the country.

During the Spring and Autumn Period and the Warring States Period, the mutual conquering between the vassal states was continuous, and those states eventually dwindled from over a hundred to what later became known as the "Seven Powers in the Warring States Period," namely Qi, Chu, Yan, Han, Zhao, Wei and Qin States. These seven vassal states actually developed into relatively independent kingdoms, and their characters gradually formed five major systems, that is, Jin, Chu, Qi, Yan and Qin Scripts. Jin State of the Spring and Autumn Period was later divided into three kingdoms: Han, Zhao and Wei States. The character of these three kingdoms resembled each other relatively closely, so they were collectively called Jin Script.

1. 温县盟书——晋系文字

盟书是天子与诸侯、诸侯与诸侯、诸侯与大夫之间向神盟誓时写在玉石上的文字，上面记载了盟誓活动的内容。盟书通常1式2份，1份在盟府，1份则埋入地下，表示有神灵做证，不得反悔。

温县位于今河南省境内，春秋时期隶属于晋国，温县盟书上的文字属于晋系文字，对于今天的人们来说，不是很容易辨认。根据盟书文辞中"十五年十二月己未朔"推算，盟誓的时间是晋定公十五年（公元前497年）十二月二十七日，主盟人为韩氏宗主，晋国六卿中的韩简子由晋国都城返回他的都邑州城之后，为争取支持打击敌对势力所进行的一次盟誓记录。

2. 郭店竹简——楚系文字

竹简指的是中国古人写字用的细长竹片，是植物纤维纸发明以前中国古代文字最主要的书写材料。竹简的制作一般包括备料、选材、片解、刮削、杀青、编联等工序。竹简制作成形后，一般是先用绳子把单个的竹简编在一起，然后再抄写文献，也有先抄写再编联的。

从文献记载和有关的文字形体来推断，竹简早在商朝就已经出现了。中国古籍《尚书》记载："惟殷先人有册有典。"殷指的就是商

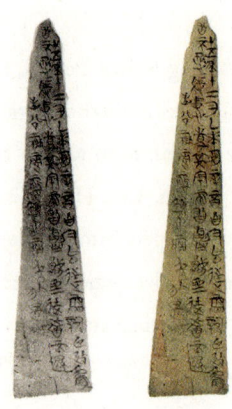

温县盟书
Wen County Allied Oath

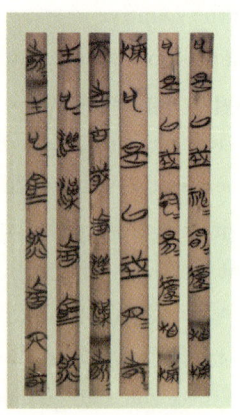

郭店竹简
Guodian Bamboo Slips

1. Wen County Allied Oath—Jin Script

The allied oath was written on jade to record the pledge taken by the emperor and the dukes or the officials. The allied oath was usually made in duplicates, with one kept in the office preserving the allied oath documents and the other buried underground, indicating that there was god to bear witness, so no one could go back on his words.

Wen County is located in today's Henan Province, belonging to the State of Jin in the Spring and Autumn Period. The characters on it belong to the Jin Script, which is not easy to recognize for today's people. The oath was taken on December 27th, the fifteenth year of the reign of Duke Ding of Jin (497 B.C.) according to the record in the allied oath. This allied oath recording an oath taken by Han Jianzi, the leader of Han family and one of the six ministers in the Jin State was made after Han Jianzi had returned to his capital city of Zhoucheng from the capital of the Jin State, intending to muster support for fighting against the enemy.

2. Guodian Bamboo Slips—Chu Script

Bamboo slips refer to slender bamboo strips used by ancient Chinese to write on, and they were the main writing materials in ancient China before the invention of plant fiber paper. The production of bamboo slips generally includes the processes of material preparation and material selection before flaking, scraping, water-removing and weaving. After bamboo slips are produced and take shape, they are usually composed of individual bamboo slips with ropes; documents are then copied, while some are copied first and then linked.

Based on literary records and related written forms, bamboo slips appeared as early as the Shang Dynasty. The Chinese ancient book *Shangshu* (*The Book of History*) records that 惟殷先人有册有典(wéi yīn xiān rén yǒu cè yǒu diǎn, Only Yin ancestors have books). Yin refers to the Shang Dynasty. This sentence suggests that the ancestors of people in the Shang Dynasty had already begun using bamboo slips to record significant events. The Chinese character 册 in

朝,这句话是说商人的先祖就已经用典册来记载大事了。甲骨文"册"字写作卌,金文"册"字写作卌,"册"字很明显是一个象形字,像是用两根绳子编联的若干根细长的竹简,而"典"字写作卌,则是在"册"字的基础上引申出来的,为双手捧册的形状,用手将竹简拿起来读,或者合起来保存。只不过竹木材质容易腐烂,商朝的典册没能保存下来,或者说现在还没有发现。

郭店竹简是考古发掘出土的楚简中先秦典籍的一次重大发现。1993年10月出土于湖北省荆门市,共有894枚,时代为战国晚期,保存相当完整,内容都是儒家、道家文献,共18种。由于抄写者的不同,郭店楚简的书写风格多有不同,但都比较清晰地展示了战国时代楚系文字的主要特征。

3. 杜虎符——秦系文字

符是中国古代朝廷传达命令、征调兵将以及用于各项事务的一种凭证。用金、银、玉、角、竹、木等不同原料制成,用时双方各执一半,合在一起可以验证符的真假。杜虎符是现存最早的一件调兵凭证,一个虎形符从中间剖为左右两半,右半边留存于朝廷,左半边交地方官吏或统兵将帅保管,使用时两半相合,表示命令验证可信,进而可以调动兵马。

杜虎符
Du Tiger-Shaped Tally (*Fu*)

the oracle bone scripts is written as 册, and written as 册 in bronze scripts. It is obviously a pictographic character, like a number of slender bamboo slips woven with two ropes. The Chinese character 典 is written as 典, which is derived from the character 册. It keeps the shape of holding a book with both hands, holding the bamboo slips by hand for reading, or holding them together for preservation. However, bamboo materials rot easily, and the Shang Dynasty's books have been unable to be preserved or have not yet been found.

The Guodian Bamboo Slips are a major discovery of the bamboo slips of Chu in the pre-Qin Period unearthed in archaeological excavations. They were unearthed in Jingmen City, Hubei Province in October 1993. They had 894 pieces belonging to the late Warring States Period, and they were well preserved. Their contents are all Confucian and Taoist documents, totaling 18 kinds. Due to the different copyists, the writing styles of Guodian Bamboo Slips are different, but they clearly show the main features of Chu scripts in the Warring States Period.

3. Du Tiger-Shaped Tally (*Fu*)—Qin Script

Fu is one type of certificate used by the ancient Chinese court to convey orders, recruit and transfer soldiers, as well as conduct various affairs. It was made of different materials such as gold, silver, jade, horn, bamboo, and wood. Each party held one half of the certificate, which together could verify the authenticity of the *Fu*. Du Tiger-Shaped Tally (*Fu*) is the earliest existing certificate of troop deployment. It is split into two halves from the middle, the right side intended to be kept by the emperor while the left side was handed over to local officials or commanders of armies. When used, the two halves are combined into one, indicating that the command is verified, and thus military forces can be mobilized.

杜虎符以老虎为形，用威猛的虎来鼓舞战士的斗志，在虎的颈部有一个穿孔，可以系绳。这件兵符上有错金铭文9行40字，其中有10个字为"兵甲之符，右在君，左在杜"，"君"指国君，"杜"是一个地名，明确标明虎符左右两半在何处保管。

从上面的晋系、楚系、秦系文字可以看出，诸侯之间的文字差异比较大，这严重影响了各地区之间在经济、文化等方面的交流。秦始皇统一全国后，迅速进行了统一文字的工作，六国文字与秦国文字不一致的异体字都被废除。

秦始皇要用秦国文字统一全国文字，首先需要对秦国文字本身作一番整理，拿出一种标准字体来。这种标准字体就是小篆，由春秋战国时代的秦国文字逐渐演变而成。小篆的字体整体呈长方形，字体结构讲究平衡对称，笔画横平竖直，粗细基本一致。

4. 铜方升——刻有皇帝诏书的量器

升是古代测定谷物体积的一种量器。始皇诏方升呈长方形，一边有手柄，外壁一侧竖刻秦始皇二十六年诏书，诏书共三行40字，简要说明了统一度量衡的历史背景和统一要求。诏书内容大意是：秦始皇二十六年，皇帝兼并了天下各国诸侯，百姓安居乐业，下诏书给两位丞相，要求把混乱的和不统一的度量衡都统一起来。

铜方升

Oblong Bronze Sheng

Du Tiger-Shaped Tally (Fu) takes the shape of a powerful tiger to inspire soldiers' morale. There is a hole in the tiger's neck that can be tethered. There are inlaid gold inscriptions with nine lines and 40 characters on this military symbol, of which ten characters are "兵甲之符，右在君，左在杜"(bīng jiǎ zhī fú，yòu zài jūn，zuǒ zài dù, the commander's tally, the right half kept by the emperor and the left half kept in Du). The character 君 refers to the emperor, and the character 杜 is a place name, clearly indicating where the left and right halves of the Tiger-Shaped Tally are kept.

From the above scripts of Jin, Chu and Qin, we can see that there were great differences between the vassal states, which seriously affected the economic and cultural exchanges between different regions. After Qin Shi Huang (First Emperor of Qin) (259 B.C.-210 B.C.) unified the whole country, he quickly carried out the work of unifying characters, and the variant characters which were inconsistent with the characters of the Qin State in the six kingdoms were subsequently abolished.

Qin Shi Huang wanted to unify the national characters with Qin characters. First of all, he needed to sort out the Qin characters and come up with a standard font. This standard font was small seal script, which had gradually evolved from Qin characters of the Spring and Autumn and Warring States Periods. The overall character of small seal script was rectangular, with balanced and symmetrical character structure, horizontal and vertical strokes with typically the same thickness.

4. Oblong Bronze Sheng—A Measuring Vessel Engraved with Qin Shi Huang' s Edict

Sheng was a measuring vessel used to measure grain volume in ancient times. This Oblong Bronze Sheng is a rectangle, with a holder on one side, and an outer wall engraved with Qin Shi Huang's edict. The edict was issued in the 26th year of his reign, with a total of three lines and 40 characters, briefly describing the historical background and unification requirements of the unified measurement. The main content of this edict states that, in the 26th year of his reign, Qin Shi Huang unified China by defeating all other states, and people lived and worked in peace and contentment. Qin Shi Huang wrote an edict to two prime ministers, demanding that measures and weights should be made uniform.

这个铜方升便是秦朝颁行的标准量器,秦始皇二十六年是公元前221年,也是秦始皇统一全国的元年。统一之初就颁发诏书,可见统一度量衡的重要性和急迫性。除了直接刻在器物上,有时还把诏书制作成铜诏版,再把铜诏版镶嵌到大的铁权上,即使铁权生锈皇帝的诏书也能长久保存。

5.峄山刻石——小篆的代表

秦始皇统一全国后,为了加强对全国的控制,多次到各地巡视。公元前219年,他出巡到山东省的峄山时,登高远望,激情满怀,对群臣说道:"朕既到此,不可不加留铭,遗传后世。"丞相李斯当即用小篆书写颂扬秦始皇统一全国功绩的文字,派人刻成石碑,并立在峄山上,这就是著名的峄山刻石。

李斯曾任秦朝的丞相,在秦统一文字时做出了突出贡献,他主持了小篆的标准制作和在全国的推广。许慎在《说文解字》中说:李斯等人制作标准字样时,是在秦国原来文字大篆的基础上进行省改创制而成的,而小篆的名称也是为了尊崇大篆而谦称为"小篆"的。为

峄山刻石拓片

The Rubbing of the Stele of Mount Yishan

The Oblong Bronze Sheng is the standard measuring vessel issued by the Qin Dynasty. The 26th year of Qin Shi Huang's reign was 221 B.C., and it was also the first year of Qin Shi Huang's unification of the whole country. At the very beginning of the national unification, imperial edicts were issued, which showed the importance and urgency of unifying weights and measures. In addition to the edicts that were inscribed on implements, some were made into a copperplate edict, and then laid on a big iron weight. Even if the iron weight rusted, the emperor's edicts could be preserved for a long time.

5. The Stele of Mount Yishan—The Representative of Small Seal Script

In order to strengthen control over the country, Qin Shi Huang conducted frequent inspections around the nation. In 219 B.C., he arrived at Mount Yishan in Shandong Province. Ascending afar, he said to his courtiers passionately, "There should be an inscription recording my being here to tell the later generations." Prime Minister Li Si immediately wrote an inscription in small seal script, extolling Qin Shi Huang's achievements of unifying the country. Then he directed people to carve it into stele and erect it on Mount Yishan, thus creating the famous Stele of Mount Yishan.

Prime Minister Li Si made a prominent contribution to the unification of characters in the Qin Dynasty. He presided over the standard production of small seal script and its corresponding promotional work throughout the country. Xu Shen said in his book *Shuowen Jiezi* (*The Explanation of Script and Elucidation of Characters*) that the standard model of written characters made by Li Si and others was created from the original script of Qin, big seal script, and the name of small seal script was also a modest appellation of the big seal script. In order to promote the unified characters, Li Si wrote *Cang Jie Pian* with seven chapters by

了推广统一的文字，李斯亲自作《仓颉篇》七章，作为学习小篆的课本，供人临摹。

遗憾的是，峄山刻石原石已毁，现在的碑为宋代人翻刻，现藏在西安碑林。秦朝的小篆遗留下来的真迹很少，峄山刻石因笔画匀整、圆润流畅、风格秀丽而深受人们的青睐，可以毫不夸张地说，峄山刻石是秦小篆的代表作。

6. 瓦当文字——别具一格的小篆

到了汉代，隶书取代小篆成为主要字体，小篆的实用功能大大削弱，装饰性功能逐渐突出。

瓦当俗称瓦头，是中国古代建筑中覆盖建筑檐头筒瓦前端的遮挡，是古建筑的重要构件，起着保护木制飞檐和美化屋面轮廓的作用。瓦当上最初制作有图案，后来出现文字。瓦当文字盛于秦汉时期，秦汉宫殿楼台屋顶瓦当上的文字，多为小篆字体，排列组织和谐匀称、布局讲究，具有极高的艺术观赏性。

"汉并天下"瓦当
Eaves Tile of "Han Bing Tian Xia"

himself as a textbook for learning small seal script and for people to copy.

Unfortunately, the original stele was destroyed and what we see now is the stele duplicated in the Song Dynasty, and it is now collected in the forest of steles in Xi'an, Shaanxi Province. Authentic works of small seal script from the Qin Dynasty are rare, and the Stele of Mount Yishan is widely appreciated for its neat strokes, smoothness and beautiful style. Thus, we can say with no exaggeration that it is the masterpiece of the small seal script of the Qin Dynasty.

6. Inscriptions on the Eaves Tile—A Distinctive Style of Small Seal Script

During the Han Dynasty, small seal script was replaced by clerical script. The practical function of small seal script greatly weakened, but its decoration function gradually stood out.

The eaves tile, commonly known as watou (tile head), was a shield covering the front end of the eaves in ancient Chinese architecture. As an important component of ancient architecture, it played a role in protecting wooden eaves and beautifying the roof outline. Originally, there were patterns on the eaves tile, and then characters began appearing. The inscriptions on eaves tiles were popular in the Qin and Han Dynasties, when most of the characters on the palace buildings were small seal script, with harmonious and symmetrical arrangement as well as exquisite layout, demonstrating high artistic and aesthetic standards.

长生无极　　　　长生未央　　　　长乐未央　　　　羽阳千秋
chǎng shēng wú　chǎng shēng　　chǎng lè wèi　　yǔ yáng qiān qiū,
jí, Immortality　wèi yāng,　　　yāng, Boundless　Yuyang Palace
　　　　　　　Everlasting Life　Happiness　　　Eaves Tile

竹泉宫当　　　　蕲年宫当　　　　巨杨冢当　　　　万岁冢当
zhú quán gōng　qí nián gōng dāng,　jù yáng zhǒng　wàn suì zhǒng
dāng, Zhuquan　Qinian Palace　　dāng, Yang Burial　dāng, Long Live
Palace Eaves Tile　Eaves Tile　　　　　　　　　　　Burial

瓦当文字四个字的较多，章法布局端庄美观，且具有突出的思想内涵，是形式与内容高度统一的艺术品。瓦当文字分标名类和吉祥语类两大类别。标名类是在瓦当上写明建筑物的名称，即宫殿、官署的名称，如"蕲年宫当""羽阳千秋""竹泉宫当"等。吉祥语类瓦当是表达人们祈祷吉祥的愿望，如"长生未央""长乐未央"等。除此以外，陵墓建筑物上用的是"冢"字瓦当，如"万岁冢当""巨杨冢当"等。

7. 墓志盖——长久使用小篆的石刻

墓志是指刻有死者生平事迹的石刻，一般放置于死者的棺柩前面，埋在墓穴中。墓志大都有盖，盖上刻有标题，即墓主人所处的朝代、官职、姓氏等信息，盖下为墓志，刻有墓志铭，详细记载死者官职、姓名、族源、生平事迹、卒葬时地、配偶子嗣及对死者的赞颂言辞等。

Most of eaves tiles were inscribed with four characters, with dignified and beautiful composition layouts and prominent ideological connotations. Altogther, they were works of art with highly unified form and content. The inscriptions on eaves tiles can be divided into two categories: the labeling category and the auspicious words category. The labeling category was intended for clearly writing the names of buildings on eaves tiles, namely, the titles of palaces and official departments, such as 蕲年宫当(qí nián gōng dāng, Qinian Palace Eaves Tile), 羽阳千秋 (yǔ yáng qiān qiū,Yuyang Palace Eaves Tile) and 竹泉宫当(zhú quán gōng dāng, Zhuquan Palace Eaves Tile). The auspicious words category was used to express people's wish for luck, such as 长生未央(chǎng shēng wèi yāng, Everlasting Life), and 长乐未央(chǎng lè wèi yāng, Boundless Happiness). In addition, the eaves tiles of mausoleum buildings were decorated with the character of 冢(zhǒng,Tomb), such as 万岁冢当(wàn suì zhǒng dāng, Long Live Burial) and 巨杨冢当(jù yáng zhǒng dāng, Yang Burial).

7. Inscription on the Tombstone Lid—Stone Inscription always in Small Seal Script

An inscription on the tombstone refers to the stone inscription engraved with the life story of the deceased, usually placed in front of the coffin and buried in the tomb. Most of them have a lid engraved with titles—about the dynasty, official position, surname, and other information of the tomb owners. Placed under the lid, the inscription on the tombstone is inscribed with epitaphs detailing the official position, name, ethnic origin, life story, burial time and place, spouse, children of the deceased, and praise for him.

北宋韩琦夫妇墓志盖拓片
The Rubbings of the Inscription on the Tomb Lid of Han Qi and His Wife in the Northern Song Dynasty

墓志内容的书写以楷书居多，墓志盖多用小篆书写，这种惯例一直保持到清朝末年，直到墓志的消失。墓志盖可以说是小篆字体使用时间最长的载体之一。

韩琦是北宋时期著名的政治家，死后葬于河南省安阳市。他的墓志于2009年发掘出土，长、宽都是155厘米，是目前发现的尺寸最大的墓志。墓志盖由北宋时期的政治家、书法家文彦博用小篆书写，共5行20字，即"宋故司徒兼侍中赠尚书令魏国忠献韩公墓志铭"。韩琦妻子崔氏的墓志盖上共有小篆字体9个，即"宋安国夫人崔氏墓铭"。

在中国，天南海北的人可能由于高山大河的天然地形阻绝而不相往来，但他们可以念一样的书，学习一样的历史和文化，通过汉字进行全面对话而没有任何障碍。中国汉字的这种超越语音的优越性，和秦始皇用小篆统一全国的文字密不可分。

秦朝统一文字是中国历史上第一次运用行政手段大规模地规范文字的产物。它结束了春秋战国以来汉字的混乱局面，促进了文化交流与民族融合，是汉字发展史上的一个里程碑。更重要的是，文字的统一带来交流的方便，为以后中国的大一统国家模式奠定了良好的基础。

The epitaph is mostly written in the regular script, and the inscription on the tomb lid is usually written in small seal script. This convention lasted until the epitaph disappeared by the end of the Qing Dynasty. The inscription on the tomb lid can be said to be one of the longest-used carriers of small seal script.

Han Qi was a famous politician in the Northern Song Dynasty, buried in Anyang City, Henan Province after his death. His inscription on the tombstone was excavated in 2009. It is 155 centimeters long and wide, and it is the largest inscription on a tombstone ever found. His inscription on the tomb lid was written in small seal script by Wen Yanbo, a politician and calligrapher in the Northern Song Dynasty, with a total of 5 lines and 20 characters: "宋故司徒兼侍中赠尚书令魏国忠献韩公墓志铭" (the epitaph of Han Qi, well-known as minister, privy counselor and chief secretary in the Song Dynasty). The inscription on the tomb lid of Han Qi's wife whose surname is Cui has a total of nine characters in small seal script: "宋安国夫人崔氏墓铭" (the epitaph of Lady Cui, renowned for Anguo Lady in the Song Dynasty).

In China, people all over the country may be separated from each other by the natural terrain of mountains and rivers, but they can read the same books, learn the same history and culture, and have a comprehensive dialogue through Chinese characters without any obstacles. The ability of Chinese characters to transcend pronunciation is largely attributed to the First Emperor of Qin and his unification of the whole country with small seal script.

Unifying characters by the Qin Dynasty was the first time for a dynasty to take administrative means to standardize them in large scale in Chinese history. It ended the chaotic state of Chinese characters since the Spring and Autumn Period and the Warring States Period, promoted cultural exchange and ethnic integration, and served as a milestone in the history of the development of Chinese characters. More importantly, the unification of characters has brought convenience for communication, which laid a crucial foundation for China's unified national model in the future.

三、隶书

隶书起源于战国时期，因简便方正、通俗易写，在汉朝正式取代小篆，成为官方字体。从此以后，汉字的象形性特征彻底消失，汉字的笔画逐渐定型。在汉字形体演变的过程中，由小篆变为隶书，是最重要的一次变革。这次变革使汉字的面貌发生了极大的变化，对汉字的结构也产生了很大影响，可以说是汉字形体上最重要的一次简化。

小篆变为隶书，首先是字体结构从竖向发展朝着横向转变，其次是笔画有很大的变化，圆笔变为直笔，连笔改为断笔，笔画可以有粗细，所有这些，都使得书写更加便利、快捷、实用。

小篆和隶书对比举例
Examples Comparing Small Seal Script and Clerical Script

III. Clerical Script

Originating from the Warring States Period (5th century B.C. and 221 B.C.), clerical script was simple, square, popular, and easy to write; it replaced the small seal script and became the primary script of the Han Dynasty. Later, the pictographic features of Chinese characters vanished, and the strokes of Chinese characters were gradually categorized. During the morphological evolution of Chinese characters, the replacement of small seal script by clerical script is one of the most important reforms; the reform exerted a great influence on the structure of Chinese characters and was the most significant simplification in form.

Compared with small seal script, the font structure of clerical script changed from the vertical to the lateral direction, followed by a great change in strokes from round to straight, unbroken to broken, and from identical to varied in thickness. These developments led to a faster, more convenient, and more practical writing style.

1. 黑夫木牍——中国最早的家书

木牍是指写在较宽的木板上的文字，比竹简要宽，一枚竹简一般写一行，而一块儿木牍可以写好几行。黑夫木牍是迄今为止中国发现最早的家信实物，写信人是秦国的两个士兵黑夫与惊，他们是兄弟俩，收信人是他们的大哥衷。

公元前225年，秦国大将王翦带着60万秦军杀到楚国边境，那时候最大规模的战争拉开序幕。黑夫和惊是秦军中的两名普通士兵，他们写的,或者说找人代写的这封信有500多字，还原了一个秦国士兵的真实面貌：他们打仗穿的衣服都是自己的，花的钱也要家里寄，冒死作战的动力在于得到官府的封爵。

当时，黑夫和惊在离家乡400多里的淮阳与楚国作战，他们兄弟俩的结局现在已不得而知，史书上只留下了此战后楚国灭亡的记录。这封家书是在他们的大哥衷的墓葬中被发掘的，一封家书出现在墓葬中，可能是黑夫与惊终于还是战死沙场了。哥哥去世时特地把这封信带到了地下。衷能拥有专门的墓葬，显然不是普通人家可以做到的，由此看出，黑夫和惊兄弟俩在战场勇猛作战所换来的爵位荣耀应该是被家人分享到了。

黑夫木牍
Wooden Tablet

1. Wooden Tablet-The Earliest Letter Home in China

Wooden tablet refers to writing on a board wider than the bamboo slip. While typically only a single line could be written on a bamboo slip, several lines could fit on a wooden tablet. Wooden tablet by Heifu is the earliest letter home discovered in China to date. The senders of the letter are two military brothers, Heifu and Jing, and the recipient is their elder brother, Zhong.

In 225 BC, Qin general Wang Jian, together with 600,000 soldiers, fought along the border of the State of Chu. Their advancement started a massive war in Chinese history. Both sides exhausted all their resources preparing for the protracted war and left no buffer. The five-hundred-word letter by two ordinary soldiers Heifu and Jing reveals the true features of a Qin soldier: the clothes they wear to war are handmade; the money spent is sent from home. Their motivation and fervor stemmed from the possibility to rise in rank.

At that time, Heifu and Jing fought against the State of Chu in Huaiyang (one county currently in Henan Province), over 400 li from their hometown. It is unknown whether they died in combat, but history books recount that only Chu perished after the war. The letter home was excavated in the tomb of their elder brother. It was likely that Heifu and Jing had perhaps died in combat, leaving the letter with their elder brother in the tomb. An ordinary family could not afford a special tomb for Zhong, but they nevertheless inherited honor from the bravery of the two brothers.

2. 正始石经——中国的罗塞塔碑

罗塞塔石碑（Rosetta Stone）是一块刻有三种文字的石碑，是打开古埃及象形文字之门的唯一钥匙。罗塞塔石碑制作于公元前196年，上面刻有古埃及国王托勒密五世登基的诏书。石碑上用古希腊文字、古埃及象形文字和当时的通俗体文字刻了同样的内容，这使得近代的考古学家得以对照各语言版本的内容后，解读出已经失传很久的埃及象形文字的意义与结构。

中国也有类似的石碑，上面用三种文字刻写了重要的儒家经典书籍。实际上，这不是三种文字，而是汉字在不同时期的三种形体，石碑就是刻于公元241年的正始石经。

石经是指刻写在石头上的儒家经典。在印刷术发明之前，书籍的流传主要依靠一代一代的人用手抄写，由于抄写者的水平有高有低、文字形体也存在变化，在长期的传抄过程中出现错字就在所难免，从而影响对书籍的理解。为了宣扬儒学，朝廷会召集名儒对儒家经典进行修订，并将修订后的典籍刻在石碑上，立于全国最高学府作为学习的标准范本，便于全国学子抄写或者纠正自己手中的典籍。

正始石经拓片（局部）
The Rubbing of Zhengshi Stone Scripture(Partial)

2. Zhengshi Stone Scripture: Rosetta Stone in China

The Rosetta Stone, a stone tablet inscribed with three writings, is the key to unlocking the secrets of ancient Egyptian hieroglyphics. The Rosetta Stone was made in 196 BC, inscribed with the decree of King Ptolemy V of ancient Egypt. The same content is engraved with ancient Greek writing, ancient Egyptian hieroglyphics, as well as the common language of the time, which has helped modern archaeologists interpret the meaning and structure of the long lost Egyptian hieroglyphics by comparing the content across these three forms of writing.

China also has a similar stele, the Zhengshi Stone. It is inscribed with important Confucian classic books in three kinds of characters in 241 BC. In fact, they are three different forms of Chinese characters used in different periods.

Stone scripture refers to the Confucian classics inscribed on stone. Before the invention of printing, the circulation of books mainly relied on hand-copying from generation to generation. Due to the different skill levels of transcribers and the morphological change of Chinese characters, the occasional appearance of mis-written characters is inevitable in the long process of transcription, thus affecting the understanding of the book. In order to promote Confucianism, the court often convened well-known Confucian scholars to revise the Confucian classics, and the revised classics were engraved on the stone. The stele would be placed in the highest-level educational institutions as a standard model of learning for students to transcribe or correct the classics in their hands.

魏正始二年,官府把《尚书》《春秋》等儒家经书刻在石碑上,因碑文每个字都用古文、小篆和隶书三种字体书写三遍,所以也叫三体石经。看石经右边第一列中间"月"字的写法,三种字体的差异还是挺大的。刊刻石经的主要目的是弘扬儒学,同时也有校正文献内容与文字、书体的功能。石经上的隶书字体便是当时通用的、已经相当成熟的规范字体。

罗塞塔石碑从发现到解读用了20多年的时间,并且耗费了法国天才语言学家商博良多年的精力。而中国的正始石经,只要认识易认的隶书,另外两种字体稍加对比、思索便可以认识,这要归功于汉字传承的连续性。

3.石台孝经——皇帝亲自书写的经典

石台孝经由唐玄宗李隆基亲自作序、注解并书写,刻于唐玄宗天宝四年。碑文用隶书书写,工整秀美、多姿丰艳,有盛唐气息。原石由四块黑色细石合成,长方柱体,四面刻字,碑座底下有三层石台,所以被称为石台孝经,现藏于西安碑林。

西安碑林石台孝经
The Stele of Filial Piety in Steles Forest, Xi'an

In the second year of Zhengshi, the State of Wei, the Confucian classics were inscribed on stele like *The Book of Documents* and *Spring and Autumn*. The inscription was carved with three styles of the classical pre-Qin script, the small seal script and the clerical script, so the stele was called Three-script Stone Classics. For instance, the writing of 月 (yuè, moon) in the first right column shows great variation. The main purpose for inscribing the stone classics is to advocate Confucianism, and to revise the content, characters and the script of books. The clerical script used in the stone classics at the time was the accepted, established, and standard font.

It has taken over 20 years to discover and interpret the Rosetta Stone, and has consumed the energy of renowned French linguist Jean François Champollion for years. However, the Zhengshi Stone Classics in China is easy to identify and interpret thanks to the continuity and inheritance of Chinese characters.

3. The Stele of the Filial Piety—A Classic Written by the Emperor Himself

The Stele of the Filial Piety was prefaced, annotated and written by Emperor Xuanzong (Li Longji) of the Tang Dynasty, and engraved in 745 A.D. It was written in clerical script, featuring neat and graceful handwriting, and exhibited a stately and dignified style true to the prosperous age of the Tang Dynasty. The original stele is composed of four black fine stones with rectangular columns and inscriptions engraved on all sides, and there are three layers of stone tables under the stele base. Named the Stele of the Filial Piety, it is now held in the Forest of Steles in Xi'an, Shaanxi Province.

《孝经》是中国流传久远且影响广泛的儒家经典之一，很多学者都为这部经典作注解。唐玄宗时期，考虑到《孝经》注解纰漏较多，唐玄宗就在以往学者的注解中采集菁华，成书后颁布天下，并亲自用隶书书写，刻于石碑。

中国自古以来注重孝道，人们常说一句话"百善孝为先"。皇帝认为家国一体，以孝治家和以孝治国是紧密联系的。唐玄宗希望通过提倡孝道，把皇家的内部秩序整顿好，并使它成为治国的重要做法。唐玄宗对《孝经》的整理、注释以及推广在文化建设上是有一定贡献的，集儒家经典大成的《十三经注疏》中只有一位皇帝留下了著作，就是唐玄宗的《孝经注》。

石台孝经拓片（局部）
The Rubbing of Stele of the Filial Piety (Partial)

The Classic of Filial Piety is a Confucian classic that has one of the longest histories and widest influence in China, and many scholars have made annotations of it throughout the centuries. During the period of Emperor Xuanzong of the Tang Dynasty, there still remained many errors in the annotation of *The Classic of Filial Piety*; thus, Emperor Xuanzong collected the core meanings of previous scholars' annotations in order to publish his own consolidated and updated book, personally writing it in clerical script and engraving it on the stele.

Since ancient China revered filial piety, it was often said that "filial piety is the foundation of all virtues". The emperor believed that the family and country are a whole, and the rule of family by filial piety and the rule of state by filial piety are closely linked. Emperor Xuanzong hoped that by advocating filial piety, the royal internal order would be well-organized and gain traction as an important way to govern the country. Emperor Xuanzong's collation, annotation, and promotion of *The Classic of Filial Piety* was an important contribution. Among the *Thirteen Classics Explanatory Notes and Commentaries* (a collection of Confucian classics), only one was written by an emperor, that is, Emperor Xuanzong's *The Annotation of the Classic of Filial Piety*.

四、楷书

隶书在发展过程中不断变化，向着楷书演变，至隋唐时期趋于成熟，成为官方认可和社会通行的标准字体。从表面上看，楷书对隶书的改变似乎不大，但是楷书的笔画书写起来比隶书更加方便，所以汉字形体由隶书变为楷书也是一次重要的变化。

楷书字形方正，讲究横平竖直。《辞海》说它"形体方正、笔画平直，可作楷模，故名楷书"。后来人们把汉字称为"方块字"，就是针对楷书讲的。楷书出现后，汉字的结构基本上固定下来，之后的1000多年总体上没有太大的变化。

1. 多宝塔碑——楷书的代表之作

颜真卿是唐代著名的书法家，他对前人书法进行深入研究，吸取他们的长处，创造了新的时代风格，他的书体被称为"颜体"，后世学习"颜体"书法的人不计其数。

多宝塔碑，全称大唐西京千福寺多宝塔感应碑，由颜真卿书写，唐天宝十一年刻于陕西兴平县千福寺，内容主要记述和尚楚金禅师创建多宝塔的经过。

多宝塔碑拓片（局部）
The Rubbing of Duobao Pagoda Stele (Partial)

IV. Regular Script

The clerical script has been changing in the course of development. It evolved towards the regular script and matured in the Sui and Tang Dynasties, becoming the standard font recognized by the government and accepted by society. Though on the surface, the regular script doesn't appear significantly different from the clerical script, the strokes of regular script are actually easier to write than clerical script. The subtle change of Chinese character form from clerical script to regular script is also an important one.

The regular script is straight and square, and pays attention to the horizontal and vertical dimensions of the character. *The Word-Ocean Dictionary* points out that "the regular script gained its name with square shape and straight strokes, which can serve as a model." Later, people called Chinese characters "square characters," an alternate name for the regular script. After the appearance of the regular script, the structure of Chinese characters has stayed constant, and there has not been much change over the last thousand years.

1. Duobao Pagoda Stele—A Representative Work of Regular Script

Yan Zhenqing was a famous calligrapher in the Tang Dynasty. He studied his predecessors' calligraphy thoroughly, absorbed their strengths, and created a new calligraphy style of the age, called "Yan Zhenqing style," which attracted countless people of later generations to learn his technique.

The full name of Duobao Pagoda Stele is "Duobao Pagoda Induction Stele in Qianfu Temple in Xijing in the Tang Dynasty." The inscriptions were written by Yan Zhenqing, and engraved in Qianfu Temple in Xingping County, Shaanxi Province in the eleventh year of the reign of Li Longji in the Tang Dynasty in 196 B.C., which recorded how monk Chu Jin built the Duobao Pagoda.

2. 圣旨——皇帝旨意的体现

楷书在唐代以后一直处于官方的正体地位。历代的政府文书、科举试卷、档案、书籍抄录等官方用字场合全用楷书。该圣旨是朝廷颁给南京工部右侍郎刘俊的圣旨,时间是明成化十八年,是刘俊官职升为通议大夫时朝廷所颁。

中国古代讲究夫贵妻荣,圣旨上不仅详细罗列了刘俊八次升迁的官职,也对刘俊的妻子支氏进行了褒奖,封号由恭人加封为淑人。

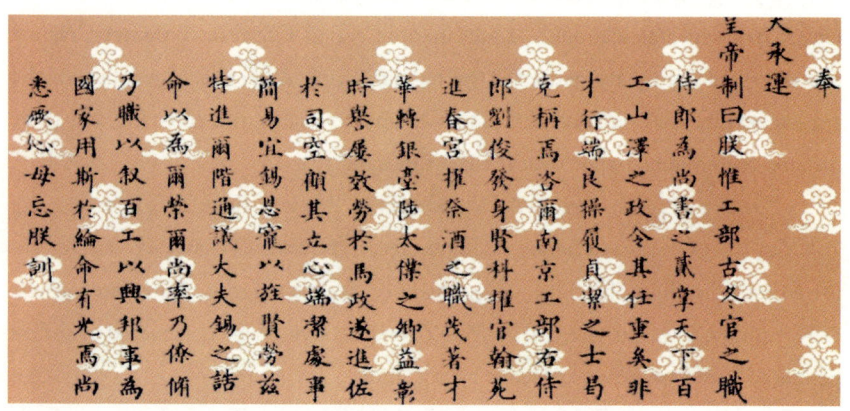

明朝圣旨(局部)

The Imperial Edict of the Ming Dynasty(Partial)

2. Imperial Edict: The Embodiment of the Emperor's Will

As shown below the court issued an imperial edict in regular script to Liu Jun when he was promoted to the vice chairman of the Ministry of Works on December 13th, 1482. By this time, regular script had been the standard script ever since the Tang Dynasty for formal occasions such as court documents of the past dynasties, imperial examination papers, archives, and transcribed books.

In ancient China, a husband's gain was also his wife's. The imperial edict showed us not only Liu's eight promotions of official positions, but the honorary titles from the 4th grade to the 2nd grade bestowed on his wife with her maiden family name Zhi.

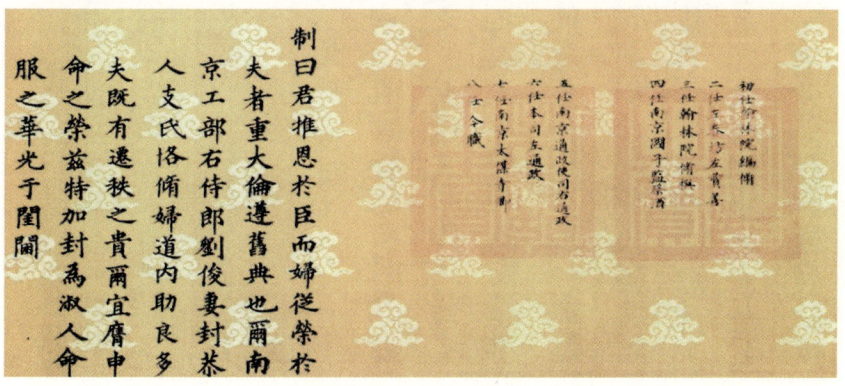

明朝圣旨(局部)
The Imperial Edict of the Ming Dynasty(Partial)

清朝考卷
The Imperial Examination Paper of the Qing Dynasty

3. 清朝考卷——楷书字体的用武之地

科举是中国古代通过考试选拔官吏的制度。科举始于隋朝,直至清光绪三十一年,前后经历1300余年,是世界上延续时间最长的选拔人才的办法。科举应试的规范书体是楷书。

这份清朝考卷是清朝最后一位状元刘春霖的殿试考卷,用楷书书写。他是清光绪三十年甲辰科状元,也是中国历史上最后一名状元。刘春霖善于书法,尤其以小楷最为著名。他的小楷笔力清秀刚劲,深

3. The Imperial Examination Paper of the Qing Dynasty: The Promised Land of the Regular Script

The imperial examination was the system used for selecting officials by examination in ancient China. Beginning in the Sui Dynasty and ending in 1905 of the Qing Dynasty, the system became the world's longest-lasting (over 1300 years) selection of talents. The standard character form of the imperial examination is regular script.

This Qing Dynasty examination paper was written by the final "Number One Scholar" Liu Chunlin of the Qing Dynasty, written in regular script. Liu Chunlin became the Number One Scholar of the Qing Dynasty in the thirtieth year of the reign of Emperor Guang Xu in the Qing Dynasty in 1904, and he was the last person in Chinese history to hold such a title. In this document, he displayed great skill in calligraphy, especially the regular script in small characters. His characters shown here are handsome and bold, and thus were highly and widely praised. He was the inspiration behind a popular compliment of the time that stated, "Learn regular script in big characters from Yan Zhenqing, but learn regular script in small characters from Liu Chunlin."

4. Transformation Record of Chinese Characters

After more than 3000 years of development and evolution, the shape of Chinese characters has undergone several changes, such as oracle bone scripts, bronze scripts, small seal script, clerical script, and regular script. Overall, Chinese characters have undergone tremendous change in both structure and writing style. However, no matter how they change, the evolution of Chinese characters is clearly visible, and the relationship between them nevertheless carries on. It is not

受世人推崇，当时有"大楷学颜（颜真卿），小楷学刘（刘春霖）"的美誉。

4. 汉字变形记

经过了3000多年的发展演变，汉字经历了甲骨文、金文、小篆、隶书、楷书等几种形体的演变，无论在结构上还是书写风格上，都发生了巨大的变化。但无论如何变化，汉字的演变脉络是清晰可见的，它们之间的关系是一脉相承的，只要认识现代汉字，了解以前的汉字也不是难事，2000多年前的古籍也并非高不可攀。对汉字字形的演变过程进行了解，有助于人们更好地理解汉字的构造。

5. 汉字简化

从汉字形体发展演变的历史可以看出，汉字简化实际上自古就有，而且从来没有停止过。纵观汉字形体的发展历程，简化是总的趋势。小篆是大篆的简化，隶书是小篆的简化，楷书是隶书的简化，都是对前代文字不同程度的简化。

为了适应社会发展及实际需求，历朝历代都有简化字的产生与使用，并传承至今。古代许多书法作品当中就有大量简化字，民间非正式场合也大量使用简化字，这些字在当时被称为俗体字。

中华人民共和国成立后，政府推进语言文字改革，即汉字简化，这是中国文字史上的一次重大改革。

汉字简化并未改变汉字的整体形态风格，只是以过去的汉字简化为基础，整理在群众中长期且广泛流行的、已经社会化了的简化字，是由俗体字到正体字的地位转变。

简体字 Simplified	学习	奋斗	团结	乐观
繁体字 Traditional	學習	奮鬥	團結	樂觀
英文 English	Study	Endeavor	Unity	Optimism

简体字和繁体字对比

Comparison Between Simplified and Traditional Characters

difficult to understand ancient characters, nor is it impossible to read ancient texts from over 2000 years ago, so long as we can recognize modern Chinese characters. Understanding the evolution of Chinese character forms will help us better understand not only the structure of Chinese characters, but the cultural lineage they've inherited.

5. The Simplification of Chinese Characters

We can see from the history of the development and evolution of Chinese character form that the simplification of Chinese characters dates back to ancient times and never ceased. Looking at the overall transformation, simplification is the general trend to varying degrees. For instance, large seal script was simplified to small seal script, which in turn was replaced by clerical script, which ultimately led to regular script.

In order to adapt to social development and other demands, the dynasties in Chinese history witnessed the emergence and use of more simplified Chinese characters. The tradition has been inherited to this day. Many simplified characters were used on informal non-government occasions and in numerous ancient calligraphy works. They are called the vulgar character.

After the founding of the People's Republic of China, the Chinese government continued to implement language and character reforms. The most recent simplication was a major reform in Chinese writing history.

The simplification of Chinese characters does not change the overall morphological style of the language, but rather it demonstrates the re-simplification and collation of the long-standing and widely popular characters. The process represents the change.

第三章

汉字的构形

Chapter III

Configuration of Chinese Characters

汉字古老而悠久，是中国文化系统中重要的象征元素。沿着汉字的足迹追根溯源，人们会惊喜地发现，汉字除了记录汉语之外还承载着丰富的古代文化内涵，从中可以了解到先民们创造文字的智慧，观察到古人在生活劳作、民风习俗、思维方式、审美观念与思想情趣等诸多方面留下的历史印记，这里面有传说的神秘、君王的意志、文人的情怀、艺人的奇想，还有无数人民的大智慧。

汉字的历史是一部别有风味的中国文化史，为人们展现出一幅幅中国文化的生动图景；也是一部独具东方特色的文明史，为人们呈现出一个个东方文明的伟大成就。对汉字的结构进行分析，明白当初它们是怎样构造出来的，造字时的用意是什么，可以帮助人们更好地理解、掌握汉字。

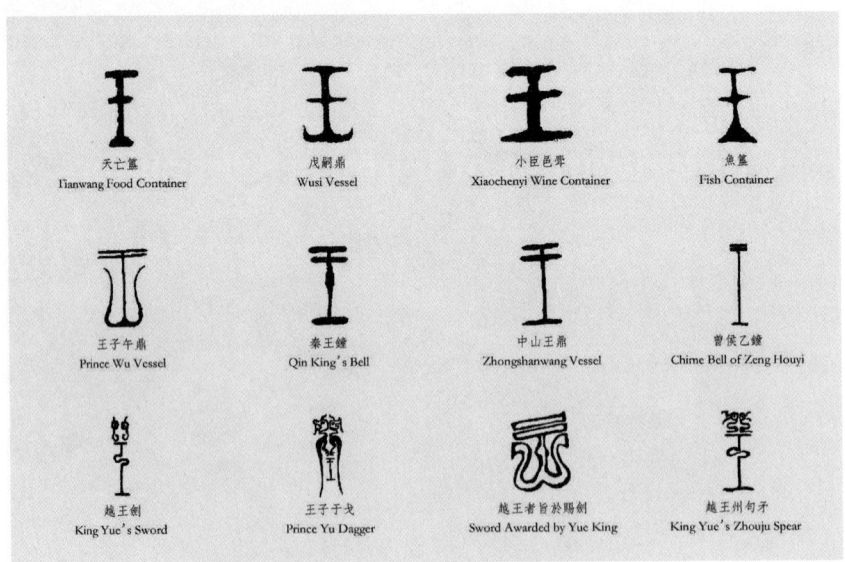

各式王字（左面）

Different Forms of the Graph for King (Left)

Chapter III Configuration of Chinese Characters

Chinese characters have a long history, representing an important symbolic element in the Chinese cultural system. Tracing the development of Chinese characters, we will find that they not only record Chinese, but also carry a rich ancient cultural connotation, through which we can understand the wisdom of ancestors, and also observe the historical imprints left by our ancestors in terms of their living and working habits, cultural customs, thinking mode, aesthetic idea ideological interests, among other aspects, which might include legendary mysteries, emperors' will, literati feelings, artists' whimsy, and the great wisdom of countless Chinese people.

The history of Chinese characters is a unique cultural history of China, presenting vivid pictures of Chinese culture. It is also a history of civilization with unique oriental characteristics, presenting great achievements of oriental civilization. Analyzing the structure of Chinese characters, we can understand how they were constructed as well as the intention behind the characters so as to help people better understand and master them.

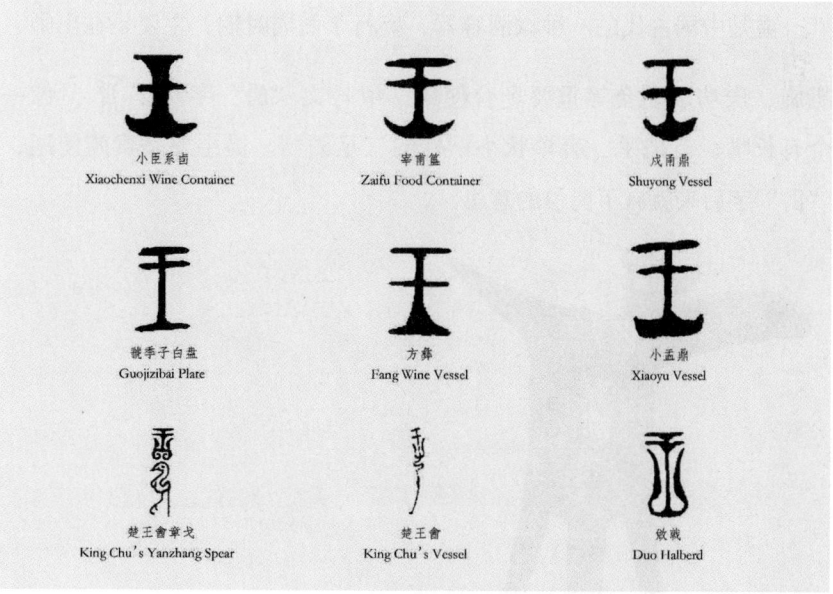

Different Forms of the Graph for King (Right)

一、造字方法

汉字自产生以来,数量一直在增加,东汉时期出现的中国第一部字典《说文解字》收录汉字9353个,1990年出版的《汉语大字典》收录汉字54678个。如此庞大的汉字体系是如何创造出来的?这引起了古代学者对汉字造字方法的思考,许慎在《说文解字》中总结、阐述了古人创造汉字的几种方法——"六书",分别是象形、指事、形声、会意、转注、假借。

象形即用简单的线条描摹客观事物的形状,使人一看就能把字形与具体事物联系起来,知道它所代表的事物。如 ☉(日)、☽(月)、⛰(山)、川(水)、🐟(鱼)、🏺(爵)等字。

甲骨文的"鱼"字写成 🐟 或 🐟 等,非常形象,鱼的头、鳍、鳞、尾各个部分全部勾勒出来。后来逐渐演变为"魚",鱼身成了田字,鱼尾为四点,简化字"鱼"的鱼尾又由四点变为一横。

爵是中国古代的一种饮酒容器,盛行于商周时期,主要是在出师、凯旋、庆功、宴会等重要场合使用。甲骨文"爵"字写作 🏺,像一个有长嘴、有把手、有伞状小铜柱的三足酒器。爵主要是贵族使用,"爵"字后来就有了爵位的意思。

青铜爵
Bronze Wine Vessel with Three Legs

Ⅰ. Methods of Creating Chinese Characters

Since Chinese characters emerged, their number has been steadily increasing. The first Chinese dictionary in the Eastern Han Dynasty, *Shuowen jiezi* (*The Explanation of Script and Elucidation of Characters*) contains 9,353 Chinese characters, while *The Grand Chinese Dictionary* published in 1990 includes 54,678 Chinese characters. How did such a huge character system come into being? Ancient scholars were interested in inquiring into the method behind making Chinese characters. Xu Shen, the writer of *Shuowen jiezi* (*The Explanation of Script and Elucidation of Characters*) , summarized six types of creating Chinese characters as "Liu Shu" (Six Categories of Chinese Character Creation): pictographic characters, self-explanatory characters, pictophonetic characters, associative compound characters, mutually explanatory characters, and phonetic loan characters.

In pictographic characters, simple lines are used to describe the shape of objects, so that people can associate the character pattern with the specific thing when they look at the character, and thus determine what the character represents. Such as ☉ 日 (rì, sun), ☽ 月 (yuè, moon), ⛰ 山 (shān, mountain), 水 (shuǐ, water), 鱼 (yú, fish), 爵 (jué, wine vessel with three legs).

The character 鱼 in the oracle bone script is written as or , which is a visual depiction of the fish's head, fins, scale, and tail. Later, it gradually evolved into the character 魚. The fish's body became the character 田 (tián, field), and the fish's tail became four points. Then in the simplified character 鱼, the fish tail changed from four points into one horizontal stroke.

Popular in the Shang and Zhou Dynasties, 爵 was a kind of drinking container in ancient China, and it was mainly used for important occasions such as the dispatchment of troops to war, triumphant returns, celebrations, and banquets. The character 爵 in the oracle bone script is written as , like a three-legged wine vessel with a long mouth, a handle, and an umbrella-shaped small copper column. At that time, 爵 was mainly used by the nobility, and the character 爵 later carried the meaning of the rank or title of a noble.

指事指的是利用本有的象形符号加些简单的指示符号实现表意功能的一些字。比如（上）━、━（下）二字，一长横代表水平线，一短横是指示性符号，短横在水平线以上就是"上"字，短横在水平线以下就是"下"字。

会意是把两个及两个以上的独体汉字或汉字构件放到一起，根据各自的含义组合成一个新的汉字，产生新的意思，造出的字就是会意字。甲骨文"休"字，写作 ⺅、⺅ 等，由"人"和"木"两个独体字组成，像一个人待在大树的枝叶之下，或依靠一棵大树，描绘了古人在野外劳作时在大树下歇息的场景。

这个"鼓"字刻在一块陶片上（如下图所示），是甲骨文里很常见的一个字，有左右结构，有时候还是左中右结构，实际是一样的，因为商代的字有时候不完全定型。中间圆圆的那一部分是鼓，鼓的底下那一块表示一个木头做的鼓座，而上面是一个像"山"字的装饰。商朝人特别喜欢做这种装饰，好多东西上都有这样的装饰。

　　这个字的右边是一只手拿着一个鼓槌，左边也是一只手拿着一个鼓槌。那个时候不像现在可以坐凳子，那个时候都是跪坐在地上，鼓也很低，两只手敲鼓或者拿着鼓槌击鼓，这就形成了"鼓"字。

形声字是由两个字或偏旁部首组合成的新字，其中一个是意符，表示意义类别，另一个是声符，表示读音。如"盂"和"雩"两个字，两个字都是以"于"字为声符，表示这两个字的读音与"于"相同或

陶器上的"鼓"字
The Character 鼓(gǔ, drum) Carved on Pottery

Self-explanatory characters were created by combining existent pictographic parts with simple indicative symbols. For example, the characters ⸺ 上(shàng, up) and ⸺ 下(xià, down): the long stroke represents the horizontal line, and the short stroke is the indicative symbol. When the short stroke is above the horizontal line, it is the character 上(shàng, up), and when the short stroke is below the horizontal line, it is the character 下(xià, down).

In associative compound characters, two or more single-part Chinese characters, or parts of these characters are combined to form a new character with a new meaning based on its respective single-part characters. The resulting Chinese character is an associative compound character. The character 休(xiū, rest) in the oracle bone script is written as 伏 or 休, which consists of two single-font characters: 人(rén, person) and 木(mù, wood), just like a person lounging under the branches of a tree or lying by a tree. This character depicts a person who is exhausted after work and is leaning against a tree for a rest.

Engraved on a pottery piece, the character 鼓(gǔ, drum) is a very common character in the oracle bone script. It has a left-right structure, but sometimes is written with a left-middle-right structure. The left-middle-right structure is actually synonymous to the left-right structure, because the characters in the Shang Dynasty were not completely fixed. The middle part of the circle is the drum, and the bottom part of the character represents a wooden-made drum base with a decoration of the character 山(shān, mountain), a favorite decoration of the people in the Shang Dynasty; consequently, many items were decorated with this pattern.

On both sides of the character are two hands holding two drumsticks. Unlike today, people at that time always kneeled directly on the ground rather than sitting on a stool, and the drums were also placed very low. Thus, when beating the drum, people kneeled on the ground with their hands holding the drumsticks. Therefore, this is the origin of the character 鼓(gǔ, drum).

The pictophonetic character refers to a new character composed of two characters or components. One of them is a semantic symbol, indicating the meaning category, and the other is a sound symbol, indicating the pronunciation. For example, the characters 盂(yú) and 雩(yú) both take the character 于(yú) as the sound symbol, indicating that the pronunciation of these two characters is

相近。甲骨文"盂"字写作 ⛿、⛿，下面是表示盛放物品的容器"皿"字，是意符，那么"盂"字就是吃饭和盛水的用具。"雩"的甲骨文写法是 ⛿，上面的"雨"字是意符，表示和雨有关，商朝人还不能正确了解雨形成的现象，当长久不下雨引发干旱的时候，他们就会祭祀上天，祈求降雨，"雩"字的意思就是为求雨而举行的祭祀活动。"雩"字在演变的过程中，下面的"于"字变形成了"亏"字。

形声字具有表意和标音两种功能，是最能产生新字的造字方法，虽然在甲骨文中出现较晚，但逐渐成为新的文字产生的主流趋势。到了商代晚期，人们也更多地用形、声结合的方法增添新字，形声字所占比例日渐增大。

转注指同一部首的字可以互相解释，比如"老"与"考"。假借即借用已有的字，表示同音而不同义的字。比如，⛿（我）的本义是指古代的一种兵器，后来被借为单数第一人称代词。

严格来说，前面的象形、指事、会意、形声是造字的方法，后面的转注和假借不产生新的汉字，属于用字的方法。

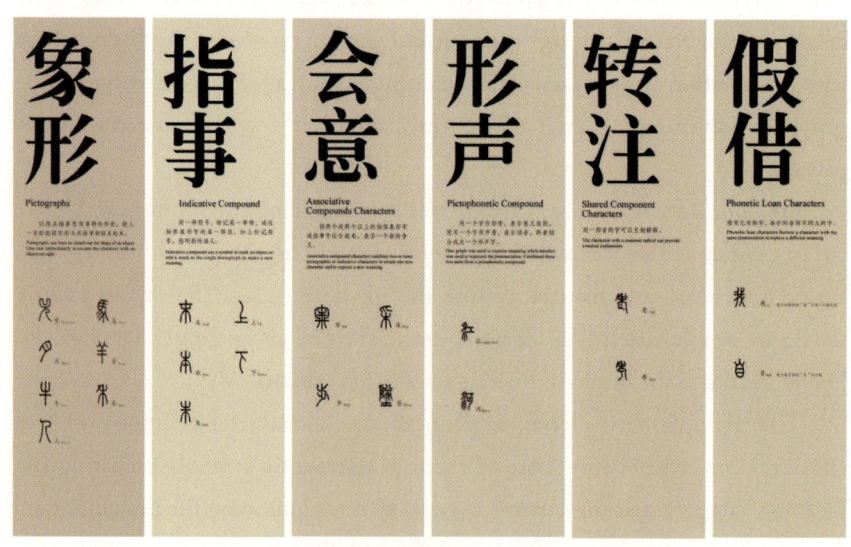

汉字造字法
Methods of Creating Chinese Characters

similar to, or the same as, that of character 于. The character 盂(yú) in the oracle bone script is written as 𝌀 and 𝌁, and the bottom part 皿 means the container, which is the semantic symbol of the character. So the character 盂(yú) refers to a utensil for eating and drinking water. The character 雩(yú) in the oracle bone script is written as 𝌂, and the character 雨(yǔ, rain) above is a semantic symbol, indicating that it is related to the rain. During the Shang Dynasty, people did not yet understand the phenomenon of rain formation and after a long period of drought, people would make sacrifices to the God of Heaven, praying for rain; thus, the character 雩(yú) fittingly means sacrificial activities for rain. During the evolution of Chinese characters, the bottom part 于(yú) of 雩(yú) has been transformed into the character 亏(kuī).

Pictophonetic characters have two functions: one is ideographic and the other phonetic. Pictophonetic formation is the most productive method for creating new characters. Although it appeared late in the oracle bone scripts, it gradually became the mainstream in the formation of new characters.In the late Shang Dynasty, people also created new characters by combining ideographic symbols with phonetic symbols, and the proportion of pictophonetic characters increased.

Mutually explanatory characters refer to the shared component characters such as 老 (lǎo, old) and 考 (kǎo, test). Phonetic loan characters indicate which characters are homonyms with different meanings. For example, the original meaning of 𢦏 我 (wǒ, I) refers to an ancient weapon, which was later borrowed as a single first-person pronoun.

Strictly speaking, pictographic characters, self-explanatory characters, pictophonetic characters, and associative compound characters are methods of making characters, while mutually explanatory characters and phonetic loan characters are methods of using characters.

二、人与人体

认识和了解自身是人类认识世界的第一步，很多最常见的字都是根据人体的形象、动作创造出来的。这些字不是简简单单的符号，而是蕴含了丰富的古代文化信息和生活在那个时代的人们最朴素的意识观念。

1. 人

小时候刚学到"人"字，以为是一个站立的人形，突出了人的双腿，这种意识在心里根深蒂固了好多年，直至看到了甲骨文。甲骨文"人"字是一个侧立的人形，竖立的曲笔表示人的头、身和腿，旁边一短笔表示倾斜下垂的手臂。现在的汉字非常规范，一个字只有一种写法，而甲骨文时期，很多字形还不固定，有的字有多种写法，有的字字形朝左、朝右没有区别。

中国最早的字典《说文解字》对人的解释是："人是天地间品性最高贵的生物。"人之所以为人，和其他动物最根本的区别在于能够直立行走和使用工具。甲骨文"人"字突出了人的直立形象，直立行走解放了人的双手，使得人可以腾出手来使用工具进行生产劳动，而弯腰垂臂的形象更像是双手在田野劳作。

"人"字的演变
Evolution of the Character "人"

甲骨文 Oracle Bone Script	金文 Bronze Script	小篆 Small Seal Script	隶书 Clerical Script	楷书 Regular Script
竹	㇉	尺	人	人

Ⅱ. Human and Human Body

Knowing oneself and one's body is the first step to understanding the world. Most common characters are created on the basis of the human body's shape and movements. These characters are not simple symbols, but contain a plethora of ancient cultural information and the simplest ideology of people living in that era.

1. 人(rén,human)

At first sight, many people interpret the character 人 (rén, human) as a man standing upright with two long legs, a notion that has been rooted in people's mind for many years. But the oracle bone script for 人 gives us a different picture: a side-standing man with arms outstretched. The vertical stroke represents the human's head, body and legs and a short stroke next to it indicates the tilted arm. Nowadays, Chinese characters are very standardized. There is only one way to write a character. However, in the period of oracle bone scripts, many character patterns were not yet fixed. Some characters were written in multiple ways, with no difference between some characters turning to the left or right.

Shuowen jiezi (*The Explanation of Script and Elucidation of Characters*), the earliest Chinese dictionary, writes that: "Human is the most intelligent creature in the world." Having the ability to walk upright and use tools is the main difference between human beings and other animals. The Chinese character 人(rén, human) in the oracle bone script highlights the erect image of a human. Walking upright liberates human hands, allowing people to free their hands to use tools for productive labor, while the image of bending over and hanging their arms is more like the scene of humans working in the fields with their hands.

其实,古人并没有把自己看得异常高贵而把人字造得非常复杂,简简单单的两笔便将人的特征勾勒了出来,微微弯曲的脊背不仅仅表示在弯腰劳作,也表示他们懂得敬畏——敬畏上天、敬畏自然。"人"字做偏旁的时候写作"亻",如伸、伴、侣、仆等,都与人或人的活动有关。

2. 天

中国的古籍《山海经》记载了一则神话故事,故事的主人公叫刑天,他的真实名字已不得而知,因为和天帝争神座,被砍掉了脑袋。但是刑天仍然不肯屈服,把双乳变成眼睛,把肚脐变成嘴巴,左手握盾,右手持斧,战斗不止。因为没有头,所以人们称他为刑天。刑有杀、割的意思,刑天就是把头砍下的意思。

从这个传说可知,天的本义为人的头部,甲骨文、金文的"天"字像一个正面而立的人,突出了人圆圆的头部,后来头的形象简化成两横或者一横。人们站在旷野,头顶便是浩瀚的天空,天就有了天空的含义。

古人认为天是有意志的神,是万物的主宰,有至高无上的权威,所以历代最高统治者被称为"天子",即天之嫡长子。他们为了巩固自己的地位和政权,自称他们的权力受命于天,是秉承天意治理天下,是上天委任于人间的代理人,只受天命约束。他们还把自己比作龙,号称"真龙天子",并且宣扬自己生下来就有许多祥瑞征兆,叫作"天子气"。

"天"字的演变
Evolution of the Character "天"

甲骨文 Oracle Bone Script	金文 Bronze Script	小篆 Small Seal Script	隶书 Clerical Script	楷书 Regular Script
呆 秂	大 天	页	天	天

Our ancestors did not seem to think too highly of themselves and made this character 人 too complicated. They outlined the character 人 with only two simple strokes. The slightly bent back not only conveys the meaning that they were working, but also indicates that they worshiped heaven and nature. When the character 人 is used as a Chinese character component, it is written as 亻, such as the character 伸(shēn, stretch), 伴(bàn, company), 侣(lǚ, partner) and 仆 (pú, servant), which are all related to humans or their activities.

2. 天(tiān, sky)

There is a myth story recorded in an ancient Chinese text, *Shan Hai Jing* (*The Classic of Mountains and Rivers*). Once upon a time, there was a human who fought with the emperor of heaven for the throne. He was defeated, and his head was cut off as punishment. However, he still refused to yield and continued to fight, turning his breasts into eyes, his navel into a mouth, with his left hand holding a shield and the right hand holding an axe. Later on, people called him Xing Tian, indicating that his head was cut off, because the characters 刑天(xíng tiān) means cutting off the head in Chinese.

From this legend, we know that the original meaning of the character 天 (tiān, sky) is the head of a human. The character 天 in the oracle bone script and bronze script is like a person standing with a round head. Later, the image of the head was simplified into one or two horizontal strokes, just like someone standing in the wilderness with a vast sky over his head. Since then, the character 天 carries the meaning of the sky.

The ancient believed that heaven is the god of will, the master of everything, and has supreme authority. Therefore, the highest rulers of all dynasties were called 天子 (tiān zǐ), or the eldest son of Heaven. In order to consolidate their status and power, they claimed that they received instructions from heaven, and they were appointed by god to follow only god's will, governing the world like agents. They also boasted that they were 真龙天子(zhēn lóng tiān zǐ, real dragons), and publicized that they were born with many auspicious phenomena, which was described as 天子气 (tiān zǐ qì, imperial bearing).

3. 口

"口"字的本义就是嘴巴，形状像人张开的嘴巴，为了与方形符号口和丁字（甲骨文写作 ▢）相区别，所以突出了微微上翘的嘴角。嘴巴的首要功能是吃饭，一个家庭里有多少人，就有多少张口需要吃饭，所以中国人说家里有多少人时一般说有几口人，比如说，老李家有六口人。吃饭问题好像是中国自古以来就需要解决的大事，中国人见面的问候语一般是"你吃饭了吗"，而不是"今天天气很好"之类的话语。

除了吃饭，人类还要用口说话、交流，"曰"字就产生了，甲骨文"曰"字写作 ㅂ，上面那一短横像口中呼出的气体，因说话的内容不是形象具体的实物，难以描摹，所以人们就用一短横来表示。在中国古代的书面语中，人们更多地用"曰"字来表示说话，而很少用"说"字。记载思想家孔子言行的书籍《论语》开篇第一句就写到：子曰："学而时习之，不亦说乎？有朋自远方来，不亦乐乎？人不知而不愠，不亦君子乎？""子曰"的意思就是"孔子说"。"曰"字和"日"字还是有明显区别的，"曰"字偏胖，"日"字偏瘦。

人需要通过说话来交流，动物也需要用嘴巴发出声音来传递信息，人们为牛的叫声创造了"牟"字，甲骨文写作 ，当"牟"字已经变

"口"字的演变
Evolution of the Character "口"

甲骨文 Oracle Bone Script	金文 Bronze Script	小篆 Small Seal Script	隶书 Clerical Script	楷书 Regular Script
ㅂ	ㅂ	ㅂ	▬	口

3. 口(kǒu, mouth)

The character 口(kǒu, mouth) depicts an opening mouth. In order to distinguish it from the square symbol □ and the character 丁(dīng, written as ⛊ in the oracle bone script), it highlights the slightly upturned corners of the mouth. The main function of the mouth is to eat. Chinese sometimes use 口(kǒu, mouth) as a unit to count people, e.g. one person means 一口. So, in Chinese, when describing how many people there are in a family, people will ask, 你家里有几口人(nǐ jiā lǐ yǒu jǐ kǒu rén , How many people are there in your family?). If there are six people in Lao Li's family, we would say, 老李家有六口人(lǎo lǐ jiā yǒu liù kǒu rén , There are six people in Lao Li's family). Food has always been a priority and a basic need for people since ancient times, which can explain why Chinese people generally greet each other by saying, 你吃饭了吗(nǐ chī fàn le ma, Have you had your dinner?) instead of 今天天气很好(jīn tiān tiān qì hěn hǎo ,It is a fine day today).

Apart from eating, human beings talk and communicate with the mouth, so the character 曰(yuē, say) was created. The character 曰 is written as ᗛ in the oracle bone script, and the short horizontal stroke on the top represents the gas exhaled in and out when speaking. In the written language of ancient Chinese, people used the character 曰 more to express their speech and seldom used the character 说 (shuō, say).

The first sentence of the book *The Analects*, which records Confucius's words and deeds to reflect his thoughts, is "子曰：学而时习之，不亦说乎？" (zǐ yuē：xué ér shí xí zhī ， bú yì yuè hū ? Confucius said: "It is a pleasure to review frequently while learning.") "有朋自远方来，不亦乐乎？ " (yǒu péng zì yuǎn fāng lái ， bú yì lè hū ? Isn't it such a delight to have friends coming from afar?) "人不知而不愠，不亦君子乎？ " (rén bú zhī ér bú yùn，bú yì jūn zǐ hū ? To tolerate those who misunderstand me, and to get along with those unwise, isn't this clement enough to be called a gentleman?). In this sentence, the Chinese characters 子曰 mean "Confucius said." There is still a distinct difference between the characters 曰(yuē, say) and 日(rì, sun). The character 曰 is wider and the character 日 is thinner.

People need to communicate by speaking, and animals also need to use their mouths to make sounds to transmit information. People created the character

得看不出有"口"字时,人们又加了口字偏旁创造了新字"哞"来表示牛的叫声。同理,人们用"咩""鸣""吠"分别来表示羊、鸟、犬的叫声。"口"字的典型形状是中间空,只要形状像口的事物都可以称为口,如瓶口、伤口、洞口等。

4. 齿

齿就是牙齿,甲骨文的"齿"字像人口中上下相对的两排牙齿的形状。从这个齿字可以看出古人造字的智慧所在,有些字很难孤立地画出来,或者孤立地画出来容易跟别的字相混,所以在造字的时候,需要把某种与其有关的事物,如周围环境、所附着的主体或所包含的东西等一起表示出来。再看"齿"字,不仅仅有牙齿的形状,牙齿周围还附带有口的形状,光有四颗牙齿的形象无法使人确定这个字就是牙齿,所以需要把牙齿所在的嘴巴也表现出来,这个形象也是成语"唇齿相依"的真实写照。同理,"舌"字的甲骨文写作舌、舌,为了确保舌头被认知,不仅要有舌头的形象,也要把舌头所在的口腔表示出来。

再仔细地看看这几个甲骨文"齿"字,就会发现四个轮廓形状的牙齿,连带外面嘴巴的形状,都有一种美在里面,这种美就是对称美。

对称美是中国人一直追求着的造物里的一种独特的美,在许许多多中国的文化国粹中,似乎都能看到对称美的存在,建筑、绘画、诗歌、瓷器、楹联、图章、书法等都讲究对称,反映着中国人的阴阳平衡概念,这也是中国人的生活美学。

"齿"字的演变
Evolution of the Character "齿"

甲骨文 Oracle Bone Script	金文 Bronze Script	小篆 Small Seal Script	隶书 Clerical Script	楷书 Regular Script
囧	齿	齒	齒	齿

牟 to describe the cow's moo, which is written as 牟 in the oracle bone script with a 口 inside it. As time went by, people added the 口 to 牟 to make up a new character 哞(mōu) in a way to indicate the cow's moo when the 口 was invisible from 牟. In the same way, people use 咩(miē), 鸣(míng), 吠(fèi) to denote the sound of sheep (baa), birds (chirp), and dogs (woof). The character 口(kǒu, mouth) has a blank in the middle, which is a common feature shared by many words. Therefore, a series of vocabularies like 瓶口(píng kǒu, bottle neck), 伤口（shāng kǒu, wound）, 洞口（dòng kǒu, hole）came into being and would be classified similarly so long as they feature the blank inside.

4. 齿(chǐ,tooth)

The character 齿(chǐ, tooth) is tooth, and the oracle bone script of 齿 is like a person's two rows of teeth. This character shows the wisdom of ancient people. Sometimes it is difficult to draw some characters in isolation, or it is easy to confuse them with other characters. Therefore, when creating such characters, it is necessary to express something else related to them, such as the surrounding environment, the attached subject or other contents. Taking the character 齿 as an example; it shows both teeth and lips as a whole, because it would otherwise be difficult to confirm the meaning of the character based on four teeth images alone, which can be seen as a vivid description of the idiom "lips and teeth are interdependent." In the same way, 舌 (shé, tongue) is written as 舌 and 舌 in the oracle bone script. In order to ensure that the tongue is recognized, this character not only has the image of the tongue, but also the mouth where the tongue is located.

If you take a closer look at the several versions of 齿 in the oracle bone script, you will find symmetrical beauty inside them.

In terms of object-creating, symmetry is significant in Chinese aesthetics and perceptions of beauty, and symmetrical beauty can be seen in many forms of arts, such as architecture, painting, poetry, porcelain, couplets, seals, and calligraphy, all of which reflect that Chinese people pursue a balance between yin and yang within their aesthetics of life.

众所周知,中国人对于建筑里的中轴线,有着千年不变的恪守,这正是源于骨子里对于对称美的钟爱。北京故宫的建筑风格就很好地体现了对称美,故宫在建造中突出了一条南北中轴线,宫内重要建筑都在这条中轴线上,其他建筑分东西对称分布。

齿由 ▨ 逐渐演变为 ▨ 的形状,人们又加了声符"止"表示读音,这就构成了后来的繁体字"齒",现在简化为"齿"字。龋齿是一种常见的牙科疾病,在中国有一种通俗的说法叫"虫吃牙"或"蛀牙",这种说法可以上溯到商朝,甲骨文的"龋"字写作 ▨ 、▨ 。那时的人们

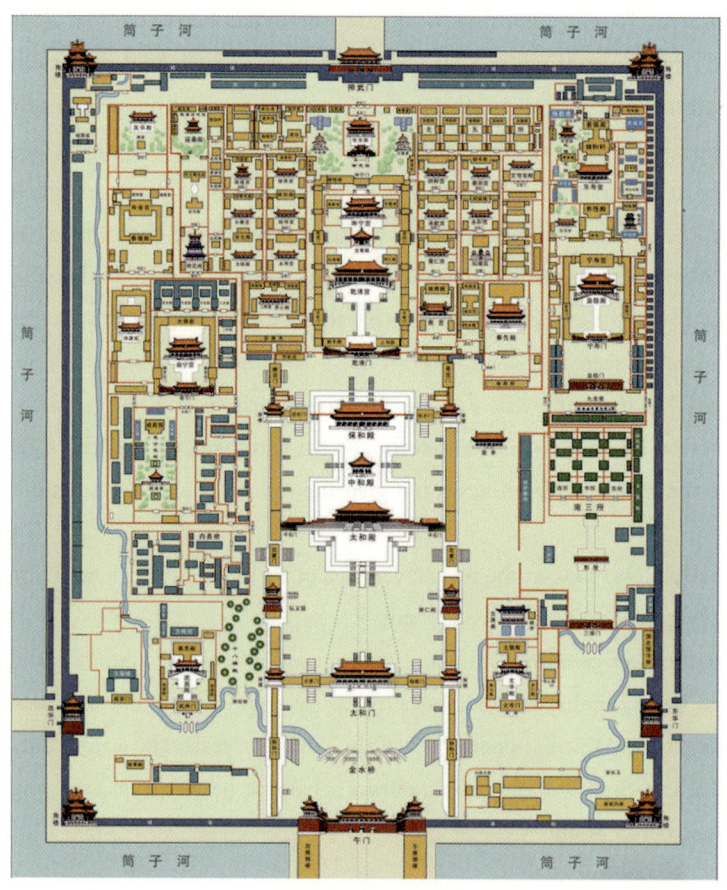

北京故宫平面图
The Floor Plan of Beijing Forbidden City

A well-known example is the central axis in Chinese-style architecture, featured in designs even several thousand years ago, stemming from a great fascination in symmetry by Chinese people. The architectural style of the Forbidden City in Beijing is an apt example embracing symmetrical beauty. Architects paid particular attention to the north-south axis of the Forbidden City and all the primary palaces were built along this axis. Secondary buildings are built with east-west symmetry.

⊞ is the original form of 齒(chǐ, tooth), which later became ⊠. Then people added the sound symbol 止(zhǐ, stop) to indicate the pronunciation, and the traditional 齒 was created, which was simplified into 齿(chǐ, tooth), in modern times. Dental cavity is a common dental disease. There is a popular saying in China called 虫吃牙(chóng chī yá, worm is eating teeth) or 蛀牙(zhù yá, tooth decay), which can be traced back to the Shang Dynasty. 齲(qǔ, dental cavity) is written as ⊞ and ⊠ in the oracle bone script. At that time, people

对于龋齿还没有科学的认知，患病的牙齿表面一般会被腐蚀出一个个小窟窿，形状非常像被虫子蛀过，"龋"字就被写成了一种虫子 🜻 在啃噬牙齿的形象。"龋"字的右边"禹"字就是一种虫的名字。

5. 自

甲骨文的"自"字像一个人鼻子的形状，是"鼻"字的初形，本义就是指鼻子。日常生活中，人们在向他人表达"我自己"这个概念的时候，习惯于用手指着本人脸部中央位置，即鼻部位置，于是"自"渐渐成了第一人称代词。人们只好在"自"字下增加一个声符"畀"字，另造了一个"鼻"字来表示鼻子的意思。

所有动物中狗的鼻子是最灵敏的，中国古人数千年前就发现了这一现象，这从一个字就可以得到很好的证明。这个字就是"臭"，甲骨文写作 🜻、🜻，"臭"字的下半部是一个"犬"字，犬就是狗，上半部是一个大大的鼻子的形象，即"自"字，就是为了突出狗的嗅觉灵敏这一特点。

人们看到"息"字时，一般会认为"息"字和心脏应该有一定的联系，因为现在的"息"字由"自"和"心"两个字组成。事实上，这只是一种字体演变过程中因字形变化而引起的误解。甲骨文"息"字写作 🜻、🜻，在鼻子下面有相对称的、短的斜线，有学者称为指示性符号，用来表示两个鼻孔呼吸时进出的气体。这些符号在演变的过程中逐渐变成了"心"字，这样才形成了现在的"息"字。有两个成语"仰人鼻息"和"息息相关"还保留着"息"字的本义。

"自"字的演变
Evolution of the Character "自"

甲骨文 Oracle Bone Script	金文 Bronze Script	小篆 Small Seal Script	隶书 Clerical Script	楷书 Regular Script
ᄇ	自	自	自	自

had no knowledge of tooth decay, but the many holes in decayed teeth closely resembled the bite marks of worms. Thus, the character 齲 was written as a worm mimicking the image of a worm(𠂇), eating a tooth. The character 禹(yǔ) on the right side indicates a worm.

5. 自(zì,self)

People breathed through the nose and created the character 自(zì, self) to denote one's nose. Thus, 自 in the oracle bone script is like a nose. Generally speaking, when people express the concept of "myself," they are used to pointing at the central part of the face — the nose—so 自 gradually started to refer to oneself as the first person pronoun. At this time, people had to add a sound symbol 畀(bì) under the character 自—鼻 to indicate the meaning of the nose.

Ancient Chinese people found the dog's nose to be the most sensitive of all animals. Accordingly, the character 臭(xiù, smell), whose oracle bone script is 𦣻, 𦣺, features the lower part犬(quǎn, dog) and the upper part resembling自(zì, self/oneself/one's own), just like a big nose, to highlight that dogs are sensitive to smell.

When people see the character 息(xī, breathe/pant), comprising of two parts 自(zì, self/oneself/one's own) and 心(xīn, heart), they generally think the word 息 should be related to the heart. In fact, this is just a misunderstanding caused by glyph changes in the evolution of the font. 息 was written as 𦣻, 𦣺in the oracle bone script, which has some symmetrical and short slashes under the nose. Some scholars call them indicative symbols, which were used to denote air when breathing. These symbols gradually changed into 心 in the process of evolution, thus forming the character 息. There are two idioms: 仰人鼻息 (yǎng rén bí xī, One has to depend on others to live) and 息息相关 (xī xī xiāng guān , One is closely related with another), which still retain the original meaning of the character 息.

中国古代有五种非常残酷的刑罚，叫作五刑。其中有一种刑罚早在甲骨文中就可以找到证据，即劓刑，"劓"字甲骨文写作 ⿰自刀 、⿰自刀 ，一个鼻子的旁边立着一把刀，意思显而易见，就是用刀把鼻子割掉。劓刑虽然轻于死刑，但使人身体致残，不仅给人造成肉体上的痛苦，而且使人无脸见人，也造成了极大的心理痛苦。后随着社会的进步，类似劓刑的残酷刑罚逐渐被废除。

6. 左、右

人们习惯用灵巧来形容双手，人类通过双手使用工具，进而劳动生产、改善生活、推动历史的前进，可见双手对于人类的重要性。甲骨文"左""右"二字分别像人的左手、右手的形状，用三个手指代表五个手指。在造字过程中，古人一般用三来表示数量多的意思，比如说人很多就用"众"字表示，树木很多就用"森"来表示。甲骨文字形不是很固定，手指朝左、朝右没有严格的区别，"左""右"二字往往混用，只有当左、右并称的时候，𠂇为左，𠂉为右，才有非常明显的区别。随着字体的演变，为了区分两者，人们分别加了"工"和"口"两个部首组成新字来区别"左"、"右"二字。

"左"字的演变
Evolution of the Character "左"

甲骨文 Oracle Bone Script	金文 Bronze Script	小篆 Small Seal Script	隶书 Clerical Script	楷书 Regular Script
𠂇	𠂇	𠂇	左	左

There were five forms of cruel punishment in ancient China, called the Five Penalties. 劓刑 (yì xíng , cutting off the nose) was one of them. The oracle writing of 劓 is 𤿥, 𤿦, just like a sword standing beside a nose; accordingly, it refers to the cutting of the nose with a sword. Although cutting off the nose is not as serious as the death penalty, it still caused physical disability, inflicting great pain on one's body and enormous shame on one's mind. With the development of society, such penalties were gradually abolished.

6. 左、右(zuǒ yòu, left and right)

People are used to applying the adjective "dexterous" to describe one's hands. The importance of hands for human beings can be seen from the fact that human beings use tools with both hands to do productive labor, improve their lives and advance the progress of history. The oracle writing of 左(zuǒ, left) and 右 (yòu, right) are like the shape of one's left hand and right hand, respectively, with three fingers representing five fingers. In the process of character creation, the ancients generally used three to express the meaning of a large number. For example, a large number of people are denoted by the character 众 (zhòng, public) and a large number of trees are denoted by 森(sēn, forest). The shape of the oracle bone script is not fixed. There is no rigorous distinction between the left and right fingers. It is hard to distinguish 左 and 右 in most cases. Only when left and right are shown together can there be a very obvious distinction, with 𠂇 being the left and 又 being the right. With the evolution of the font, people added the two words 工(gōng, labour/work) and 口(kǒu, mouth) in order to distinguish 左 and 右.

"右" 字的演变
Evolution of the Character "右"

甲骨文 Oracle Bone Script	金文 Bronze Script	小篆 Small Seal Script	隶书 Clerical Script	楷书 Regular Script
㕣	㠯	㕚	右	右

当两只手同时出现的时候，许多有趣的事情就发生了。一名年轻的姑娘得到了一块美玉，就产生了"弄"字，即👐，后来演变为👐，像双手持玉在把玩。她高高兴兴地回家去，结果在路上碰到了歹人，歹人突然从路旁冲出用手抢夺她手中的这块儿美玉，"争"字就出现了，即👐，繁体字写作爭，看起来像是两只手从上、下两个方向在争夺一件物品。正在关键时刻，一个高大威猛的义士出现了，开始与歹人搏斗，"斗"字就产生了，即👐，繁体字写作"鬥"，像两人相对而徒手搏斗。最后，义士抢回了美玉，并把它还给了这名女子，女子感激地接受了，"受"字就产生了，即👐，👐字看起来像是两只手在传递一件东西，有学者认为这件东西是"舟"，"舟"同时作为声符。👐字看起来既可以表示接受的意思，也可表示授予的意思，为了区别这两个义项，人们又在受字旁加了一只手"扌"，另造"授"字表示授予的意思，可以这么说，一个"授"字当中就有三只手。当然，一个字里也可以有四只手，例如"兴"字，繁体字是"興"，甲骨文写作👐，金文写作👐，像是四只手在合力抬起一件比较重的东西，这里用四只手代替众多的人。

7. 止

甲骨文"止"字是一幅脚掌的剪影，像脚趾头张开的脚掌形状，以三个趾头代替五个趾头，表示脚的意思，而同时期的陶文👐，则显示了一只更加形象的脚，甚至可以说是一幅脚的图画。有的甲骨文简化为线描，淡化脚掌形象，突出三趾叉开的形状。当"止"用来表示停止的意思后，人们又造"趾"来表示脚的本义。

当不同数量的"止"出现的时候，新的故事又开始了。一名信使从都城往地方传送商王的命令，一开始是跑步前行，这时"走"字出

When both hands appear at the same time, many interesting things happen. A young girl received a piece of jade, creating the character 弄(nòng, get), originally written as 𢆉, and later evolving into 弄, which represented a piece of jade being placed into her hands. People then say she met a robber on her way home. The robber suddenly rushed out from the roadside to rob the jade from the girl. Then the character 争(zhēng, contend/vie/strive) was created as 𠂇, and its traditional version is 爭, which resembles two hands fighting for one item, with one hand atop the other. At this critical moment, a tall, mighty, and righteous man showed up and began to fend off the robber. The character 斗(dòu, fight) was created as 鬥, whose traditional Chinese character is written as 鬥, like two people fighting with each other. Finally, the righteous man defeated the robber and returned the jade to the girl. The girl accepted it gratefully. In this way, the character 受 (shòu, accept) was born as 受. The shape of 受 looks like two hands passing something between them. Some scholars think it is 舟(zhōu, boat), and 舟 is also seen as a sound symbol. It seems that the character can mean both acceptance and grant. In order to distinguish the two meanings, people add a hand 扌 to form another word 授(shòu, grant) to indicate grant. It can be said that there are three hands in the character 授. Of course, there can be four hands in a single word, such as 兴(xìng, rise/get up). The traditional Chinese character of 兴 is 興, the oracle writing of it is 興, and its form of the bronze script is 興, like four hands in a joint effort to lift a heavy thing. In this word, the four hands symbolize many people.

7. 止(zhǐ, stop)

The oracle writing of 止(zhǐ, stop/toe) is a silhouette of the foot with three toes splaying out instead of five, indicating the meaning of foot. Meanwhile, the character's pottery writing of the same period— 止 , shows the foot more vividly. Some oracle scripts are simplified to line drawing, which fades the image of the foot and highlights the shape of the three splitting/splaying toes. When the character 止 was used eventually to mean stop, people created 趾(zhǐ, toe) to indicate the meaning of the original character.

When 止 is used multiple times, new words are created. A messenger carried the orders of the king in the Shang Dynasty from the capital to the surrounging areas by running at the start of his journey. At this time, the character, 走(zǒu, walk), was written as 走, whose oracle writing resembles a person swinging his arms and walking in big strides. The character 走 in the bronze script is written as

现了,甲骨文写作 ,像一个人摆动双臂大跨步行走的样子,金文"走"字写作 ,下面加了"止"代表脚,突出脚运动的状态。在古代"走"表示跑的意思,成语"走马观花"就是指骑在奔跑的马上看花,现在的走一般表示步行的意思。跑累了就缓慢行走,边休息边行走,"步"字便产生了,甲骨文写作 、 ,金文写作 ,像一前一后两只脚在行进的样子,意思就是常说的步行。正走着,前面突然出现了一条小河,而又没有舟船可用,只好徒步过河,"涉"字出现了,甲骨文写作 、 ,中间是弯弯的一道水流,两边是两只足形,一左一右或者一前一后,表示徒步蹚水过河,后来水作为偏旁放在左边,就构成了现在的"涉"字。过河之后发现夕阳西下,而命令必须在天黑之前送到,"奔"字就出现了,金文写作 ,由一个挥舞双臂的人和三个代表脚的"止"组成,在"走"字的基础上多了两个"止",表示跑得特别快的意思。

"止"字的演变
Evolution of the Character "止"

甲骨文 Oracle Bone Script	金文 Bronze Script	小篆 Small Seal Script	隶书 Clerical Script	楷书 Regular Script
ᐯ	ᐯ	ᐯ	止	止

🦵 with 止 being added at the bottom to highlight foot movement. In the ancient times, 走 means running. However, the idiom, 走马观花 (zǒu mǎ guān huā, riding on a horse while appreciating the flowers), means riding on the running horse while admiring the beauty of the flowers. When he felt tired, the messenger slowed down. Then the character, 步(bù, step), was born with 𝑌 , 𝑌 as its form in the oracle bone script and 𝑌 as its form in the bronze script, both of which represent two feet moving forward in tandem. Just as the messenger was walking, he came to a small river. There was no boat available so he had to cross the river on foot. Thus, the character 涉(shè, wade/ ford) came into being written as 𝑌 , 𝑌 in the oracle bone script, representing a stream in the middle and one foot on each side, depicting how the messenger waded across the river. Later on, the stream is placed on the left side of the character as a radical to form the current word, 涉. After crossing the river, the messenger noticed that the sun began to set and was reminded that he was supposed to deliver the orders before dark. The character, 奔 (bēn/bèn, run/go straight towards), came into shape as 🦵 in the bronze script, comprised of an arm-waving man and three 止 to express that he was running.

三、自然万物

几十万乃至百万年以前，当人类的祖先来到这个世界的时候，他们面对着阳光空气、田土山川，看过了日出日落、月圆月缺，经历了春夏秋冬、寒来暑往，目睹了自然界的鬼斧神工，自然万物的生生不息，高山沟通天地，土地生养五谷，大火烹煮食物，雨水滋润万物。人们在认识自然并总结规律的过程中创造了相对应的文字符号，汉字也成为自然万物的忠实记录者。

1. 日

日的本义是指太阳，是人们最为依赖的天体，人们日出而作日落而息，对太阳有着无比的崇拜。早期的"日"字像太阳的形状，字体为圆形，甲骨文"日"字因用刀契刻而不便刻成圆形，所以大多时候刻成方形。"日"字中间有一点或者一短横，是为了与表示圆形或方形的符号相区别。因为在文字产生之前，很多符号已经产生并长期使用，如用来表示数目一（一）、二（二）、三（三）、四（亖）和方（囗）、圆（〇）概念等的许多符号。

"日"本来指太阳，因人们只有在白天看得见太阳，日也用来表示白昼的意思，而白昼会一天一天周而复始地过去，所以日后来也指时间，"时"字就是以"日"字为偏旁组成的。

"日"字的演变
Evolution of the Character "日"

甲骨文 Oracle Bone Script	金文 Bronze Script	小篆 Small Seal Script	隶书 Clerical Script	楷书 Regular Script
⊟	⊙	⊙	日	日

III. Nature

Hundreds of thousands or even millions of years ago, when the ancestors of human beings came into the world, they faced the sun and the air, the mountains and rivers. They saw sunrise and sunset, the full moon and the waning moon; they experienced spring, summer, autumn and winter and saw the magic and mystery of nature. The mountains connect the sky and the ground; grains grow on the land; fire is used to cook food, and the rain moistens everything, all of which shows that everything in nature changes constantly. People created characters and symbols through observation of nature. Therefore, Chinese characters are also regarded as the faithful recorder of all things in nature.

1. 日(rì, sun/day)

日 refers to the sun, the celestial body on which people rely most. People work and rest as the sun rises and falls as a way to show their incomparable worship of the sun. In the early days, the character of 日 was like the shape of the sun, and the font was round. When 日 was carved in oracle bone with a knife, its shape was changed from a circle to a square because carving a circle took too much effort in the bone. The character 日 has a dot or a short cross in the middle in order to distinguish itself from the circle or the square, the reason being that many simple symbols were used for a long time before, such as symbols used to represent the numbers one (—), two (二), three (三), four (亖) and concepts of square (□) and circle (○).

日 originally refers to the sun, because people can only see the sun during the day, and it is also used to indicate daytime. Time will go round and round day by day, so 日 is also used to indicate times in the past. For example, the character 时 (shí, time) is made up of 日 as its radical.

2. 月

当太阳下山之后,月亮会悄悄地爬上天空,给人们带来或明或暗的光亮,而且,古人也发现月亮的形状和太阳总是圆形的情况不一样,月亮的形状一直在变化,有时圆有时缺,但圆的时候少而缺的时候多。人们所造的月字就非常形象地反映了这种自然现象,甲骨文"月"字看起来就是一个"弯弯的月亮",既不是新月也不是满月。

月亮绕地球运行一周大约是30天,所以古人又用月来计算时日,平均30天为一个月,一年12个月。中国自古以来就是一个农业大国,人们根据月亮的运行规律制定了历法用来指导农业生产,这种历法就叫农历,从夏朝开始使用,已有4000多年的历史。农历是根据月亮圆缺变化的周期制定的,阳历是以地球环绕太阳运行的周期制定的,在中国,日为"阳",月为"阴",所以农历也叫阴历。中国人最隆重的节日是过年,也叫春节,就是农历或者说阴历的每年正月初一。

月亮在每个月的十五日达到最圆的状态,尤其是每年的八月十五日最大最圆,而这时候秋季正好过了一半,又是丰收的季节,所以古代中国人把每年的农历八月十五日定为中秋节。在这一天,人们庆祝丰收、举家团圆、供奉月神,吃一种外形像圆月的美食,这种美食叫月饼。

月饼
Moon Cake

2. 月(yuè, moon/month)

When the sun goes down, the moon will creep up, bringing people blurry light. Moreover, the ancient found another way to represent the moon's shape, which differs from the sun's unchanging round shape. You can only see a full or almost-full moon several nights in a month while the waning moon is visible for the majority of the remaining nights. The character of 月 vividly reflected this natural phenomenon. The character 月 in the oracle bone scripts looks like a "curved moon," which is neither a new moon nor a full moon.

It takes the moon approximately 30 days to orbit around the earth, so the ancient used one full orbit, or a month, to calculate the time. There are 30 days in a month on average and 12 months in a year. China has largely been an agricultural country since ancient times. People formulated a calendar to guide agricultural production according to the position of the moon. This is referred to as the lunar calendar. It has been used since the Xia Dynasty and has a history of more than 4,000 years. The lunar calendar is based on the changing cycle between the crescent and full moon. Conversely, the solar calendar is based on the cycle of the earth's orbiting around the sun. In China, 日 is yang and 月 is yin, so the lunar calendar is also called the yin calendar. The grandest festival for Chinese people is the Lunar New Year, also known as the Spring Festival, which is the first day of the first month of the lunar calendar or yin calendar.

The moon is the fullest on the 15th of each month, especially on the 15th of August every year, which is considered both mid-autumn and harvest season. As such, the ancient Chinese designated the 15th day of the eighth lunar month every year as the Mid-Autumn Festival. On this day, people celebrate harvest, reunite with their families, worship the moon god, and have moon cakes, a kind of delicious food shaped like a full moon, while appreciating the bright moon light.

"月"字的演变
Evolution of the Character "月"

甲骨文 Oracle Bone Script	金文 Bronze Script	小篆 Small Seal Script	隶书 Clerical Script	楷书 Regular Script
☽	☽	𐊰	月	月

"月子"并不是月亮之子的意思,而是指医学上所说的产褥期,主要是指从分娩结束到产妇身体基本恢复至孕前状态的一段时间。这段时间在中国大约是一个月的时间,俗称为"坐月子",是中华养生文化中一项重要的内容。

日月的运行引起了昼夜的交替变化,由"日""月"二字分别组成了具有重要内涵的两个字"阳""阴"。山的南面容易接受阳光的照射,人们用"阳"表示山的南面或水的北面,用"阴"表示山的北面或水的南面,由此产生了许多带"阳"字或"阴"字的地名。如古都洛阳在河南省洛河之北,贵州省省会贵阳在贵山之南,还有辽宁省省会沈阳,湖南省的衡阳等。然而有趣的是,地名中带"阳"字的远远多于带"阴"字的,可能是人们更喜欢"阳"所带来的积极意义。

河南省汤阴县,因在汤河之南,故称汤阴。汤阴虽然是一个县,却是博大精深的中国文化经典《周易》的发祥地。周文王姬昌被商纣王幽禁于此,他在被囚禁的漫长岁月里,潜心研究,演绎八卦,并提出"刚柔相对,变在其中"的富有朴素辩证法的观点,最终著成《周易》一书,也叫《易经》,后被列为五经之首。

"阴""阳"也是中国古代哲学的一对非常重要的概念。中国古代哲学认为宇宙中有通贯所有物质的两大对立面,自然界中的一切现象都存在着相互对立而又相互作用的关系,就用阴、阳这个概念来解释自然界两种对立和相互消长的物质势力,并认为阴阳的对立和消长是事物本身所固有的,进而认为阴阳的对立和消长是宇宙的基本规律。

月子(yuè zǐ, sitting month) does not refer to the son of the moon, but to the puerperal period in medicine which is the time from the end of childbirth to the return of the maternal body to the pre-pregnancy state. This period of time is approximately one month in China, commonly known as "sitting month/the confinement" and is seen as an important part of Chinese health culture.

The cycles of the sun and the moon are responsible for the cycles of day and night. The characters 日 and 月 represent the words yang and yin, respectively, with important connotations. The south side of the mountain is easily exposed to sunlight. People use yang to indicate the south side of the mountain or the north side of the water, and yin to indicate the north side of the mountain or the south side of the water, resulting in many geographic names featuring the characters yang or yin. For example, the ancient capital Luoyang in Henan Province is named for its location north of Luohe River; Guiyang, the capital of Guizhou Province, is in the south of Guishan Mountain; similarly,Shenyang, the capital city of Liaoning Province and Hengyang in Hunan Province, also get their names in the same way. However, it is interesting to note that "yang" appears far more frequently in geographic names than yin, which may indicate that people prefer the positive meaning that yang carries.

For example, Tangyin County in Henan Province is named for its location south of Tanghe River. Although Tangyin is just a county, it is the birthplace of the epic and profound Chinese cultural classic *Zhou Yi* (*The Book of Changes*). King Zhouwenwang (King Wen of the Zhou, Jichang)was once confined in this place by King Shangzhouwang (King Zhou of Shang) In his long years of imprisonment, he devoted himself to researching and interpretating the Eight Diagrams and he proposed 刚柔相对，变在其中(Everything changes constantly between yin and yang), a perspective with clear dialectic thought. He completed the writing of *Zhou Yi*, also known as *The Book of Changes*, which ultimately became listed as the first among the five classics that would emerge.

Yin and yang appear frequently in ancient Chinese philosophy, which claims that there exist two opposites in the universe that connect all materials, and all phenomena in nature have an opposite, yet united relation. Ancient people believed that the continual growth and decline of yin and yang were inherent in everything, and that this relationship constituted the basic law of the universe.

阴阳对立即指世间一切事物或现象都存在着相互对立的阴阳两个方面，如天与地、男与女、动与静等，其中天为阳，地为阴；男为阳、女为阴；动为阳，静为阴。对立的阴阳双方又是互相依存的，任何一方都不能脱离另一方而单独存在，如没有动就无所谓静。

3. 山

甲骨文"山"字像由多个高耸山峰组成的山岭形状，远远望去像地平线上起伏连绵的群峰的线描，用三座山峰来代表众多的山峰。在中国古代，很多山已经不仅仅是自然的山，而被赋予了更深层次的含义。唐代刘禹锡在《陋室铭》中写到："山不在高，有仙则名。水不在深，有龙则灵。"意思是说，山有名不在它的高矮，而在于有没有仙人居住。"仙"字是因道教而产生的一个字，道教是中国的本土宗教，追求长生不老、得道成仙、济世救人。"仙"字由"人"和"山"两个字组成，强调在山上修行的人。从"仙"字可以看出道教修炼的重要场所便是高山，一些山也因道教而名扬天下，四大道教名山分别是四川的青城山、江西的龙虎山、湖北的武当山和安徽的齐云山。

佛教传入中国以来，也选择了同样的路径，逐渐形成了佛教四大名山，即山西五台山、四川峨眉山、安徽九华山、浙江普陀山，分别供奉文殊菩萨、普贤菩萨、地藏菩萨、观音菩萨。

"山"字的演变
Evolution of the Character "山"

甲骨文 Oracle Bone Script	金文 Bronze Script	小篆 Small Seal Script	隶书 Clerical Script	楷书 Regular Script
ᗑ	♠	山	山	山

Yin-yang, a couple in opposition, indicates that there are two opposite aspects in all things or phenomena in the world, such as heaven and earth, man and woman, movement and stillness, where heaven is yang and earth is yin, man is yang and woman is yin, movement is yang and stillness is yin. Yin and yang are interdependent. That is to say, yin and yang cannot exist without each other. If there is no movement, there will be no stillness.

3. 山(shān, mountain)

The character 山 in the oracle bone scripts is shaped like a mountain with a number of towering peaks. It looks like a line drawing of rolling peaks on the horizon, with three peaks representing many. In ancient China, many mountains were not just seen as part of the natural landscape, but as having a deeper cultural meaning. Liu Yuxi of the Tang Dynasty wrote in *Loushiming* (*The Humble Chamber*) that, "It is not the height of this mountain, but the saints that live here that make it famous; it is not the depth of the river, but the dragons within that make it divine." The character 仙(xiān, immortal) is a character created by Taoism. Taoism is a local religion in China, which pursues immortality and salvation. The character 仙(xiān, immortal) is made up of the characters 人 (rén, man/human being) and 山(shān, mountain), representing a man who practices Taoism in the mountain. From the character 仙(xiān, immortal), we can see that the important places for Taoist cultivation are in the high mountains. Some mountains are famous for Taoism. The four famous Taoist mountains are the Qingcheng Mountain in Sichuan, Longhu Mountain in Jiangxi, Wudang Mountain in Hubei and Qiyun Mountain in Anhui.

When Buddhism was introduced to China, it also claimed the mountain as a spiritual place, and gradually formed the four famous mountains of Buddhism, namely Wutai Mountain in Shanxi, Mount Emei in Sichuan, Jiuhua Mountain in Anhui, and Putuo Mountain in Zhejiang. They are dedicated to Manjushri, Samantabhadra, Bodhisattva, and Guanyin Buddha.

"丘"字的演变
Evolution of the Character "丘"

甲骨文 Oracle Bone Script	金文 Bronze Script	小篆 Small Seal Script	隶书 Clerical Script	楷书 Regular Script
ᗰ	巫	皿	丠	丘

4. 丘

丘泛指因地势而自然形成的小而低矮的山，山体多为土质，中国的南方有广袤的丘陵地带。字典里还有另外一种有趣的解释，即四周隆起、中央下凹的地形叫作"丘"，这种解释来自于史书对于孔子名字由来的记载。

众所周知，孔子是中国古代的大思想家、教育家。世界上很多人都知道孔子，但不一定知道他的真实名字。孔子姓孔名丘，子是对他的尊称，如道家的老子、庄子，地位仅次于孔子的儒家代表人物孟子，墨家的墨子等。孔子名丘在中国第一部纪传体通史《史记》中有详细的记载：孔子诞生于公元前551年，诞生之前他的父母叔梁纥和颜氏曾到附近的尼丘山向神明祷告过，而且，孔子刚出生时头顶是凹下去的，所以就给他取名叫"丘"，字仲尼。"伯、仲、叔、季"是中国古代用在名字中表示排行的常用字，从"仲尼"二字中可以看出，孔子排行老二，他在家里肯定还有个哥哥。

后来，丘和山都可以表示山的概念，东晋诗人陶渊明在作品《归园田居》中写到："少无适俗韵，性本爱丘山。"丘和山连用，两者已经没有分别，泛指山的概念，即隐居山林，安享田园生活。

5. 水

水是人们日常生活不可或缺的重要物质，远古先民定居时肯定选择附近有水源的地方，尤其是流动的水源。人类的各大文明几乎都是起源于大的河流，古巴比伦文明起源于底格里斯河及幼发拉底河，古埃

4. 丘(qiū, hillock/mound)

丘(qiū, hillock/mound) refers to small, low-lying mountains made of varying soils. There are vast hilly areas in southern China. Another interesting explanation can be found in the dictionary— the terrain with ridges around and hollows in the center is called 丘, which was actually written to explain the name of Confucius in the historical records.

As we all know, Confucius was a great thinker and educator in ancient China. Many people around the world may know Confucius, but they may not know his real name. Confucius' (Kong Zi) family name was Kong, his given name was Qiu, and he was also referred to as Zi as a sign of respect, just as the Taoists Lao Zi and Zhuang Zi; Men Zi(Mencius), ranking second only to Confucius; the representaive figure of Confucianism and Mo Zi of Monism. Qiu, as the given name of Confucius, is detailed in China's first biographical historical record of *Shi Ji (Records of the Historian)*. Confucius was born in 551 BC, and before his birth, his parents, Shu Liangge and Yan, had prayed to the gods in the nearby Mount Niqiu. When Confucius was born, the top of his head was sunken, so he was named "Qiu" and Zhongni was given as his second name. 伯，仲，叔，季 (bó, zhòng, shū, jì) are common words used in ancient China to indicate birth order. From 仲尼 (zhòng ní), we can deduce that Confucius was the second-born, and there must be an elder brother in his family.

Both the characters 丘(qiū, mound) and 山(shān, mountain) have come to mean mountain. The poet Tao Yuanming in the Eastern Jin Dynasty wrote in his work, "Gui Yuan Tian Ju" ("Returning to My Farm"), "I could not adapt to the folk life when I was young, and I loved life in the mountains ("丘" and "山") best." In this case, there is no difference between these two characters as they both referred to a mountain, but when these two characters were used together as "丘山," it referred to the secluded life in the mountainous and rural areas.

5. 水(shuǐ, water)

Water is an indispensable and important element in people's daily life. When the ancestors chose where to live, they often settled near water sources, especially the rivers. Almost all human civilizations originated along the banks of large rivers. Examples can be seen from the ancient Babylonians along the Tigris and Euphrates, the ancient Egyptians along the Nile, the ancient Indians along the

及文明起源于尼罗河，古印度文明起源于印度河及恒河，华夏文明起源于黄河。甲骨文的"水"字像水流动的形状，曲线旁边的小点或短线像水滴，水滴多少不等。甲骨文"水"字看起来更像是一幅简笔画，就是一条蜿蜒曲折的水流的形状，有一种灵动的美。水字做偏旁时一般写作"氵"，如江河湖海、汹涌澎湃等字词，都和水有关。

水总是停留在卑下的地方，造福万物、滋养万物，从不与万物争高下，古人从水那里学到了很多高尚的品格。中国古代的大思想家老子在《道德经》里提出了著名的"上善若水"，大意是最完善的人就应该像水一样，能尽其所能地贡献自己的力量去帮助别人，而不会与别人争功争名争利。

中国古代另一位思想家孔子对水是另一种描述，《论语》记载："子在川上曰：逝者如斯夫，不舍昼夜。"甲骨文"川"字写作 、 ，与甲骨文"水"字一样，都像水流动的形状，后来才表示有河岸的水流。孔子站在河岸边，看着日夜不停流逝的河流，发出了响彻古今的感慨：自然界、人世间、宇宙万物，无一不是逝者，无一不像河里的流水，昼夜不停地流逝，一经逝去，便不会重返。

中国人也用山、水来描写父母的爱，即"父爱如山，母爱如水"。父亲如大山，给人依靠，母亲如泉水，使人放松。父爱深沉稳重如山，母爱

"水"字的演变
Evolution of the Character "水"

甲骨文 Oracle Bone Script	金文 Bronze Script	小篆 Small Seal Script	隶书 Clerical Script	楷书 Regular Script
				水

Indus and Ganges, and the ancient Chinese along the Yellow River. The character 水 is written as the shape of flowing water in the oracle bone inscription. The small dots or short lines beside the curve are like water droplets. The droplets are of varying number. Furthermore, the character 水 in the oracle bone inscription looks more like a simple line-drawing, a shape of a winding stream with dynamic beauty. When used as a radical, this character is generally written as 氵, indicating the relation to water, such as in 江河湖海(jiāng hé hú hǎi , rivers, seas, and lakes), and 汹涌澎湃(xiōng yǒng péng pài, surging waves).

  The ancients learn many virtues from water because it always stays in a humble place, benefiting and nourishing all things and never competing with them. Lao Zi, a great ideologist in ancient China, put forward the famous philosophic theory "The highest good is like water" in *Daode Jing*(*The Classic of the Way and Its Virtue*), meaning that the perfect person should behave like water by contributing their own strength while trying their best to help others without competing for merit, fame, or profit.

  Confucius described water in another way. According to *Lun Yu* (*The Analects*), "Confucius sighed at the riverside, 'the passage of time is like a river flowing day and night.'"The character 川(chuān, river）in the oracle bone inscription is written as 𝕴 and 𝕵 , the same as 水(shuǐ, water) in the oracle bone inscription, both like the shape of flowing water, which later indicated the water flowing beside the river banks. Confucius stood on the river bank, watching the flowing rivers and sighed with the feeling that nature, the world, and everything in the universe are changing as time goes by like the flowing water in the river, running day and night. Once it passes away, it will not return.

  Chinese people also use mountains and water to describe the love of their parents, that is, "a father's love is like a mountain, while a mother's love is like water." The father figure is like a mountain, providing a source of reliability, while the mother figure is like a spring, providing peace and comfort. Mountains are as powerful as the love of fathers which is deep and steady, and water is as soft as the love of mothers which is expressed continuously. Mountains are powerful, while water is flowing continuously, so the father's love is deep and steady like the mountains, and the mother's love expresses warmth and softness like the water.

温馨柔和如水，山有力，水绵长，所以父爱如山，母爱如水。事实上，严父慈母，山水辉映，水中有山的影子，山下有水在流淌，父爱母爱一样，都是世界上最伟大的爱。

6. 昔

"昔"字的本义是从前、往日、故去，和"今"的意思相对。甲骨文"昔"字像日漂浮在波浪之上，有的则在水波之下，像是被汹涌的波浪所淹没，表示洪水滔天的意思，除了天上的太阳和地上的洪水，不见别的物体。相传上古时期，曾经一度洪水泛滥，陆地大多被淹没，引起了巨大的灾难。后来人们提起过去，总是会想起那一段洪水成灾的日子，于是就造了这个"昔"字。

在很多文明中都有史前大洪水的记录，每个文明对待这场洪水的方式都不相同。在中国，记载这场洪水最著名的就是"大禹治水"，面对洪水，中国人没有退让逃避，没有听天由命，而是靠勤劳和艰苦的斗争精神与洪水作斗争，他们在首领大禹的带领下疏通河床、开凿渠道，花费了13年的时间治理了肆虐的洪水。为了不耽误时间，大禹"三过家门而不入"，这是一种舍小家为大家的精神，这是一种敢于和自然作斗争的精神，这种精神是中华民族精神的重要内涵。

大禹治水
Yu the Great Taming the Flood

In fact, the strict father and kind mother often appear like the mountains and water, or the shadow of the mountains in the water, or the water flowing at the foot of the mountain. Therefore, the love of both father and mother is the same, intertwining to produce the greatest love in the world.

6. 昔(xī, past)

The character 昔 originally meant the past, and its antonym was 今(jīn, now). In the oracle bone script, 昔(xī, past) is like the character, 日(rì, sun), floating on or washed under the waves. We cannot see any objects besides the sun in the sky and the flood on the earth. According to a legend, there was once a catastrophic flood that destroyed the land. When people mentioned the past, they remembered the days of this tragic flood and captured this memory in the character 昔(xī, past).

Many civilizations recognize this legendary flood, although each of them has different ways of recording it. In China, the most famous story of this event is "Yu the Great Taming the Flood". In this story, Chinese people did not escape or yield to their fate, but faced the flood. Yu the Great spent thirteen years leading his men in dredging all the rivers. In order not to waste time, Yu the Great was so dedicated that he passed his home three times without entering and continued his work instead. This story embodies the ways in which national interest should take priority over everything else, as well the importance of facing the difficulties of nature.

"昔"字的演变
Evolution of the Character "昔"

甲骨文 Oracle Bone Script	金文 Bronze Script	小篆 Small Seal Script	隶书 Clerical Script	楷书 Regular Script
				昔

"云"字的演变
Evolution of the Character "云"

甲骨文 Oracle Bone Script	金文 Bronze Script	小篆 Small Seal Script	隶书 Clerical Script	楷书 Regular Script
![]	![]	![]	![]	云

7. 云

甲骨文"云"字像云气在天上回旋飘动之形,本义指云气。后来"云"被借为说的意思,有成语"人云亦云",意思就是人家怎么说,自己也跟着怎么说,用来形容只会随声附和,没有自己的主见。云由空中水气凝聚而成,积聚时间长了就成了雨水,人们又在"云"字上面加个"雨"字新造一个字"雲"来表示云的意思。汉字简化后,"云"又恢复了它的本义。

云有虚无缥缈、转瞬即逝的特点,所以人们用"浮云"表示无实际意义的事物,多用于不在意的事物。孔子说过:"不义而富且贵,于我如浮云。"即用不正当的手段得来的富贵,对于我来讲就像是天上的浮云一样。

8. 雨

甲骨文的"雨"字像从天空纷纷降落的雨滴的形状,上面一横或两横表示天空,有的雨滴非常形象,随风飘落的情景都被描摹了出来。

大雨过后,天空往往会出现彩虹。古人对彩虹这种自然现象尚不能给出科学的解释,他们认为彩虹是一种类似龙的动物,有很长的身体,身体两端有两个头,并且都张着巨大的口,常常在下雨后出现,横跨在高高的天空,低下两头吸饮水气。甲骨文的"虹"字写作 ,正是古人想象中虹的形象,像腰腹呈拱形的、有两个头的神龙。

7. 云(yún, cloud)

The character 云 in the oracle bone script resembles the shape of whirling and fluttering clouds in the sky. Later, 云 was used in an idiom, "echo others' words," which means having no opinions of your own, but simply following others. People added the character 雨(yǔ, rain) to 云 to form the character 雲, to capture the formation of clouds and the continual condensation that would inevitably lead to rain. After the simplification of Chinese characters, the character 云 was restored to its original meaning.

Clouds have the characteristics of nothingness and fleetness, so people use 浮云(fú yún, floating clouds) to express there is no practical means for something. Confucius said, "Riches and honors acquired by unrighteousness, to me, are like the floating clouds," which means that wealth obtained unjustly is worth nothing.

8. 雨(yǔ, rain)

The character 雨 in the oracle bone script is like the shape of falling raindrops, with one or two horizontal strokes above to represent the sky. Some raindrops are very vivid in the character, depicting a scene of raindrops falling in the wind.

Rainbows often appear after the heavy rain. The ancient could not give a scientific explanation to the natural phenomenon of the rainbow, so they believed that the rainbow was a kind of dragon with a long body, two heads at both ends, and a huge mouth, that often appeared after the rain. Legends claim that the dragon arches in the sky and bends its two heads to drink the water. The character 虹(hóng, rainbow) in the oracle bone script is 𩔹 which perfectly captures the image of the rainbow in ancient people's imagination, like a mythical double-headed dragon with an arched waist stretching across the sky.

"雨" 字的演变
Evolution of the Character "雨"

甲骨文 Oracle Bone Script	金文 Bronze Script	小篆 Small Seal Script	隶书 Clerical Script	楷书 Regular Script
雨	雨	雨	雨	雨

人们后来又造了一个形声字"虹",由"虫"和"工"两个字组成,一个表意,一个标音。由彩虹吸水现象命名的"虹吸"原理在很多方面都有应用,中国人很早就懂得了这个原理,农民用竹筒制作虹吸管把峻岭阻隔的泉水引到山下灌溉农田,古人还应用虹吸原理制作了唧筒,用于战争中的灭火。

9. 木

甲骨文"木"字像一棵树的形状,上面像树枝,中间像树干,下面像树根。木的本义指树木,是木本植物的通称。甲骨文"林"字写作 ⚹,由两个"木"字组成,表示树木众多,本义是指成片的树木。甲骨文"森"字写作 ⚹,由三个"木"字组成,像树木茂密丛生的样子,现在一般"森林"两字连用。

人们后来分别在"木"字的上端和底部加了一个指示性符号,即一横,新造了两个字"末"和"本","末"字表示树梢、末端的意思,"本"字表示树根的意思。秋天到了,树上结满了圆圆的果实,甲骨文"果"字写作 ⚹,由于果实难于单独表示,连生长果实的树木也被描写出来,金文时演变成 ⚹。果实熟了,人们迫不及待地开始采摘,甲骨文"采"字写作 ⚹,像一只手在采摘果实,但也有人认为在采摘树叶,有的甲骨文写法比较简略,如 ⚹,省去了树上的果子,像一个人用手去采摘树上的东西。不论采摘的是果实还是树叶,采摘的这个动作还是活灵活现地表现了出来。

"木"字的演变
Evolution of the Character "木"

甲骨文 Oracle Bone Script	金文 Bronze Script	小篆 Small Seal Script	隶书 Clerical Script	楷书 Regular Script
✦	✦	✦	木	木

Later, people created a phonetic word 虹(hóng, rainbow), composed of 虫(chóng, worm) and 工(gōng). One is the ideographical expression, and the other is the phonetic symbol. The principle of "siphon", named after the phenomenon of rainbow absorbing water, was understood by Chinese people long ago. Farmers used bamboo tubes to make siphons to guide the spring water that was blocked by the mountains to irrigate farmlands. The ancients also used the principle of siphoning to make Jitong (fire pumps) used for firefighting in the war.

9. 木(mù, wood)

The character 木 in the oracle bone script is like the shape of a tree, with branches above, trunks in the middle, and roots below. This character referred initially to trees and was used as a general term for woody plants. The character 林(lín, forest) in oracle bone script is written as 𣎴 ,consisting of two 木 characters, which means that there are many trees. The character 森(sēn, forest) in the oracle bone script is written as 𣏕 and is made up of three characters of 木(mù, wood), to resemble the appearance of dense trees. Now, the word 森林(sēn lín, forest) is used in general.

Later, people added a horizontal stroke to the top and bottom of the character木(mù, wood) to form the characters 末(mò, end) and 本(běn, root). The character 末means the tip of a tree, and the character 本(běn, root) means the root of a tree. To represent the round fruits that grew on trees in the autumn, the character 果(guǒ, fruit) was introduced. In the oracle bone script, it is written as 𣎴 . The difficulty in expressing a fruit without context was resolved by describing fruits alongside trees. This character was transformed in bronze script as 𣎴 . When the fruit is ripe, people can't resist picking it, and that is why the character 采(cǎi, picking) in the oracle bone script is written as 𣎴 , which is like a hand that is picking fruit, but others think the hand is picking leaves. Some oracle bone characters are abbreviated, such as 𣎴 , leaving out the fruit of the tree, like a man picking things from the tree by hand. Whether the man is picking fruits or leaves, the action of picking is vividly expressed.

10. 燕

甲骨文的"燕"字像张开翅膀在天空自由飞翔的燕子的形象，本义指燕子。因燕子全身黑色，玄有黑色的意思，所以古人把燕子称作玄鸟。《诗经》有"玄鸟生商"的记载，这是一个关于商朝祖先诞生的美丽传说。相传古代有个叫简狄的女子，在洗澡时看到一只玄鸟飞过，并产下一颗卵，简狄把卵取来直接吞食。她因而怀孕，并生下了一个男孩，那个男孩就是商朝人的祖先。

过去人们都认为《诗经》里的这个记载是后人附会的，而从甲骨文里可以看出，这个概念早就存在于商朝人的脑子里。甲骨文里一旦出现"亥"字，即 ᚠ，上面就会出现一只鸟，如 ᚠ、ᚠ 等。通过甲骨文得知，"亥"是商朝人的祖先，商朝人的祖先一出现就有一只鸟，这是商朝人对自己族氏起源的一个推想。

燕子
Swallow

10. 燕(yàn, swallow)

The character 燕 in the oracle bone script is like the image of a swallow who spreads its wings and flies freely in the sky. Because the swallow is black, the character 玄 is used and together, the ancient arrived at 玄鸟 (a black bird). *Shi Jing (The Book of Songs)* has a record of 玄鸟生商 (xuán niǎo shēng shāng, the black bird gives birth to Shang), which is a beautiful legend about the birth of the ancestors of the Shang Dynasty. According to legend, there was a woman named Jian Di in ancient times who, while taking a bath, saw a black bird flying and laying an egg. The woman took the egg and swallowed it. After that she became pregnant and gave birth to a boy, who was the ancestor of the Shang Dynasty.

People used to believe that this story in *Shi Jing (The Book of Songs)* was incorporated by later generations, but when studying the oracle bone script, they discovered the story had long existed in the minds of the Shang Dynasty people. The oracle bone script character 亥 (hài) is 丂, and once this character appears we can see a bird perching upon it, such as in 匊 and 亥. According to oracle bone script, 亥 (hài) was the ancestor of the Shang people and birds marked the birth of the ancestors of Shang people. This was a common origin myth during the Shang Dynasty.

"燕"字的演变
Evolution of the Character "燕"

甲骨文 Oracle Bone Script	金文 Bronze Script	小篆 Small Seal Script	隶书 Clerical Script	楷书 Regular Script
燕		燕	燕	燕

从下表中可以看出,商朝人已经认识、了解了很多种动物,但是能把这些字准确无误地造出来,却不是一件容易的事。尤其是陆地上的爬行动物,大多都是四条腿,有头有尾,最大的难点在于如何通过简单的笔画来区分它们。

这些字大部分都是象形字,有的描绘正面形象,有的勾勒侧面形象,但都抓住了动物最典型的体态特征。例如:"蛇"字突出了蛇的尖圆的头部和弯曲的身体;"虎"字突出了老虎锋利的牙齿和身上的条形花纹;"豹"字突出了豹子身上的圆形斑点;"马"字突出了马的长脸大眼、鬃毛飞扬的形象;"兔"字突出了兔子长耳短尾的特征,容易使人想到一个歇后语"兔子的尾巴——长不了";"鼠"字突出了老鼠的尖牙以及拖在地上的细长尾巴;"象"字突出了象的长鼻子;"鹿"字突出了鹿的分叉的鹿角;"兕"字突出了头顶的尖角;"豕"和"犬"看起来很像,主要区别就在尾巴上,豕尾下垂,犬尾上卷。

还有一些字比较特殊,比如"牛"和"羊",这两个字选取了牛和羊头部的典型特征,牛的角是向上的,羊的角是向下弯曲的,异常简单明了。"鸡"字原来是一只鸡展翅的形象,后来加偏旁"奚"组成形声字"雞"。

龙是中国人的最爱,虽然现在都知道龙根本不存在,但"龙"字在甲骨文中就已经大量出现,写法多达数十种。从字形看,龙是古人根据蛇、兽等动物的特征创造出来的形象,被赋予了特殊的神性,是商人崇拜的对象。后来成为中华民族的图腾,直到现在,中国人仍然自称为龙的传人。

From the table below, we can see that during the Shang Dynasty, people began classifying many kinds of animals, but representing these different species uniquely and accurately in characters was difficult. Generally, a reptile on land can be represented by four legs, a head, and a tail. The challenge was how to distinguish different reptiles by using simple strokes.

Most of these characters are hieroglyphs, some depicting the full-face image, some outlining the side image, but they all capture the most typical physical characteristics of those animals. For example , 蛇(shé, snake) have pointed heads and curved bodies; 虎(hǔ, tiger) have sharp teeth and stripes on their bodies; 豹 (bào, leopard) have round spots on their bodies; 马(mǎ, horse) have long faces, big eyes, and manes; 兔(tù, rabbit) have long ears and short tails; 鼠(shǔ, rat) highlight the fangs and the slender tail that drags on the ground; 象(xiàng, elephant) highlight the long noses; 鹿(lù, deer) highlight the bifurcated antlers; 兕(sì, female rhinoceros) have sharp horns on the top of their heads; The character 豕 (shǐ, pig) and 犬 (quǎn, dog) are very similar, but the main difference is on the tail. For example, the pig's tail sags, and the dog's tail curls.

There are also some special characters, such as the character 牛 (niú, cattle) and the character 羊(yáng, goat). These two characters manifest the typical features of the head of the cow and the sheep. The horn of the cow is upward curved and the horn of the sheep is downward curved. The character 鸡(jī, chicken) was originally an image of chicken spreading its wings, and later the radical of 奚(xī) was added to form a phonogram 雞(jī, chicken).

The dragon is a favorite creature of the Chinese people. Although the dragon does not exist, the character 龙(lóng, dragon) often appears in the oracle bone script, and there are dozens in the writting style. According to the font, the dragon is an image created by the ancient people based on the characteristics of snakes and other animals. It is endowed with a special divinity and is the object of worship by Shang Dynasty people. Later, it became the totem of the Chinese nation. Until now, Chinese people still refer to themselves as descendants of dragons.

甲骨文里的动物举例（一）
Examples of Animals in Oracle Bone Scripts

虎 (hǔ, tiger)		豹 (bào, leopard)	
兔 (tù, rabbit)		鼠 (shǔ, rat)	
龙 (lóng, dragon)		凤 (fèng, phoenix)	
蛇 (shé, snake)		虫 (chóng, insect)	
鱼 (yú, fish)		龟 (guī, tortoise)	
马 (mǎ, horse)		兕 (sì, the female rhinoceros)	
牛 (niú, cattle)		羊 (yáng, sheep)	

Chapter III Configuration of Chinese Characters

甲骨文里的动物举例（二）
Examples of Animals in Oracle Bone Scripts

豕 (shǐ, pig)		犬 (quǎn, dog)	
象 (xiàng, elephant)		鹿 (lù, deer)	
鸟 (niǎo, bird)		雀 (què, sparrow)	
鸡 (jī, chicken)		雉 (zhì, pheasant)	

从一些字中可以看出商朝人和动物之间的关系，牛和羊已经被驯化了，并且出现了圈养它们的场所，养牛的场所叫作"牢"，写作 ▨，像牛的周围有栅栏之类的围挡，养羊的场所写作 ▨，现在这两个字都用"牢"字来表示，成语"亡羊补牢"的"牢"字写作 ▨ 似乎更恰当一些。当然了，大多数时候还是要把牛、羊赶到野外去放牧，赶牛写作 ▨，像一只手拿着棍子之类的工具在驱赶牛群，赶羊写作 ▨，现在这两个字都用"牧"字来表示。

河南现在已经见不到大象了，实际上，3000多年前的中原地区，气候比现在要温暖湿润，这里曾有大象生存。河南省在古代曾被称为"豫州"，现在简称"豫"。字典对"豫"的解释是特别巨大的象，这便是一个很好的证明。甲骨文"为"字写作 ▨，像人的一只手牵着一头大象，表示人牵象、役使象劳动的意思，说明商朝人已经对象非常了解，并驯化了象。

商王特别喜欢打猎，打猎就要追逐猎物，追逐不同的猎物用不同的字来表示，追猪用 ▨ 字表示，就是"逐"字，追鹿用 ▨ 字表示，追犬用 ▨ 字表示，追兔用 ▨ 字表示，这些字都是在不同的动物下面加一个"止"字，止就是脚，表示追赶不同的猎物。现在这几个字的意思都用"逐"字来表示，成语"逐鹿中原"的"逐"字用 ▨ 似乎更直观一些。

除了地上的走兽，空中的飞鸟也是商朝人的猎物，用手抓鸟写作 ▨，像一只手抓住一只鸟的形象，这就是"隻"字，简化为"只"

We can understand the relationship between people and animals in the Shang Dynasty from some characters. Cattle and sheep were domesticated, and there were places where they were housed. The place where cattle are raised is called 牢 (láo, prison), written as ▨ , just like a fence around the cattle. The place for raising sheep is written as ▨ , which is also 牢. In Chinese, there is an idiom 亡羊补牢 (wáng yáng bǔ láo, it's never too late to mend the sheepfold after the sheep have been stolen). The sheepfold is 牢 in Chinese, and it is appropriate to write as ▨ . Often, the caretakers of these animals must drive the cattle and sheep out to pasture to graze and as such, driving the cattle was written as, ▨ like a hand holding a stick to drive the cattle. Herding sheep was written as ▨ . Now these two characters are used together in 牧(mù, pasture).

Elephants are no longer native to Henan. However, more than 3,000 years ago in the Central Plains area, the climate was warmer and more humid than it is now and elephants thrived. In ancient times, Henan Province was once called 豫州(yù zhōu), and even now it is still referred to as 豫(yù). The dictionary's interpretation of 豫 is a particularly huge elephant. The character 为(wéi) in the oracle bone script is written as ▨ , like a person holding an elephant in one hand, indicating that a person leads an elephant to work for us. This character suggests that during the Shang Dynasty, people were familiar with elephants and domesticated them.

The King of the Shang Dynasty loved hunting and this was reflected in multiple characters in the oracle bone script that capture the hunting of various prey. For instance, chasing pigs is written as ▨, and that is 逐(zhú, chase) in modern Chinese, chasing deer as ▨ , chasing dogs as ▨ and chasing rabbits as ▨. These characters all include the character 止(zhǐ, foot) beneath the different animals to express that the animal is being chased. Now the meaning of these characters can be expressed by the character 逐(zhú, chase), and this character, used in the idiom 逐鹿中原 (zhú lù zhōng yúan, fight for the world), is expressed by ▨ , which seems more intuitive.

In addition to the animals on land, the birds in the air were also the prey of the Shang Dynasty people. The character ▨ means to catch a bird with one's hands and as such, the character resembles an image of a hand holding a bird. Eventually, that character became 隻(zhī), which was simplified further to 只(zhī).

字。鸟飞在空中,商朝人用弓箭射鸟,写作 ,像一支箭射向一只飞鸟的形象,就是"雉"字。箭的制作需要成本,在打猎时为了能够回收箭矢,古人会制作带有丝绳的箭,但绳子不会太长、太重,便于在箭射出后顺着绳子找回箭矢或猎物,如 字,左边的部分像是缠有丝绳的箭。

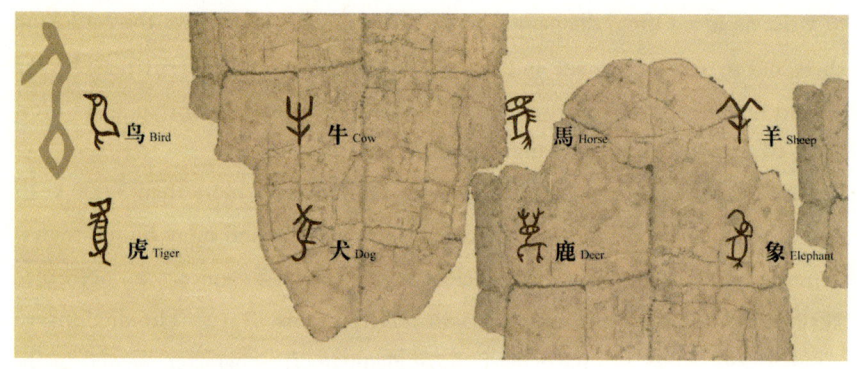

独体象形字内容
Single Pictographic Characters

The Shang Dynasty people used bows and arrows to shoot flying birds out of the air and expressed this scene with the character 𦥑 which resembles the image of an arrow shooting at a flying bird represented as the character 雉 (zhì, pheasant). In order to recover the arrows while hunting, the ancients attached silk ropes to the arrows. The silk ropes were designed to be short and light so that the hunter could easily draw in the rope to retrieve the downed prey or the missed arrows. Like the character 矰, the left part is like an arrow wrapped around by a silk rope.

四、衣食住行

古今中外，衣食住行都与人们的生活休戚相关，它们不仅仅是人类生存的需要，更是人类文明的见证。从古至今，衣食住行的发展经历了从单一到丰富、从简陋到华丽、从缓慢到快捷的蜕变过程，而每一个时期的衣食住行，都见证了当时社会的文明程度，这在汉字的形体上也有所反映。古人服饰的特点和材质、饮食习惯和烹饪器具、建筑形式和居住习俗、出行方式和交通工具都能从汉字的构形中体现出来，为人们解读古人造字时期的生活提供了一条捷径。

1. 衣

甲骨文"衣"字是一件古代上衣的轮廓图形，上为衣领，左右为衣袖，中间是交衽的衣襟，本义是指上衣。古代称上身衣服为衣，下身衣服为裳，现在合称衣裳，泛指衣服、服装。

"衣"字做偏旁的时候写作"衤"，凡是由"衣"组成的字，大多与衣服、布匹有关，如衬、衫、裘、袂等。古时候生活资料极度匮乏，人们捕获野兽，把肉吃掉以后，通常会把动物的皮毛保存下来，用于冬季御寒，用动物皮毛做的衣服就是裘，写作 ，看起来像一件上衣的

古代服装
Ancient Clothes

Chapter Ⅲ Configuration of Chinese Characters

Ⅳ. Clothing, Food, Housing and Transportation

Clothing, food, housing and transportation are not only essential for survival, but also a testament of the development of human civilization. From ancient times to the present, the development of these basic needs has undergone a process of transformation from simple to complex, shabby to luxurious, slow to fast, and each period of development has mirrored the different degrees of civilization. These developments are also reflected in the evolution of Chinese characters. In a way, many aspects of ancient living can be seen from the structure or configuration of Chinese characters, the materials and characteristics of clothing, eating habits and cooking utensils, architectural forms and residential customs, as well as travel and transportation tools, all of which help to provide us with insight into the lives of ancient people.

1. 衣(yī, upper garment)

In the oracle bone script, 衣 looks like a sketch of a traditional Chinese upper garment: the upper part is the collar, the lower left and right parts are the sleeves, and the middle part is the front of the garment where the two pieces meet. In ancient times, the upper garment was called 衣, and the lower garment was called 裳(shang). At present, 衣 and 裳 are put together as 衣裳, a general term for clothing.

When 衣 serves as a component of a character, it is written as 衤. Characters with 衣 as a component are most often related to cloth and clothing such as in 衬(chèn, lining), 衫 (shān, unlined upper garment), 裘 (qiú, fur coat), or 袂 (mèi, sleeves). In ancient times, important resources were often scarce. People caught animals not only to obtain meat for food, but also pelt to keep warm. Clothes made of fur are called 裘 (qiú, fur coat), written as 裘 , looking like the shape

"衣" 字的演变

Evolution of the Character "衣"

甲骨文 Oracle Bone Script	金文 Bronze Script	小篆 Small Seal Script	隶书 Clerical Script	楷书 Regular Script
				衣

形状，衣服的外边有茸茸的毛，金文写作 ，加了一个"求"字构成了形声字，就形成了现在的"裘"字。裘又可用作姓氏，大概是与裘氏祖先出身于制皮工匠有关吧。

2. 丝

丝绸之路是古代连接东西方的著名贸易要道，简称丝路，而丝绸则是丝绸之路最具代表性的货物。古代罗马人甚至称中国为"丝国"，而穿中国的丝绸衣服则成为古罗马贵族的社会时尚。公元1世纪左右，罗马城的豪华市区设有专售中国丝绸的市场。甲骨文里已经出现了"丝"字，像两束蚕丝的样子。而且，甲骨文里也出现了"蚕"字和"桑"字，桑即桑树，为蚕提供食物。

"丝"字的演变
Evolution of the Character "丝"

甲骨文 Oracle Bone Script	金文 Bronze Script	小篆 Small Seal Script	隶书 Clerical Script	楷书 Regular Script
丝(甲骨文)	丝(金文)	丝(小篆)	丝(隶书)	丝

of a garment with the fur on the outside. In the bronze script, the component 求(qiú) is added to indicate its pronunciation as seen in 裘 . Now, we have the pictophonetic character 裘, which can also be used as a surname, probably reflecting that their ancestors were leather craftsmen.

2. 丝(sī, silk)

The Silk Road was a famous trade route linking the East and West in ancient times, and silk was the most representative good of the Silk Road. China was even called the "silk country" by ancient Romans who considered Chinese silk clothing fashionable among Roman aristocracy. Around the 1st century AD, in the luxury urban district of Rome, a special market was installed for selling Chinese silk. 丝(sī, silk) appeared as early as in the oracle bone script, resembling two strands of silk. Moreover, in the oracle bone script, there are also the characters蚕(cán,silkworm) and 桑(sāng, mulberry). The leaves of 桑 are food sources for silk worms.

3. 禾

不论是甲骨文还是金文，"禾"字都真实地再现了禾的形象，下面像茎与根，上面像叶子和穗，尤其是突出了沉甸甸的、下垂的禾穗。禾当时指的是谷子，也叫粟，去皮以后就是小米，谷子是那时主要的粮食作物。直到今天，中国北方地区仍然大量种植谷子，小米依旧深受人们喜爱。

谷子熟了，人们开始在地里忙着收割，一手抓住一把谷子，一手执镰拉割，就产生了"秉"字，如 、 、 ，表示手里拿着一束禾。成语"秉烛夜谈"的意思就是手拿点燃的蜡烛深夜交谈。如果手里拿着两束禾，就产生了"兼"字，如 。人们喜欢用"德才兼备"来形容一个人同时具有优秀的品德和杰出的才能。人们也喜欢用"鱼与熊掌不可兼得"来形容两件事或两个目的不可能同时达到，这个典故出自儒家经典《孟子》一书："鱼，我所欲也，熊掌，亦我所欲也；二者不可得兼，舍鱼而取熊掌者也。生，亦我所欲也，义，亦我所欲也；二者不可得兼，舍生而取义者也。"中国古代思想家孟子用人们生活中熟知的具体事物打了一个比方，在生命和义两者不能同时得到的情况下，孟子宁愿舍弃生命而要义，这也是成语"舍生取义"的来源。

谷子成熟了，收割了，然后搬运回家，那时候的运输工具很有限，更多的时候需要人们把粮食扛回去，甲骨文的"年"字写作 ，由"禾"和"人"组成，像一个微微前倾的人背负着沉重的禾谷，表示运输收割好的庄稼，本义指庄稼的收成。因为禾谷一年成熟一次，所以年

"禾"字的演变
Evolution of the Character "禾"

甲骨文 Oracle Bone Script	金文 Bronze Script	小篆 Small Seal Script	隶书 Clerical Script	楷书 Regular Script

3. 禾(hé, standing for grain)

Whether in the oracle bone script or in the bronze script, 禾 vividly reproduces the image of crops. The lower part looks like stems and roots, and the upper part looks like leaves and ears which are characterized as heavy and drooping. 禾 usually referred to the millet, a staple food at that time. Until now, millet is still popular among Chinese people, and it is widely planted in northern China.

When millet ripens, people are busy harvesting it in the field, with one hand grabbing a handful of millet and the other hand cutting. This was how the character 秉(bǐng, holding) was invented. 秉 (秉 秉) looks like a man holding a stalk of grain in his hand. The idiom 秉烛夜谈(bǐng zhú yè tán) means holding a lit candle and talking late at night. If you hold two bunches of stalk grain in hand, you will have the character 兼 兼 (jiān, holding two things at the same time). People like to use 德才兼备 (dé cái jiān bèi, the combination of virtue and talent) to depict a person with excellent moral character and outstanding talent. People also like to use 鱼与熊掌不可兼得(yú yǔ xióng zhǎng bù kě jiān dé, You can't have fish and bear paw at the same time/You cannot have your cake and eat it too) to describe two things or two purposes that cannot be achieved at the same time. This allusion comes from *The Classic Book of Mencius*, "Fish is what I want. So is bear paw. But if I cannot get both, so I would take bear paw instead of fish. Life is what I cherish, so is justice. If I cannot have both at the same time, I would sacrifice my life to uphold justice." By employing common elements of daily life, Mencius was good at using analogies to shed light on more profound thoughts. Between life and justice, Mencius would rather abandon life and take up justice. This was how the idiom 舍生取义(shě shēng qǔ yì, to give up one's life for justice) came into being.

When the millet ripens, it needs to be harvested and taken home. In ancient times, manpower was needed to carry the millet crops since there were few tools available to do this job. In the oracle bone script 年(nián, year) was written as 年, composed of 禾 and 人(rén, person), signalling a man who bent his back forwards slightly to carry the heavy grains. Since millet ripens only once a year,

又用来表示时间,即地球绕太阳运行一周的时间,而年也成为中国最为隆重的节日,叫"过年"。

4. 酉

中外考古学家在对河南贾湖遗址发掘出土的陶器进行残留物分析时发现,残留物的化学成分与现代稻米、米酒、葡萄酒等的化学成分相同。这也是目前世界上最早的酒的证据,将中国造酒历史向前推进到了距今近9000年。酒的酿造离不开容器,甲骨文"酉"字像一个酒坛子的形状,中间加一横,表示坛子里有液体、酒汁,本义是指酒坛子或者酒壶。"酉"字后来借用为干支名,为地支中的第十位。在汉字中凡是以"酉"为偏旁的字大都与酒有关,如酗、醉、酿、配等。

当"酉"字表示别的意思之后,人们给"酉"加了个偏旁"氵"新造一个酒字,即 ,强调酒坛中酒的液态性质。当有事情令人烦恼

陶罐
Pottery

the character 年 is used to indicate the duration, when the earth revolves around the sun.

4. 酉(yǒu, wine container)

After conducting an analysis, archaeologists at home and abroad have found that the chemical components of the residue in the pottery unearthed from the Jiahu Site in Henan bear resemblance to that of modern rice, rice wine, and grape wine. This is also spectacular proof that China had some of the earliest wines in the world and Chinese wine history could be dated back as early as 9,000 years ago. When the wine is ready, a container is needed to hold it. 酉 in the oracle bone script looks like a wine jar. A horizontal stroke is added in the middle of 酉, indicating liquid or wine in the jar. So, the original meaning of 酉 refers to the wine jar or wine pot. The character 酉 was later used as the name of the tenth Earthly Branch, a traditional Chinese system of sequence. Characters with 酉 as a component often refer to wine, such as 酣 (hān, heavy drinking), 醉(zuì, drunk), 酿(niàng, wine-making), 酌 (zhuó, to drink), or 配(pèi, to mix a drink).

When 酉 is used to refer to something else, the component 氵 is added to 酉 to form a new character 酒（jiǔ, wine). Previously, 酒 was used to highlight the liquid in the jar. When someone is bothered, he may attempt to drown his sorrows with wine. While drinking wine heavily, some might quote the ancient poem that reads, "What can dispel my sadness? The only solution is the Dukang wine." This line is from the poem, "A Short-Song Ballad", by Cao Cao, a great thinker and militarist in the Eastern Han Dynasty (25 AD-220 AD). Legends suggest that the earliest wine maker was 杜康(Dù Kāng), a name that has now been long associated with wine. Even now, there is still Du Kang wine on the market.

"酉" 字的演变

Evolution of the Character "酉"

甲骨文 Oracle Bone Script	金文 Bronze Script	小篆 Small Seal Script	隶书 Clerical Script	楷书 Regular Script

时，很多人借酒浇愁，喝酒时还不忘引用一句古诗"何以解忧？惟有杜康"。这句古诗出自东汉丞相曹操所作《短歌行》，诗中所说杜康，原来指传说中最早造酒的人，后来成为一种酒的品牌，直到现在，市场上仍然有杜康酒。

由于受到生产力水平和思想意识的影响，商朝人异常崇信鬼神，凡事都要请求祖先神灵的指导和保佑，所以祭祀鬼神的活动特别多。丁、丅、示，这几个字是"示"字的甲骨文写法，表示被祭祀对象的牌位，就是神牌。"示"字作偏旁时写作"礻"，比衣字偏旁"衤"少一个点。凡是以示为偏旁的字，如福、禄、祝、礼等，都与祭祀、祈福有关。

甲骨文"福"字写作 畐 、 畐 ，像在神主牌位前面摆放用于祭祀的酒，有的字还写出了恭恭敬敬捧着酒的双手,金文写作 福 ，和现在"福"字的写法已经很接近了。酿造酒需要多余的粮食，所以古人用酒象征生活的丰富完备，向祖先神灵供奉酒以报答神灵的护佑，或者请求神灵的护佑。福指神灵所降赐的福气，又引申为一般的幸福、好运气，与"祸"的意义相对。中国人在过年的时候喜欢贴倒着的"福"字，"倒"和"到"谐音，表示"福"到了，即"幸福"、"福气""好

倒"福"字
The Resupinate Character

Due to outdated beliefs and ideologies, many people in the Shang Dynasty (about 1600 BC-1046 BC) were rather superstitious. They would call on gods and spirits for guidance and protection in anything they were going to do, so sacrifice-offering ceremonies were often held. 丁, 干, and 示 are characters in the oracle bone script that approximate the modern word, 示(shì), symbolizing the memorial tablet of the object to be worshiped. As a component, 示 is written as 礻, which is different from the component 衤, which stands for clothes as mentioned above. Characters with the component 示 include 福(fú, blessing), 禄(lù, happiness), 祝(zhù, to pray), 礼(lǐ, manners) and so on, and these characters are all related to sacrifices and blessings.

福 in the oracle bone script is 畐 or 福. It looks like a jar of wine placed before a memorial tablet. Sometimes, the character 福 was written as a man respectfully holding the jar of wine with both hands. The bronze script of the character 福 was written as 福 which is very close to the writing of 福 now. Wine making involves abundant grains, so wines were used to symbolize prosperity by the ancient people who offered wine to their ancestors to repay the gods' protection or to ask for blessings from the gods. Though 福 refers to blessings of the gods, it can also be used for happiness or good fortune in general, opposite to 祸(huò, misfortune). Therefore, when celebrating the New Year, people often paste an upside down 福 on doors because the characters 倒(dào, upside-down) and 到(dào, to arrive) have the same pronunciation, so an upside down 福 sounds the same as 福到了(fú dào le, your luck has arrived). Whether it is now or

运"降临了，无论是现在还是过去，都寄托了人们对幸福生活的向往，也是对美好未来的祝愿。

5. 家

"家"字由"宀"和"豕"两部分组成，"豕"是猪的意思，金文"家"字里的猪非常形象，甲骨文"家"字突出了猪硕大的腹部和下垂的尾巴。"宀"字写作⌂，像是房子的形象。考古工作者对西安半坡村仰韶房屋遗址进行了复原，在圆形的基址上建墙，墙上覆盖圆锥形屋顶，就像此类房屋的轮廓图。人在房屋内的席子上休息，就构成了"宿"字，写作⌂，现在人们还把住的房屋叫宿舍。

房屋和猪如何就构成了家的概念，长期以来一直在困扰着人们，人们对此也有多种解释。《说文解字》认为，"家"字是个形声字，"宀"下面的"豕"是"豭"的省写，"豭"音jiā，就是公猪的意思。从甲骨文"家"字来看，房屋下面确实不是一般的猪，而是公猪的形象，即⌂，比一般的猪⌂多了生殖器。

也有人认为，"家"字反映了古人生活方式的转变，由原来居无定所的狩猎生活演进到定居的农耕生活。猪原来是野生动物，后来逐渐被驯化为家畜，养在人们所居住的房子周围，或者所居住的院子内，而猪肉也是中国人肉食的主要来源，有房有猪是一个家庭的基本特征。⌂并不是表示房屋里面养着一头大腹便便的猪，只是表示房屋和猪之间的关系，古人写字为了节省地方就把猪移到了房子下面。直到现在，许多农村还保留这样的习俗，在居住的房子边或院子内建有养猪的猪圈。

"家"字的演变
Evolution of the Character "家"

甲骨文 Oracle Bone Script	金文 Bronze Script	小篆 Small Seal Script	隶书 Clerical Script	楷书 Regular Script
𠂇𠂇	𠂇	家	家	家

in the past, people are always longing for a happy life and a better future.

5. 家(jiā, house or family)

The character 家 consists of two parts: 宀 and 豕(zhì, pig). In the bronze script, the character for 豕 is the image of a pig, while the oracle bone script character highlights the abdomen and sagging of the pig's tail. 宀 in ancient writing was ⌂, resembling a house. Archaeologists have restored a primitive house in Banpo Village of the Yangshao Site in Xi'an. The house, built on a circular base with a conical roof atop the walls, appears like 家, or ⌂ in ancient writing. With a house, people are protected from the elements. The character 宿, written as 宿(sù) nowadays, looks like a man lying on a cushion under a roof, signalling rest or sleep. Even now, people still call their sleeping house a 宿舍 (sù shè, dormitory).

The question of how a house and a pig came to form the concept of family has long confused people and there are many interpretations for how this character came into being. It is believed in *The Explanation of Script and Elucidation of Characters* that the character 家 is a phonogram, and the component 豕 is the omissive spelling of 豭(jiā, boar). From the oracle bone script character for 家, we can find that the pig under the roof is not a usual pig, but the image of a boar 豭, because it has male genitals that cannot be seen in other representations of pigs 豕.

Some believe that the character 家 reflects the changes of the ancient ways of life that transformed from a primitive hunting lifestyle to a settled, farming life. Pigs were originally wild animals and were gradually domesticated into livestock and raised around the house or in the yards where people lived. Pork is also the main meat for Chinese people, so houses and pigs, together, stand in as a basic symbol for family. The oracle bone script 家 does not necessarily mean that a pig with a big belly, as shown in the image, must be raised in the house, but instead it draws attention to the relationship between the house and the pig. When writing this character, 豕 was positioned under 宀 to make the character more aesthetically pleasing. Even now, many rural villagers have retained the custom of building pigsties around the house or in the yard.

6. 门、户

甲骨文"门"字，有门框，有门楣，有一对门扇，是一个完整的门形，有的甲骨文省去门楣，但仍保留着两扇门的形状。"门"的繁体字写作"門"，和门的原始形象很接近。

甲骨文"户"字，像带有一边门框的一扇门，是门的一半。一般来说，有两扇门的才叫"门"，多建在庭院或大厅的入口，只有一扇门的叫"户"，多用在小房间的入口。

有时候"门"和"户"都表示门的意思，没有差别，如成语"门当户对"，旧时指男女双方的社会地位和经济情况相当，结亲很适合。有时候"门"和"户"的意义差别是很明显的，中国唐代著名诗人杜甫有句名诗"朱门酒肉臭，路有冻死骨"，诗句中的"门"就不能用"户"字代替。

甲骨文的"启"字写作 ，像人用手打开一扇门的样子，表示开门、打开的意思。如果给某人写了一封信，而不想让别人看见，就会在信封上写上"某某亲启"，就是收信人亲自打开的意思。有的"启"字加一个口旁，写作 ，繁体字是"啓"，所以"启"字又有说话、陈

"门、户"字的演变
Evolution of the Characters "门、户"

甲骨文 Oracle Bone Script	金文 Bronze Script	小篆 Small Seal Script	隶书 Clerical Script	楷书 Regular Script
甲骨文 Oracle Bone Script	金文 Bronze Script	小篆 Small Seal Script	隶书 Clerical Script	楷书 Regular Script

6. 门(mén, door), 户(hù, a door with one leaf)

The oracle bone script character for 门 was a pictogram, showing the complete image of a traditional Chinese door with its frame, lintel and a pair of "leaves". Sometimes the lintel can be omitted, but the leaves are retained to give the outline of the door. The traditional Chinese character of 门 is written as 門, which more closely resembles the original image of the door.

The oracle bone script character for 户 looks like a door with only half of the frame. Generally speaking, a door with two leaves is referred to as 门, and this type of door is typically installed at the entrance of a courtyard or hall. If there is only one leaf for the door, it is referred to with 户, and this type of door is typically installed at the entrance of smaller rooms.

On some occasions, there is no difference in usage between 门 and 户. For example, the Chinese idiom, 门当户对(mén dāng hù duì), means that marriage is suitable only if the social status and economic situation of each partner are equally matched. At other times, there are drastic differences between the meanings of 门 and 户. The famous poet, Du Fu of the Tang Dynasty (618 AD-907 AD), has a famous poem that reads, 朱门酒肉臭, 路有冻死骨(zhū mén jiǔ ròu chòu, lù yǒu dòng sǐ gǔ; "Behind the vermilion gates of the rich, meat and wine go to waste, but along the roads are bones of the poor who have frozen to death/the rich are excessively wealthy while the poor suffer stark poverty.") Here, 门 cannot be replaced by 户.

The oracle bone script of the character 启(qǐ, to open a door) was written as 𠃓, like a person opening a door leaf by hand, indicating the opening of a door or opening up, more generally. If you write a letter to someone and would not like others to read it, you may write, 某某亲启(mǒu mǒu qīn qǐ, open the letter by someone only), on the envelope, which means that only the recipient should open the letter. When this character is compounded with 口(kǒu, mouth) such as 𠮛, the traditional Chinese character for 啓(qǐ), it means speaking or presenting. 启事

述的意思，如"启事"就是公开声明某事的文字。找人的时候就写"寻人启事"，找物的时候就写"寻物启事"，这些"启事"多登在报刊上或贴在墙壁上。

7. 邑

甲骨文"邑"字上面的方形像是城郭之形，下面是跪坐的人形，"邑"字表示人们聚居的地方。从甲骨卜辞可以看出，商朝人将王朝都城称为"大邑商"。西周青铜器何尊的铭文中有武王克商的记载，"武王既克大邑商"，说明西周人也将商王朝的都城称为"大邑商"。"邑"字做偏旁时写作"阝"，放在字的右边，如都、郑、鄂、邺、邯等，意义多和地名、邦郡有关。

何尊是中国青铜器中知名度非常高的一件铜器，不仅是因为铭文里有武王克商的记载，最重要的是铭文中第一次出现了"中国"这个词，"国"字写作 或，圆圈和"邑"字上方的方框表示一个意思，即人们所居住的城邦，上下两短横进一步表示疆域，右边是武器"戈"，表示城邑、疆域需要用武力守卫，人们后来在"或"字外面再加"囗"另造"國"字，表示古代诸侯封地而建的、有武力守卫的相对独立的城邦。"國"后来简化为"国"字。

"邑"字的演变
Evolution of the Character "邑"

甲骨文 Oracle Bone Script	金文 Bronze Script	小篆 Small Seal Script	隶书 Clerical Script	楷书 Regular Script
![]	![]	![]	邑	邑

(qǐ shì, announcement) refers to making a public and typically formal declaration. When looking for someone who is missing, we write a 寻人启事(xún rén qǐ shì). When looking for something that is lost, we write a 寻物启事(xún wù qǐ shì). These 启事 are often printed in newspapers or plastered on public walls.

7. 邑(yì)

The character 邑 in the oracle bone script has a square 口 on the upper part, representing a city, while the lower part is a man kneeling on the ground, indicating a compact community where people live. According to the oracle bone scripts, the people in the Shang Dynasty called their capital city 大邑商(dà yì shāng, great capital city of Shang). Also in the inscriptions of 何尊 (hé zūn, He Goblet), an unearthed bronze ware of the Western Zhou Dynasty, there is a record of war, 武王既克大邑商(wǔ wáng jì kè dà yì shāng, King Wu conquered the great capital city of Shang), indicating that the Western Zhou Dynasty also called the capital of the Shang Dynasty, "Da Yi Shang". As a component of other characters, 邑 was written as 阝, placed on the right side of a character such as in 都 (dū, capital), 郑(zhèng, a state in the Zhou Dynasty), 鄂(è, the alternative name for Hubei), 邺(yè, an ancient name for a part of what is today's Hebei Province), or 邯 (hán, a surname). The meaning of this character in this compound form expresses that the entire character is related to a place name or state.

"He Goblet" is a famous bronze ware not only because it bears the record of King Wu defeating Shang, but because the characters 中国(China) appear for the first time. The character 国(guó) was written as 或 with the circle referring to the city wall, just as the square atop the character 邑 did. The upper and lower horizontal lines further indicate the territorial boundary. The right side of the character is 戈(gē), which refers to a weapon used to safeguard the territory. Later, People added 口(kǒu, mouth) around 或 to produce another character, 國, which refers to a relatively independent vassal state with military troops. 國 was later simplified as 国.

"车"字的演变
Evolution of the Character "车"

甲骨文 Oracle Bone Script	金文 Bronze Script	小篆 Small Seal Script	隶书 Clerical Script	楷书 Regular Script

8. 车

甲骨文"车"字非常形象，如果俯视单个的商代马车，再把它和甲骨文"车"字比对一下，就会发现有的甲骨文"车"字和这些马车一模一样。从字形看，车的车轮、车轴、车辕、轭具等一应俱全，有的"车"字还有车厢的形状。"车"字构造复杂，人们将它简化为"車"字，看起来是车的俯视图，中间的"口"应该是"舆"，就是车厢，"丨"是车轴，上下两横应该是车轮。"車"字现在简化为"车"。

考古发现证明，商朝时开始出现马匹牵引的马车，并且成为当时最重要的交通工具，商朝马车都是独辕车。除了安阳，河南洛阳、陕西西安、山东滕州、山西灵石等地的二十多个地点都发现有商代车马坑。

9. 行

商代出土马车的这些地点，有的属于王畿之地，有的是臣服于商王室的诸侯方国。这说明马车已经成为商王室与诸侯方国进行联系的重要工具，而且都城和方国之间有道路相通，并借马车来确保商王室与各地之间的密切关系。甲骨文的"行"字便是这种道路的真实写照，"行"

8. 车(chē, cart)

A cart during the Shang Dynasty would bear great resemblance to the pictogram for 车 in the oracle bone script. From this iconic character, we can see the complete components of a cart such as wheels, axles, shafts, and yokes. Some characters of 车 bear the outline of a carriage. The ancient character for 车 was complicated, so it was simplified as 車, an outline of the carriage from above. The middle □ was originally 舆(yú), the carriage, the ︱ was the axle, and the upper and lower horizontal lines were the wheels. 車 in simplified Chinese is 车.

Archaeological findings prove that horse-drawn carriages began to appear in the Shang Dynasty and became the most important means of transportation at that time. Most of the carriages were chariots with a single shaft. In addition to Anyang, Luoyang (in Henan Province), Xi'an (in Shaanxi Province), Tengzhou (in Shandong Province), and Lingshi (in Shanxi Province), more than 20 chariot pits within the territories of the Shang Dynasty have been discovered.

9. 行(xíng, go)

The sites where the horse-drawn chariots were unearthed were on the land that belonged to the royal family and the vassal states. This shows that the carriage had become an important tool to connect the royal families and the affiliated states. In order for the chariots to operate, roads had to be built. The character

商代马车

A Carriage in the Shang Dynasty

"行"字的演变
Evolution of the Character "行"

甲骨文 Oracle Bone Script	金文 Bronze Script	小篆 Small Seal Script	隶书 Clerical Script	楷书 Regular Script
㣔	㣔	行	行	行

字看起来像四通八达的十字路口，后来引申出行走的意思。

  在安阳殷墟的发掘中，多次发现商代道路遗迹。其中有一条路呈西北、东南走向，宽约10米，上面留有双向车辙的遗痕。这是一条行驶马车的大道，它位于洹北商城东南，是发现的众多道路中最宽的一条，应该是一条重要的大道。深深的车辙遗痕，是车轮反复辗压的结果，它反映了商朝都城3000多年前车水马龙的繁忙情景。

  古代的陆地交通工具主要是车，而水路的交通工具主要是舟。甲骨文的"舟"字像一只两头翘起的木船的简单形象，有船舷、船头和船尾。汉字中凡以舟为偏旁的字大都与船及其作用有关，如航、舫、舰、艇、艘等。

"舟"字的演变
Evolution of the Character "舟"

甲骨文 Oracle Bone Script	金文 Bronze Script	小篆 Small Seal Script	隶书 Clerical Script	楷书 Regular Script
舟	舟	舟	舟	舟

行(xíng) was created to reflect the road. 行 in the oracle bone script resembles a crossroad extending in all directions and later, its meaning was extended to include walking.

Often, the remains of roads from the Shang Dynasty were revealed in the excavation of the Yin Ruins in Anyang. One of the roads is approximately 10 meters wide, running northwest-southeast, and has traces of two-way ruts. This was a main road for carriages and it was located southeast of the Huanbei Capital of the Shang Dynasty. It is one of the widest road remains that have been discovered so far. The deep tracks of the ruts were the result of heavy usage in a capital city, especially by the repeated rolling of wheels, reflecting the busy and prosperous scene of the capital city in the Shang Dynasty more than 3,000 years ago.

In former times, the main transportation tools on land and water were carriages and boats, respectively. The oracle bone script character 舟(zhōu, boat) resembles a simple image of a wooden boat with head and tail up, consisting of rails, bow and stern. Characters with 舟 as a component are most often related to boats and the use of boats such as in 航(háng, to sail), 舫(fǎng, boat), 舰(jiàn, warship), 艇(tǐng, light boat), or 艘(sōu, a classifier for boats).

舟
Boat

五、各类器具

原始社会的物质生产活动基本都是直接利用自然物作为人的生活资料，对自然的开发和支配能力极其有限。为了获取更多的生活资料，人们逐渐学会了制造简单的石斧、戈、弓箭等原始工具和武器用来农耕和打猎。各类器具的发明加快了人类社会发展的步伐，也正是这些宝贵的实践经验为汉字提供了许多造字依据，并被熔铸进了汉字的构形之中。

1. 舂

古代没有碾米的机器，为谷物脱壳全靠手工操作。这种手工劳动就叫作舂。甲骨文"舂"字像人双手握木杵给臼中的粮食脱壳的样子，有的字还描绘出了飞扬的谷壳。

舂米雕塑
Sculpture of Husking Rice with a Mortar and Pestle

V. Various Appliances

In earlier periods, most resources were unprocessed and used as they were found in nature because the ability to take advantage of natural resources was limited. In order to obtain better living materials in greater quantities, people developed simple tools and weapons such as stone axes, spears, bows, and arrows for activities like farming and hunting. The invention of more complex tools has accelerated the development of human society, and it is precisely these valuable practical experiences that provide a basis for the configuration of Chinese characters.

1. 舂(Chōng, to husk rice)

In ancient times, there was no machine for milling rice, and the shelling of the grain was done entirely by hand. This activity was called 舂(chōng, to husk rice). The oracle bone script character of 舂 resembles two hands holding a pestle on top of a mortar. Some version of the character for 舂 also depicts the flying chaff.

"舂" 字的演变
Evolution of the Character "舂"

甲骨文 Oracle Bone Script	金文 Bronze Script	小篆 Small Seal Script	隶书 Clerical Script	楷书 Regular Script
舂	舂	舂	舂	舂

春米需要两种工具，一种是盛放谷物的容器，叫作"臼"，多用石头凿成，中间凹下去以盛谷物，内壁上嵌有齿状槽纹，用以增加春磨时的磨擦力。另一种工具用来撞击谷物，叫作"杵"，甲骨文有 ▎、▎ 等多种写法。但这个字在甲骨文中多借用为十二地支的第七位，就是"午"，"午时"指上午十一点到下午一点的时间，又泛指日中的时候，"午夜"则指半夜。因为杵大都用木头制成，人们又给"午"字加了个"木"字旁，新造"杵"字来表示它的本义。杵和臼配合使用除了可以春米，还有捣中药、捣蒜的功能。

春米工作结束后，人们需要把米和谷壳区分开来，这时就需要用到簸箕，甲骨文有 ᗢ 字，即"其"字，很像一只簸箕的形状，本义指簸箕，是一种用竹篾、柳条等制成的扬去糠麸或清除垃圾的器具。因簸箕多用竹子编制，当"其"字被借用为代词后，人们加"竹"字头新造"箕"字表示簸箕的意思。

簸箕

Bò Jī, Winnowing Pan

Two tools are needed to husk rice. One of these tools is a container made of stone with a recessed middle to hold the grain called a 臼(jiù, mortar). The inner surface of the mortar is rough to generate more friction for husking. The other tool used to mash the grain is called 杵(chǔ, pestle). In the oracle bone script, the character was written as ↧ or ↧. However, to express this concept, on many occasions the oracle bone script borrows the character 午(wǔ, noon), which is the seventh place of the 12th branch. 午时(wǔ shí) refers to the time from 11 am to 1 pm, or mid-day, while 午夜(wǔ yè) refers to the middle of the night. The majority of mortars are made of wood and accordingly, the component 木(mù, wood) was added to 午 to form a new character, 杵, which expressed this original meaning. The pestle and mortar are used together not only to husk rice, but also to grind herbal medicine or crush garlic.

When the husking work was done, it was necessary to separate rice from chaff with a winnowing pan. The character 其(qí,an instrument for winnowing) in the oracle bone script is written as ∀. The character looks like a dustpan, a utensil made of bamboo stalks or wicker to remove bran or garbage. Since the winnowing pan was usually made of bamboo, people added竹(zhú, bamboo) to create the character 箕(jī)for 簸箕(bò ji). In other instances, the character is used as a pronoun.

"力"字的演变
Evolution of the Character "力"

甲骨文 Oracle Bone Script	金文 Bronze Script	小篆 Small Seal Script	隶书 Clerical Script	楷书 Regular Script
↓	↓	扔	力	力

2. 力

"力"字是原始农具耒的形象,是一种松土的工具。用耒耕作必须用力,后引申为力气的意思。由于在田地里从事农耕这种费力的劳作,多是由男子所做,所以"田"加"力"用来表示男子,写作 ᛚ 或 ᛜ 。成语"男耕女织"便是这种男女分工的诠释,指的是中国古代社会中的小农经济,一家一户经营,男的种田,女的织布。

3. 网

网是捕捉鱼鳖鸟兽的工具,这种工具不遮光,又通风透水,具有很强的迷惑性,可以捕鱼、捕鸟、捕兽,是狩猎时代的伟大发明。甲骨文"网"字左右两边是木棍,中间网绳交错、网眼密布,有的稀疏,有的稠密,正是一张网的真实形状。

甲骨文"罗"字写作 ᛘ ,上面是一张网,下面是一只鸟,表示小鸟被罩在网罩里。罗的本义为以网捕鸟,如"门可罗雀",作为名词使用时指网,如"天罗地网"。

2. 力(lì, strength)

The character 力(lì, strength) is the image of a tool 耒(lěi, plough) which was used for ploughing the land in ancient times. Holding the tool requires strength and as such, the character for "strength" has been derived from that of the tool. The laborious nature of farming in the field is mostly done by males, so adding the character 田(tián, farmland) to 力 was done to form the character 男(nán, male). This combination is evident in ancient characters such as ![], or ![]. The idiom, 男耕女织(nán gēng nǚ zhī, the men plough and the women weave), is the interpretation of this division of labor between men and women in the small-scale farming economy of ancient Chinese society. Every family ran their own business as men ploughed while women wove.

3. 网(wǎng, net)

网(wǎng, net) is an instrument for catching fish, birds and other small animals. Pervious to light and ventilation, this tool was handy to trap animals, and it was a great invention in the hunting era. In the oracle bone script, the character 网 looks exactly like a net woven between two sticks with irregular spaces.

The oracle bone script character for 罗(luó, catch birds with nets) was written as ![], resembling a bird caught beneath a net. The original meaning of 罗 is to catch birds with nets such as in the idiom, 门可罗雀(mén kě luó què, birds can be caught by a net at the door — a deserted house). 罗 can also be used as a noun such as in 天罗地网(tiān luó dì wǎng, nets above and snares below-spread, a net [situation] from which there is no escape).

"网"字的演变

Evolution of the Character "网"

甲骨文 Oracle Bone Script	金文 Bronze Script	小篆 Small Seal Script	隶书 Clerical Script	楷书 Regular Script
𠕁	⋈	𠔿	网	网

4. 鬲

鬲是古代煮饭的一种炊具，最先出现的是新石器时代的陶鬲，后来又出现青铜鬲。古人已掌握了很多物理知识，在制作鬲的时候把三足做成中空的，有的鬲足粗大呈袋状，增加了受热面积，便于对鬲内的食物快速加热。而且，古人已懂得用蒸汽加热食物，并制作了一种叫作甗的器物，甲骨文写作 ，下部是鬲，上部是另一种炊具甑，鬲和甑之间用带孔的篦子隔开，在甑内放置需要加热的食物，鬲内的水加热后就可以蒸食物了。

甗

Ancient Chinese Bronze Steamer, Or Cooking Vessel

鬲

Ancient Cooking Tripod with Hollow Legs

4. 鬲 (lì, an ancient cooking tripod with hollow legs)

鬲 (lì, an ancient cooking tripod with hollow legs) is a kind of cooking utensil. In the Neolithic age, 鬲 was made of pottery clay, and later there was 鬲 made of bronze. It was crafted with three hollow legs and a large vessel to increase the heated surface area so that the food inside could be heated quickly. Furthermore, by this time people had learned to use steam to heat food. They produced an artifact called 甗(yǎn), written as 甗 in the oracle bone script. The lower part of the character is 鬲, and the upper part of the character is another cookware, 甑 (zèng, a utensil for distilling water). The 鬲 and 甑 are separated by a perforated steaming rack. Foods are placed in the 甑, which is steamed by the boiling water in the 鬲.

"鬲" 字的演变
Evolution of the Character "鬲"

甲骨文 Oracle Bone Script	金文 Bronze Script	小篆 Small Seal Script	隶书 Clerical Script	楷书 Regular Script
鬲	鬲	鬲	鬲	鬲

5. 皿

甲骨文"皿"字像一个带有底座的容器，本义是盛东西的器具。在汉字中由"皿"字组成的字大都与器皿及其用途有关，如盂、盆、盅、盖、盘、盏等。皿里面可以盛水供人洗手，就产生了"盥"字，写作 ，像器皿里有一只手，有的字还加上了溅起的水滴形，写作 ，金文的"盥"字写作 ，更加形象具体，好像是双手在流动的水下冲洗。事实上，这个字也反映了古代的一种礼仪。

西周时期有一种礼仪叫沃盥礼，是中国古代重要的礼仪。沃的意思是浇水，盥的意思是洗手，沃盥即浇水洗手，举行这样的礼需要两种器具配合使用，一种是匜，一种是盘，侍者手里拿着盛满水的匜浇水，盘用于承接洗过手的废水，类似现在用自来水洗手。现代很多的洗手间都被命名为盥洗室，既可洗手也可洗脸。

"浴"字写作 ，像一个人站在一个大盆子里面，周围的小点代表四溅的水滴，表示人在洗澡的意思，现在的"浴"字是个形声字。古人称洗身为"浴"，洗头为"沐"，洗手为"盥"，洗脚为"洗"，而现在的"洗"字也可以表示其他三个字的意思。古人往往"沐浴"连用，如遇重大事件或节日，人们要"沐浴更衣"，以示敬意。

铜匜
Bronze Washbasin

铜盘
Bronze Plate

5. 皿(mǐn, a general term for vessels)

The oracle bone script for 皿(mǐn, a general term for vessels) is like a container with a base. It is a general term for vessels. Characters with 皿 as a component most often relate to vessels and the use of vessels such as in 盂(yú, broad-mouthed jar), 盆(pén, basin), 盅(zhōng, handleless cup), 盖(gài, lid), 盘 (pán, plate), or 盏(zhǎn, small cup). When 皿 is filled with water, it can be used to wash hands. As such, 盥(guàn, to wash hands) was produced and written as ⚬, like a hand within a container. Sometimes this character was written as ⚬ by adding splashing water drops to the character. In the Bronze script it was written as ⚬, a more vivid image of hands being washed under running water. In fact, this character also reflects an ancient etiquette.

In the Western Zhou Dynasty, there was an important etiquette called 沃盥礼 (wò guàn lǐ). 沃(wò) means watering, 盥(guàn) means washing hands, and 沃盥 (wò guàn) refers to washing hands under running water. To hold such a ceremony, two kinds of utensils must be used together: one is an 匜 (yí), the other is a 盘(pán, tray). A servant might pour the 匜 full of water, while the 盘 is used to receive waste water from the process, similar to washing hands with tap water now. Now, many toilets are called 盥洗室(guàn xǐ shì), a place for hand washing, face washing, and other uses.

The character 浴(yù, to take a bath) was written as ⚬, which looks like a person standing in a large basin with splashing water drops around him. This character is a phonogram, depicting a person taking a shower. The ancient Chinese called washing the body 浴, washing the head 沐(mù), washing the hands 盥, and washing the feet 洗(xǐ). Now, 洗 and at times 沐浴 refers to washing any part of the body. In case of a major event or festival, people would bathe and change their clothes to show respect.

"皿" 字的演变
Evolution of the Character "皿"

甲骨文 Oracle Bone Script	金文 Bronze Script	小篆 Small Seal Script	隶书 Clerical Script	楷书 Regular Script
⚬	⚬	⚬	⚬	皿

"豆"字的演变
Evolution of the Character "豆"

甲骨文 Oracle Bone Script	金文 Bronze Script	小篆 Small Seal Script	隶书 Clerical Script	楷书 Regular Script

6. 豆

看到"豆"字，现在的人们一般会想到各种豆类植物。实际上，豆是古代的一种食器，甲骨文、金文的"豆"字像一个上有盘下有高圈足的容器，盘中一横表示盘中所盛的食物。

中国自古以来就是礼仪之邦，"礼"字繁体字写作"禮"，就和"豆"字有很大的关系，意为用豆盛放物品以供奉神祇，后把敬奉神祇之类的事情称为礼，现在多指礼仪、礼节。我们日常生活中常用到的一个词"非礼"来源于孔子，孔子在《论语》中说到："非礼勿视，非礼勿听，非礼勿言，非礼勿动。"意思就是，不合乎礼节的事情不看、不听、不说、不采取行动。

7. 斤

人们现在所熟知的"斤"的意思是重量单位名称，一斤500克。而甲骨文的"斤"字像一把曲柄带有尖锐刀锋的金属工具，本义指锋利的斧头。在汉字中，凡是由"斤"组成的字都与斧头及其作用有关，如斧、断、析、折等。斤字后来多用作重量单位，在古代一斤等于十六两，人们习惯用"半斤八两"来形容彼此不相上下、实力相当。

"斤"字的演变
Evolution of the Character "斤"

甲骨文 Oracle Bone Script	金文 Bronze Script	小篆 Small Seal Script	隶书 Clerical Script	楷书 Regular Script

铜豆(dòu)
Bronze Sacrificial Vessel

6. 豆(dòu, an ancient food vessel)

The sight of 豆(dòu, bean) reminds people of various sorts of legumes. In fact, 豆 used to be an ancient food vessel. In the oracle bone script and the Bronze script, the character looks like a vessel consisting of a deep-set plate on the top, a ring-like stand at the bottom, and the stroke inside the plate represents food.

China has always been known as a 礼仪之邦(lǐ yí zhī bāng, nation of etiquette). The traditional Chinese character for 礼(lǐ, etiquette) is written as 禮 and it is related to 豆, which was often used to refer to sacrifice or offering ceremonies. Now, 礼 refers to etiquette instead of god worshiping. One of the commonly used words, 非礼(fēi lǐ, indecent assault), comes from *The Analects*: "非礼勿视，非礼勿听，非礼勿言，非礼勿动"(fēi lǐ wù shì, fēi lǐ wù tīng, fēi lǐ wù yán, fēi lǐ wù dòng). It means what is not courteous should not be seen, listened to, spoken, or acted.

7. 斤(jīn)

The character 斤 that people know now is a measure of weight: one 斤 equals 500 grams. But in the oracle bone script, 斤 looks like a sharp axe with a crooked handle and its original meaning was a sharp axe. Characters with 斤 as a component most often relate to axes and their uses, such as 斧(fǔ, axe), 断(duàn, to break), 析(xī, to split), or 折(zhé, to bend). 斤 is often used as a weight unit today. In ancient times, one 斤 was equal to sixteen 两(liǎng). People used the idiom 半斤八两(bàn jīn bā liǎng, half jin and eight liang-six of one and half a dozen of the other) to describe what is commonly known as "Tweedledee and Tweedledum."

第三章 汉字的构形

在煤炭没有被发现的远古时期，人们主要靠木材生火来做饭、取暖，这时候需要伐木，"折"字就出现了，甲骨文"折"字写作 🪓，左边是折断的树木，右边是一把曲柄斧子，像是用斧头把树木拦腰斩断，本义为断。医学术语"骨折"就是骨头断了的意思。烧火需要劈开木料，"析"字就产生了，甲骨文"析"字写作 🪓，像是用斧头在纵向砍木。

斤既是一种生产工具，作战时也是一种武器。甲骨文"兵"字写作 🪓，像双手拿着一把"斤"的形象，本义指作战用的兵器，引申为手持兵器作战的士兵，进一步引申为军队、军事、战争等义，如成语"纸上谈兵"，指的是在纸面上谈论打仗，比喻空谈理论，不能解决实际问题。

8. 父

古文字的"父"字像手上拿着石斧之类的工具，石斧是石器时代一种主要的生产工具和武器。手持石斧与敌人作战或从事艰苦的野外劳动，是成年男子的责任，因此"父"是古人对从事劳动的男子的尊称，后来又成为对亲生父亲及其同辈男子的称呼。

古人认为教育孩子的责任来自于家庭教育和学校教育两个方面，而家庭教育则更看重父亲的责任，古代启蒙教材《三字经》里写到："养不教，父之过。"意思是仅仅供养儿女吃穿，而不好好教育，是父亲的过错。古代社会以男性为尊，女性读过书受过教育的很少，所以教育孩子的职责大多落在父亲身上。现在人们将"父"理解为"父辈的家长"，也就是我们平常所说的"父母"。不能教育好自己的子女，是做父母的过错。

"父"字的演变
Evolution of the Character "父"

甲骨文 Oracle Bone Script	金文 Bronze Script	小篆 Small Seal Script	隶书 Clerical Script	楷书 Regular Script
 🖋	 🖋	 🖋	 父	 父

Before coal was discovered, people mainly relied on wood as the fuel for fires to cook food and keep warm. They had to cut wood for fuel, and 折 was formed. In the oracle bone script, 折 was 𣂑, resembling a broken tree on the left and an axe with a crooked handle on the right. It looks like a tree being cut down with an axe. The original meaning was "to break." The medical term 骨折 (gǔ zhé, fracture), means the broken bone. To prepare fire wood, a tree needs to be split. As such, the character 析 (xī, to split) was formed. In the oracle bone script the character is written as 𣂐, and it resembles a man cutting wood with an axe from above.

斤 serves as both a tool in production and a weapon in combat. In the oracle bone script, the character of 兵 (bīng, the weapon using in war) was written as 𠬞. It looks like two hands holding a 斤. Its original meaning is "a weapon," but its meaning has been extended to cover the person who holds the weapon, namely a soldier. It can also be used to refer to armies, military affairs, or wars such as in zhǐ shàng tán bīng (talking about stratagems on paper), which refers to an armchair strategist indulging in empty talk.

8. 父 (fù, father)

The character 父 (fù, father) in ancient writing systems looks like a hand holding a stone axe. The stone axe was one of the most important weapons and tools in the Stone Age. Traditionally, an adult man would take on the responsibility of fighting the enemy and working in the fields with a stone axe, hence 父 became a term of address for the adult man. Gradually, it has come to mean father or male peers.

Traditional thought suggests that both the family and the school are responsible for the education of children. In a family, it is the father who should take more responsibility for his children's education. In the ancient enlightenment textbook, *The Three-Character Classic*, there is a section that reads, 养不教，父之过 (yǎng bú jiāo, fù zhī guò), which means that although the father's children are fed, it is his fault if his children are not taught properly. In the past, men enjoyed more privileges than women in education, so it was a father's duty to teach his children. More recently, however, 养不教，父之过 means that both parents should bear the responsibility of educating their children.

在商朝，还有一种大斧子，甲骨文写作 ⼤ 、⽟ ，从外形看像是一把带手柄的宽刃钺，金文写作 王 、王 ，斧钺的形状更加明显，就是现在的"王"字。在商代，斧钺是军权和王权的象征，代表权力，"王"的意义也由一件斩杀、砍头的武器演变为国家的最高领袖。在商王武丁妻子妇好的墓中，发现了两件特大的斧钺，一把龙钺，一把虎钺，每一把都是九公斤。在墓中发现九公斤重的钺主要是象征意义，很难想象妇好会拿着这么重的武器上阵杀敌，况且这还是没有手柄。别的墓中还出土过很小的钺，根本就没法杀人，多半也是象征性的。

现在的"王"字非常常见，也是中国人数较多的姓氏之一，《说文解字》中"王"字的小篆写法是 王 ，三横一竖，但三横之间不是等距的，中间一横比较靠近上面的一横，许慎给出的解释是：王，是人心所向、天下人归附和向往的英杰。然后引用西汉著名儒家学者董仲舒的说法，说三道横画分别代表天、地、人，而能够参悟、贯通这三者的人，就是王。可以说，这样的解释在现在看来并不令人满意。

铜钺
Bronze Axe

In the oracle bone script, there is another type of Shang Dynasty axe that is written as 太 and 太. These characters appear more like 斧钺(fǔ yuè), a large axe-shaped weapon with a handle. In the Bronze script, this axe is depicted in the characters 王 and 王, which resemble the modern character, 王(wáng, the king). At that time, 斧钺 was a symbol of power, representing military leadership and kingship. The meaning of 王 evolved from a weapon to the ruler of the country. In the tomb of Fu Hao, the wife of King Wuding of the Shang Dynasty, there were two particularly large and heavy 斧钺 discovered: one was a dragon-shaped 钺, and the other was a tiger-shaped 钺. These axes were likely more symbolic than practical, as it was unlikely that such a heavy weapon would be used in combat. Some similar 斧钺 had been unearthed in other tombs, only in much smaller sizes. However, these axes were also likely just symbolic as they were too small to be used effectively as a weapon.

In modern times, 王 is frequently used as a surname for Chinese people. In the small seal script, the character of 王 appears as 王 in Xu Shen's *The Explanation of Script and Elucidation of Characters*. It consists of three horizontal strokes and one vertical stroke, but the three horizontal strokes are not equidistant. The middle stroke is closer to the upper stroke. The explanation given by Xu Shen is that the king is a hero who wins the love of the crowds. Then, Xu quoted Dong Zhongshu's interpretation, a famous Confucian scholar in the Western Han Dynasty, who said that the three horizontal strokes represent the heaven, the earth, and the people, but only those who truly understand these three subjects could be made a king. These interpretations are still debated today.

9. 戈

戈是古代常用的主要武器之一,可以用来横击、钩杀,大都用铜或铁制成,装有长柄,商代已经出现了铜戈。甲骨文和早期金文的"戈"字正像这种兵器的形状。在汉字中凡由"戈"组成的字大都与武器、战争和格杀有关,如戎、戒、戍、伐等。

甲骨文"戒"字写作 ,中间是一把长戈,左右两侧是两只手,看起来像两只手紧握长戈,以防范来犯的敌人,本义为双手持戈做好战斗准备,引申为防备、警告的意思,又引申为戒除的意思,如戒烟、戒酒等。

甲骨文的"伐"字由戈和人组成,像用戈砍击人的脖子的形象,本义为武力杀戮,引申为击刺、攻杀的含义。古文字的"戍"字同样由人和戈组成,写作,与"伐"不同的是,"戍"字像人扛着或拿着戈的形象,是武装守卫的意思,本义指保卫、防守边疆。

戈
Bronze Halberd

9. 戈(gē)

戈 is one of the weapons most commonly used in ancient times. With a long handle and a horizontal blade at its head, it could be used to strike or hook. Most of them were made of bronze or iron. The bronze 戈 was produced as early as the Shang Dynasty. In the oracle bone script and early Bronze script, the character 戈 bears the shape of this weapon. Characters with 戈 as a component most often are related to weapons, war, or fighting such as in 戎(róng, army), 戒(jiè, to guard against), 戍(shù, to defend), or 伐(fá, to attack).

The character of 戒 in the oracle bone script was written as 𠁁. There is a long 戈 in the middle with one hand on the left side and the other hand on the right side. The character resembles a man holding a weapon to guard against an enemy. Its primary meaning is "to guard against," but its meaning has been extended to include "to warn," "to prohibit," or "to give up" such as in 戒烟(jiè yān, to give up smoking), or 戒酒(jiè jiǔ, to give up drinking).

The character of 伐(fá, to chop) in the oracle bone script, consisting of 戈 and 人, appears as 𠂉, which looks like a man chopping the head of an enemy with 戈. The original meaning of 伐 is "to chop," but its meaning has been expanded to include "to strike" and "to attack." 戍(shù, to defend) also consists of 人 and 戈, and was written in the oracle bone script as 𠂉. Unlike 伐, the character 戍 looks like a person carrying or holding a 戈, indicating that they are defending their land. As such, the primary meaning of 戍 is "to defend or to guard the frontiers."

"戈" 字的演变
Evolution of the Character "戈"

甲骨文 Oracle Bone Script	金文 Bronze Script	小篆 Small Seal Script	隶书 Clerical Script	楷书 Regular Script
千	戈	戈	戈	戈

"刀"字的演变
Evolution of the Character "刀"

甲骨文 Oracle Bone Script	金文 Bronze Script	小篆 Small Seal Script	隶书 Clerical Script	楷书 Regular Script

10. 刀

甲骨文"刀"字像有手柄的一把刀的形状，商代陶器上也出现了"刀"字，即 。在商代，刀很少用作武器，更多用作工具或者刑具，甲骨文就是用小的青铜刀或者玉刀刻到甲骨上去的。刀在劳动中的用途比较广泛，如农业中用于收割的镰刀等，畜牧业中用于宰杀、割肉、剔骨的尖刀，手工业中用的就更多了。刀后来也作为一种随身佩戴的防身武器。甲骨文"刃"字写作 ，是在"刀"字上加一点指明刀口所在的位置，指刀的锋利部位。甲骨文"分"字写作 ，表示用刀将物体切成两部分或几部分。

11. 射

在冷兵器时代，弓箭是最可怕的致命武器。甲骨文"射"字是弯弓搭箭的形象，本义是射箭，有的金文"射"字又加了一只手，突出射箭的动作，像一个人在用手拉弓发箭。甲骨文的"弓"字写作 ，像一把弓的形状，商代时候的箭叫作"矢"，写作 ，甲骨文的"矢"字突出了锋利的箭锋和装在箭尾的燕尾状的翎羽。"箭"和"矢"表示的意思一样，只是"箭"字出现的比较晚，是个形声字。箭射出去之后，肯定会到达一个地方，"至"字就产生了，写作 ，像箭从高空降落到地上，意思为到达。

10. 刀(dāo)

In the oracle bone script, 刀(dāo) looks like a knife with a handle. It also appeared on pottery as ▬ during the Shang Dynasty. At that time, 刀 was used as a tool or instrument as opposed to a weapon. By using a small bronze or jade knife, people carved characters into the oracle bones. Knives are widely used in productive activities, such as 镰刀(lián dāo, sickle) used for harvesting in agriculture and 尖刀(jiān dāo, pointed knife) used in husbandry for killing animals, cutting meat, and deboning. As a tool, 刀 was most used in handicraft industries. Only later was 刀 used as a self-defense weapon. The character 刃(rèn, the point or edge of a knife), appears in the oracle bone script as ⟨⟩, featuring the addition of a part of the character 刀 to indicate the position of the blade's edge. The character 分 appears in the oracle bone script as ⟨⟩, indicating that an object is cut into two or several parts with a knife.

11. 射(shè, shooting)

During the age of cold steel, bows and arrows were the deadliest weapons. The character, 射(shè, shooting), appears in the oracle bone script as an arrow on the bowstring. This character's primary meaning was "to shoot an arrow." In the bronze script, a part of a hand is added to the character of 射 to emphasize the action of shooting by making the character look more like a person drawing an arrow. The character 弓(gōng, the weapon used for shooting an arrow), appears in the oracle bone script as ⟨⟩, which resembles the shape of a bow. During the Shang Dynasty, the arrow was called 矢(shǐ, arrow) and written as ↑ to emphasize the sharp head and the dovetail-shaped feathers at the tail of the arrow. The characters 箭(jiàn, arrow) and 矢 share similar features, but the character 箭 was developed as a phonogram thereafter. The character 至(zhì, to reach) was written as ↓ looking like an arrow falling from the sky or like a signal that an arrow had reached the ground.

210　　第三章　汉字的构形

在打猎时，如果箭矢用完了怎么办，人们会继续使用弓，只不过用弓发射的是圆石头之类的东西。甲骨文的"弹"字写作  ，像在弓弦上加一颗圆形物的形状，用以表示利用弓弦发射球形东西，本义指弹丸，也指弹弓。

12. 乐

甲骨文的"乐"字由"丝"和"木"两个字组成，像木枕上系着丝弦的琴具。金文又加了一个"白"字，写作  ，后逐渐演变为"樂"，现在简化为"乐"。本义指琴类的丝弦乐器，后来引申为音乐。乐声悦耳，能使人感到快乐，所以乐字又可用作动词，读lè，有喜悦、快乐、欢喜的意思。

"乐"字的演变
Evolution of the Character "乐"

甲骨文 Oracle Bone Script	金文 Bronze Script	小篆 Small Seal Script	隶书 Clerical Script	楷书 Regular Script
			 樂	 乐

"射"字的演变
Evolution of the Character "射"

甲骨文 Oracle Bone Script	金文 Bronze Script	小篆 Small Seal Script	隶书 Clerical Script	楷书 Regular Script

If the arrows were used up while hunting, people would continue to hunt using round stones instead of arrows. The oracle bone script character for 弹(dàn, pellet) appeared as 𐂃 which resembles a pellet on a bowstring. This character came to refer to a catapult.

12. 乐(yuè)

In the oracle bone script, 乐 consisted of 丝(string) and 木(wood), and looked like a stringed instrument stretched over wood. The bronze script character of 乐 added 白(bái, white) and appeared as 𮕿. It evolved gradually into 樂 and then the simplified form, 乐. It originally referred to stringed musical instruments, but has since come to mean "music" as well. Music is pleasing to the ear and gives people varying satisfaction and as such, the character 乐 used as a verb and pronounced as lè, can mean being happy, cheerful, or joyful.

13. 磬

磬是中国古代的一种打击乐器，形状像曲尺，起源于某种片状的石制劳动工具，悬挂于架上，敲击时就会发出悦耳的声音。磬的形状后来有多种变化，也出现了玉制、铜制磬等。有单个的特磬，也有成组的编磬。甲骨文中"磬"字一边像悬石，另一边像手执槌敲击，表示敲击悬挂的乐器。磬最早用于先民的乐舞活动，后来用于历代帝王、上层统治者的殿堂宴享、宗庙祭祀、朝聘礼仪活动中的乐队演奏，成为象征身份地位的礼器。

除了琴、磬，中国古代还有多种乐器，统称八音，是中国历史上最早的乐器科学分类法。西周时期，人们已将当时的乐器按制作材料分为金（钟）、石（磬）、丝（琴）、竹（箫）、匏（笙）、土（埙）、革（鼓）、木（柷）八类，合称八音。

石编磬
Stone Chime

13. 磬(qìng, chime made by stone)

磬 was a kind of percussion instrument shaped like a trisquare and used in ancient China. This instrument originated from a kind of sheet-shaped stone tool hung on a shelf which would make a pleasant sound when struck. There were many changes in the shape over time. 磬 was originally made of stone, but later there was also 磬 made of jade and bronze. As a musical instrument, 磬 could be played by one person or by a group. In the oracle bone script, the character 磬 looks like a man striking the hanging chime stone with a mallet. This instrument was first played in the earlier music and dancing activities of ancestors, before transitioning into a symbol of status used for palace feasts, sacrificial rituals, and royal ceremonies.

In addition to 琴(qín, a seven-stringed plucked instrument) and 磬, there were many instruments in ancient China that were collectively known as 八音(bā yīn, eight sounds—eight categories of musical instruments in ancient orchestra), one of the earliest classifications of musical instruments in Chinese history. In the Western Zhou Dynasty, musical instruments were divided into eight categories according to the materials they were made of, namely 钟(zhōng, bell made of metal), 磬(qìng, chime made of stone), 琴(qín, lute made of string), 箫(xiāo, a vertical flute made of bamboo), 笙(shēng, a reed pipe wind instrument made by plants), 埙(xūn, a holed wind instrument made of mud), 鼓(gǔ, drum, made of leather), and 柷(zhù, an ancient musical instrument made by wood).

"磬"字的演变
Evolution of the Character "磬"

甲骨文 Oracle Bone Script	金文 Bronze Script	小篆 Small Seal Script	隶书 Clerical Script	楷书 Regular Script
磬		磬	磬	磬

第四章

汉字的艺术

Chapter IV

The Art of Chinese Characters

第四章 汉字的艺术

  远古先民通过对生活的观察和体验,用事物的形状轮廓、姿态特征赋予了汉字最初的生命,也因此造就了汉字独特的构形方式和独有的艺术形式。

  数千年来,华夏先民把汉字书写发展成为多种具有独特审美价值和深远文化影响的艺术创造,如中国书法、印章篆刻、汉字画等。所有这些,都体现了中华民族的艺术创造和审美旨趣,值得人们去探寻、去思考。

石鼓文-1
Shiguwen (stone-drum characters) A

Chapter IV The Art of Chinese Characters

Ancient people assigned the literal meaning to Chinese characters with the shape, outline and posture of what they observed in their lives and thus crafted the distinct configurations and unique art form of the Chinese character.

For thousands of years, Chinese ancestors developed Chinese characters as artistic creations with unique aesthetic values and profound cultural effects that were continually renewed in the forms of Chinese calligraphy, seal cutting, and Chinese painting. These forms embody the artistry and aesthetic ideals of the Chinese nation are worth experiencing and exploring.

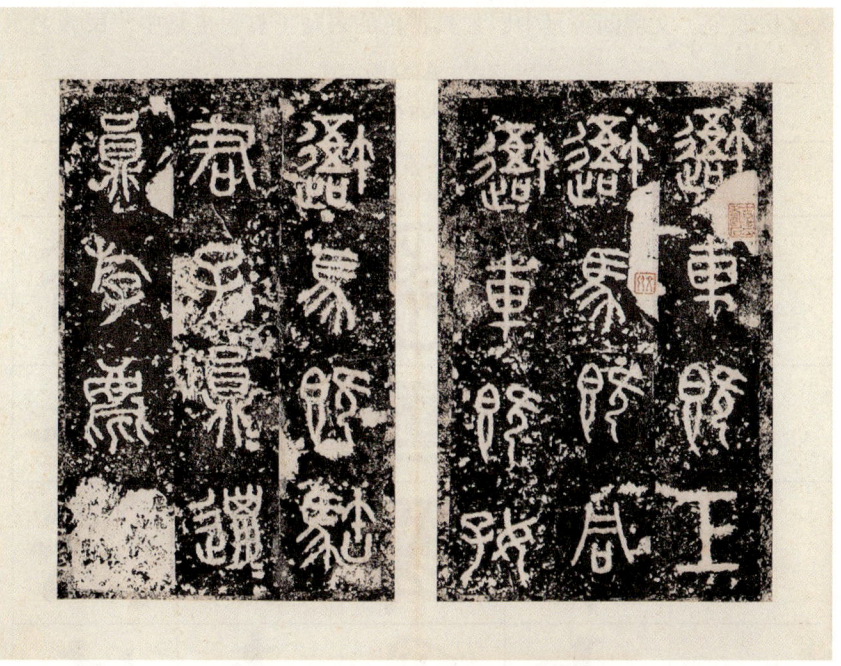

石鼓文-2
Shiguwen (stone-drum characters) B

一、书法

中国书法是一门古老的汉字书写艺术，是汉字文化的一大特色，反映了人们在书写汉字过程中的审美追求。数千年来，汉字独特的构形方式、汉字独有的书写工具、中国人独特的审美情趣等因素共同造就了汉字的书法艺术。在书法艺术的历史长河中，产生了篆书、隶书、楷书、行书、草书等不同的书体，这些书体各具特色，名家辈出，大量名作流传至今，使得汉字的书法艺术日渐繁荣。

1. 文房四宝

文房是指文人书房，笔、墨、纸、砚为文房所使用，因而被人们誉为文房四宝。文房四宝是中国独具特色的书写工具，也是中华民族艺术

中国书法五种书体对比
Comparison of Five Styles of Chinese Calligraphy

	中 Zhong	國（国） Guo	書（书） Shu	法 Fa
篆书 Seal Script				
隶书 Clerical Script				
楷书 Regular Script				
行书 Semi-Cursive Script				
草书 Cursive Script				

Ⅰ. Calligraphy

Chinese calligraphy is an ancient art of writing and a major component of Chinese character culture that reflects aesthetic pursuit in the process of writing Chinese characters. For thousands of years, the distinct configuration of Chinese characters, their unique writing tools, and the unique aesthetic taste of Chinese people among other factors have influenced the calligraphic art of Chinese characters. During the long history of calligraphic art, different calligraphy styles have been produced, such as seal script, clerical script, regular script, semi-cursive script, and cursive script. These styles have their own distinct characteristics and many famous calligraphers have created a large number of famous calligraphies that circulate today, making the calligraphic art of Chinese characters increasingly prosperous.

1. The Four Treasures of the Study

Wen Fang refers to the literators' study in which the four treasures of the study—the brush, inkstick, paper, and inkstone—are used. The four treasures of the study are distinctive Chinese writing tools and a glittering gem in art treasure

毛笔 墨锭 宣纸 砚台
Writing Brush Inkstick Xuan Paper Inkstone

宝库中绚丽的瑰宝。

当今世界上流行钢笔、圆珠笔、铅笔等各种笔，但中国书法所用的笔专指毛笔，就是用兽毛和笔管制成的笔。兽毛指兔、羊等动物毛，笔管一般用竹管制成，也有用犀牛角、象牙或金银制作的。中国目前最著名的毛笔，是浙江湖州善琏镇所产的选料严格、制作精良的湖笔。

墨是中国古代书写、绘画的黑色颜料，通过砚台用水研磨可以产生用于毛笔书写的墨水。在人工制墨发明之前，一般利用天然墨或半天然墨来作为书写材料。后代的人工墨因原料不同，可分为油烟墨、漆烟墨、松烟墨等不同种类，有的在墨面雕刻山水人物，将墨锭制成各种艺术形态。中国最有名的墨是安徽省的徽墨，徽墨具有"落纸如漆、色泽黑润、经久不褪、香味浓郁"等特点。为了方便，目前一般书画都采用墨汁，但讲究用墨的人仍采用研磨徽墨的办法来创作书画。

宣纸指的是用于创作书画作品的纸，因产自宣州府（今安徽省泾县）而得名，历代王朝都把泾县宣纸列为贡品。宣纸的特点是：质地绵韧，纹理美观，洁白细密，经久不坏，并善于表现笔墨的浓淡润湿，因而被称作"纸中之王"。宣纸价格较贵，初学习者可不用宣纸，用价钱便宜的毛边纸即可。

砚，俗称砚台，是中国文人为书写、绘画而研磨色料的工具。因为磨墨，所以有一块平坦的地方；因为盛墨汁，所以有一个凹陷。明、清

houses in China.

Today, pens, pencils and the like are popular throughout the world, but the pens used in Chinese calligraphy refer exclusively to the writing brushes made of animal hair and pen tubes. The hair used in brushes are from rabbits, sheep, and other animals. The pen tube is usually made of bamboo pipe and sometimes rhinoceros' horn, ivory, gold, or silver. The most famous writing brush in China is the Hu writing brush with strict selection guidelines for materials to ensure excellent production. These brushes are made in Shanlian Town, Huzhou City, Zhejiang Province.

An inkstick is a black pigment for writing and painting developed in ancient China. Ink for writing brushes can be produced by grinding down an inkstick on an inkstone and mixing the product with water. Prior to the invention of artificial inksticks, natural and semi-natural inksticks were often used to produce ink. Artificial inksticks of later generations can be divided into different types such as lampblack inkstick, paint smoke inkstick and pine-soot inkstick. People made inksticks into various artistic forms by carving the image of landscapes and figures on their surface. The most famous inkstick in China is the Hui inkstick of Anhui Province. This kind of inkstick features black, smooth, long-lasting color, and strong fragrance. The ink from this inkstick appears on the paper like paint when writing. Currently, common paintings and calligraphy use ink for convenience, but those who are particular about tradition still use the method of grinding the Hui inkstick to create calligraphy and paintings.

Xuan paper is the preferred canvas for Chinese calligraphy and painting. It gained its name from Xuanzhou Prefecture, which is now Jing County.It features great tensile strength,smooth surface,pure and clean texture and clean stroke, suitable for conveying the artistic expression of both Chinese calligraphy and painting with great resistance to crease and corrosion.Renowned for such unique characteristics and known as "the king of paper," it has been long enlisted as a tribute to the Court since the Tang Dynasty. The price of Xuan paper is relatively expensive, so beginners often begin writing on cheap moben paper.

Inkstone, also known as inkslab, is a tool used by Chinese literators to grind pigments for writing and painting. There is a flat surface for grinding inksticks, and a dent for holding the ink. During the Ming and Qing Dynasties, there were

时期，出现了被人们称为"四大名砚"的端砚、歙砚、洮砚和澄泥砚。

2. 篆书

篆书有大篆和小篆之分，大篆指秦以前的各种书体，小篆指秦统一后的书体。标准的小篆字体排列整齐，字形修长，线条匀称，运笔圆转，结构讲究左右对称。典型特点就是笔道圆转弯曲，用圆转匀称的线条表现了婉转流畅的美。

《三坟记》由唐代著名书法家李阳冰书写，讲述的是立碑人李季卿迁葬他三个哥哥的事情。

3. 隶书

隶书字形方扁，横画长而竖画短，笔画有了粗细变化，比篆书书写简约、便捷。曹全碑刻于东汉时期，是王敞等人为郃阳县令曹全歌功颂德而立的石碑，碑文记述了曹全的祖上以及曹全本人的功德。曹全碑碑文清秀，显示出轻盈活泼、柔和婉转的风格特点，是汉隶的代表作之一。

4. 楷书

楷书结构方正，笔画横平竖直，结构紧凑。中国历史上形成了"楷书四大家"，即唐代的颜真卿、欧阳询、柳公权和元代的赵孟頫，他们的作品到现在仍是书法爱好者临摹的首选。九成宫醴泉铭碑是欧阳询的

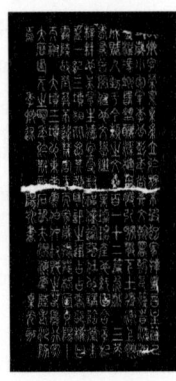

《三坟记》拓片　　　　　　　曹全碑拓片（局部）

"The Three Tombs" Rubbings　　Stele of Cao Quan Rubbings (Partial)

Duan, She, Tao, and Chengni Inkstones which, together, were known as the "Four Famous Inkstones."

2. Seal Script

Seal script can be divided into large seal script and small seal script. Large seal script refers to the various writing styles before the Qin Dynasty and small seal script refers to the writing style after the unification of the Qin Dynasty. The standard small seal script is neat, slender, well-proportioned in line, round in shape, and bilaterally symmetrical in structure. The identifying characteristic of standard small seal script is the rounding and bending of many strokes that draw out the beauty, grace, and smoothness of the character's well-proportioned lines.

"The Three Tombs," written by Li Yangbing, a famous calligrapher of the Tang Dynasty, recorded Li Jiqing's relocation of his three brothers' tombs.

3. Clerical Script

The style of the clerical script is square and flat; the horizontal strokes are long, the vertical strokes are short, and the strokes change in thickness throughout. This style is simpler and more convenient than seal script. The Stele of Cao Quan was engraved in the Eastern Han Dynasty. It is a stone tablet built by Wang Chang and others praising Cao Quan, who was a county magistrate in Heyang County. The epitaph describes the merits of ancestors of Cao Quan and Cao Quan himself. The epitaph of Cao Quan Stele is delicate and handsome, showing a light, lively, soft, and mellow style. This stele is one of the representative works of clerical script from the Han Dynasty.

4. Regular Script

The structure of the regular script is square and compact, and the strokes are horizontal and vertical. In the history of China, there were "four masters of the regular script," namely Yan Zhenqing, Ouyang Xun, and Liu Gongquan of the Tang Dynasty, as well as Zhao Mengfu of the Yuan Dynasty. Their works are still the first choice for calligraphy enthusiasts to copy. The Stele of Jiucheng Palace is a representative work of Ouyang Xun. This stele records the story of how Li

九成宫醴泉铭拓片（局部）
Jiucheng Palace Stele Rubbings (Partial)

代表作，内容记述唐太宗李世民在九成宫避暑时发现醴泉的事情。

5. 草书

草书的特点是结构简省、笔画连绵，对于普通人来说不易辨认。唐代的张旭、怀素将草书发挥到了极致。《自叙帖》是怀素流传下来篇幅最长的作品，也是他晚年草书的代表作。内容为怀素自述写草书的经历和经验，还有当时士大夫对他书法的品评。

6. 行书

行书是介于楷书、草书之间的一种书体，是为了弥补楷书的书写速度太慢和草书的难于辨认的劣势而产生的，其特点是在保持楷书形体轮廓的前提下，适当运用连笔，省减笔画。行书比楷书易写，比草书好认，是人们手写的主要字体。楷法多于草法的叫"行楷"，草法多于楷法的叫"行草"。

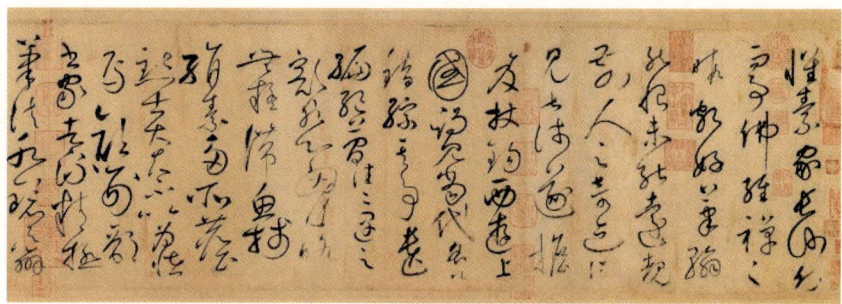

《自叙帖》(局部)
A Self Account by Myself (Partial)

Shimin, Emperor Taizong of the Tang Dynasty found the Li Spring when he summered at the Jiucheng Palace.

5. Cursive Script

Cursive script has a simple structure and uses continuous strokes. Cursive script is difficult to read for audiences unfamiliar with that style. Zhang Xu and Huai Su of the Tang Dynasty brought cursive script to the highest level. "A Self Account by Myself" is the longest work handed down by Huai Su, and this work is representative of his cursive script in his later years. This particular work recounts Huai Su's own experiences in writing cursive script as well as the scholar-officials' comments on his calligraphy at that time.

6. Semi-Cursive Script

Semi-cursive script is a kind of writing style between regular script and cursive script. It was produced with the intention of remedying the slow writing speed of regular script and the difficult recognition of cursive script. It is characterized by the proper use of semi-continuous writing to reduce strokes on the premise of maintaining the outline of regular script. Semi-cursive script is easier to write than regular script, and easier to recognize than cursive script, so it is the main handwritten font. Variations between the degrees of regular script and cursive script are referred to in different ways. Calligraphies with more regular script than cursive script are called *xingkai* and calligraphies with more cursive script than regular script are called "running script."

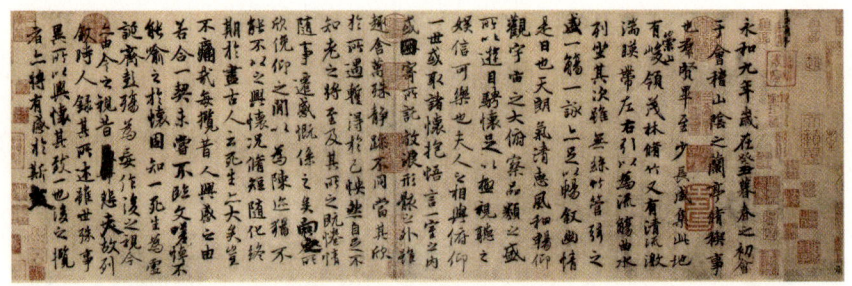

《兰亭集序》

Preface to the Orchid Pavilion Collection

王羲之是中国历史上最杰出的书法家，是当时书坛的核心人物，他的书法影响了此后整个中国书法的进程，被后人誉为"书圣"。《兰亭集序》是王羲之的代表作，被誉为"天下第一行书"，被历代学书者奉为学习行书的典范。

古人习惯说："楷如立，行如行，草如奔。"如果把楷书比作一个人站立的话，那么行书就像人在行走，草书就像人在奔跑。体现在书写风格上就是：一般楷书端严工整，书写速度比较缓慢；草书率意奔放，往往难于识读；而行书则兼楷书的工稳和草书的率意，具有简便、易识、通俗的特点。

Wang Xizhi is the most outstanding calligrapher in Chinese history and he was a core figure in calligraphic circles of his time. Wang's calligraphy has influenced the whole process of Chinese calligraphy since the appearance of his work and he has been praised as the "Sage Calligrapher" by later generations. As a representative work of Wang Xizhi, "Preface to the Orchid Pavilion Collection" is known as the "Number One Work of Semi-Cursive Script in the World," and this work has been regarded as the ideal model for learning semi-cursive script for calligraphy learners of all ages.

The ancient used to say that "regular script looks like a standing man, semi-cursive script like a walking man, and cursive script like a running man." That is, if you compare the regular script to a standing man, then the semi-cursive script looks like a walking man, and the cursive script looks like a running man. It is embodied in the writing style:regular script is generally strict and neat with a relatively slow writing speed; cursive script is unrestrained and often difficult to recognize and read; while semi-cursive script combines the neatness of regular script and the freedom of cursive script to produce a script that is simple, easy to recognize, and thus popular.

二、印章

印章起源很早,是全世界共有的古老文明,也是人们日常生活中不可或缺的文化产物。公文书信、日常琐事等很多场合都需要用到公章或私人印章。

中国商代已出现印章,战国秦汉时期是印章使用的第一次高峰,并逐渐影响了同是汉字文化圈的日本、韩国、越南,以及非使用汉字的蒙古族、满族、藏族等。十六、十七世纪,篆刻流派兴起,风格各异,在理论与实践上得到极大发展,成为专门之学,印章艺术达到第二个高峰,许多文人投入了大量的精力,自书自刻,有的还加上边款诗文,印章的材质也由铜转为石。到清末民初,专业篆刻家越来越多,所治印文更加精美,书画家用印也更加讲究,可以说是名家林立,作品异彩纷呈,使印章艺术涌现出第三个高峰。

1. 材料与工具

印章的质地古今不同,先秦以及秦汉时期多用铜和玉,也有用金银的。唐代以后,印章材料增加了象牙、犀角、陶、瓷等。元末及明代以后,多用石材,也有将水晶、玛瑙、竹根、有机玻璃等作为印材。石材中又以寿山石、青田石、昌化石、巴林石为最佳。

制作印章的工具主要有刻刀、印床、砂纸等。因镌刻的印章大小、质地、文体不同,刻刀也有大小和品种之分。用来固定印章的夹

石章料
Stone Material of Seal

刻刀
Graver

印床
Printing Bed

印泥
Seal Paste

II. Seal

The seal emerged early across ancient civilizations of the world and has been an indispensable cultural product in daily life. Official seals or private seals are used for many occasions including official documents and daily chores.

In the Shang Dynasty, seals were already popular. The use of seals peaked initially in the Warring States Period as well as the Qin and Han Dynasties. The use of seals during these periods in China gradually influenced the use of seals by the Japanese, South Koreans, and Vietnamese, who are in the same cultural circle of Chinese characters, as well as the Mongolians, Manchus and Tibetans, who do not use Chinese characters. In the sixteenth and seventeenth centuries, seal art was rejuvenated as seal-cutting schools emerged with new styles. Seal-cutting became an intensive study through the development of new theories and practices. Many literati spent a lot of energy on the renewal of seal art, and they wrote and engraved by themselves. Poems were included occasionaly alongside the seal, and seal materials, which were originally made of bronze, were beginning to be fashioned out of stone. From the end of the Qing Dynasty to the founding of the Republic of China, there was a proliferation of professional seal engravers pushing the creative bounds to produce more exquisite imprints. Calligraphers and painters also paid more attention to using inksticks. When considering the sheer number of outstanding seal art works produced by famous artists during this period, some experts have referred to this time as the third peak in seal art.

1. Materials and Tools

The material of the seal has differed from ancient to modern times. The seals of the pre-Qin period and Qin and Han Dynasties were often made of copper and jade, and some were made of gold and silver. After the Tang Dynasty, seals were also made of ivory, rhinoceros' horn, pottery, and porcelain. After the end of the Yuan Dynasty and the Ming Dynasty, stones were often used to make seals, but occasionally, crystal, agate, bamboo root, and plexiglass were also used. Among stone materials, Shoushan, Qingtian, Changhua, and Balin Stone have been the best for making seals.

The tools for making seals include gravers, printing beds and abrasive paper. Due to different sizes, materials and styles of the seal, there are also differences

具叫印床，刻印时用印床固定印章，操作起来方便省力。砂纸主要用于磨平印面。

印泥是钤盖印章的材料，主要以艾叶纤维、朱砂和蓖麻油为基本原料，经过精细加工制成，印泥的颜色一般为红色。

2. 朱文与白文

印章文字主要有两种不同的表现形式，一是朱文，文字的线条在刻的时候是突起的，印出来的文字是红色的，也叫阳文；二是白文，和朱文正好相反，文字的线条在刻的时候是凹下去的，印出来的文字是白色的，也叫阴文。当然，如果一枚印章印文部分既有白文也有朱文，我们称它为朱白相间印。

朱文印章
Zhu Wen Seal

白文印章
Bai Wen Seal

3. 印章内容

印章文字有多种字体，但以篆书居多。根据内容的不同，印章可以分为官印和私印两大类。在古代，官印一般由皇帝颁发，什么样的官职颁发什么样的印章，作为各级官员发号施令的凭据，是权力的象征。官印多为四方形，文字工整、严谨，体现国家权力的威严。

官印之外的印章大多都可称为私印，私印不像官印要求那么严格，内容比较丰富，大致可分为姓名字号印、斋馆印、收藏鉴赏印、吉语印、成语印、肖形印、花押印等。

in size and varieties of gravers. The printing bed is a fixture used to hold the seal during engraving. Abrasive paper is used to smooth the printing surface of seals.

Seal paste is a material for stamping. It is typically composed of folium artemisiae, argyi fiber, cinnabar, and castor oil. The color of the seal paste is generally red.

2. Characters Carved in Relief on a Seal (*Zhu Wen*) and Characters Cut in Intaglio (*Bai Wen*)

Typically, there are two main forms of seal characters. The first form is characters carved in relief on a seal, or yang seals. The lines of the characters protrude when they are engraved and imprint the Chinese characters in red ink. The other form is characters cut in intaglio on a seal, or yin seals. The lines of the characters are concave at the time of carving, which is exactly opposite to yang seals, and imprint the background in red and leave the characters colourless. If the characters of a seal have been carved both in relief and in intaglio, the seal is called a "red-white characters combined seal."

3. Content of Seal

There are many styles of characters on seals, but most of them are seal script. According to their characteristics, seals can be divided into two categories: official seal and private seal. In ancient times, the official seal was generally issued by the emperor. Different official positions had different seals, as they were a symbol of power and displayed the evidence of orders issued by officials at all levels. The official seals were mostly square, and the characters on them were neat and bold to reflect the majesty of state power.

Most non-official seals can be called private seals. Private seals are not as strict as official seals, and their content is often quite rich. Content of private seals might include details such as "personal name, style name and alias seal," "studio or study seal," "storage and appreciation seal," "lucky sayings seal," "idiom seal," "portrait seal," and "signature seal."

第四章　汉字的艺术

各类印章（一）
Various Seals

官印 Official Seal	琅琊相印章 Langya Prime Minister's Seal	广陵王玺 Guangling King's Seal	渭成令印 Weicheng Magistrate's Seal	武陵尉印 Wuling Commandant's Seal
姓名字号印 Personal Name, Style Name and Alias Seal	上官贤 Shangguan Xian's Seal	杜嵩之信印 Du Song's Letter Seal	潘可 Pan Ke's Seal	徐朝阳印 Xu Chaoyang's Seal
斋馆印 Studio or Study Seal	三友斋 Sanyou Study Seal	金玉堂 Jinyu Mansion Seal	古瓦量斋 Guwaliang Studio Seal	静思轩 Jingsi Veranda Seal
收藏鉴赏印 Storage and Appreciation Seal	乾隆御览之宝 Seal for the Qianlong Emperor's Inspection	乾隆御览之宝 Seal for the Qianlong Emperor's Inspection	太上皇帝之宝 Seal for Taishang Emperor's Treasure	石渠定鉴 Seal for Shiqu Appreciation

Chapter IV The Art of Chinese Characters

各类印章（二）
Various Seals

吉语印 Lucky Sayings Seal	千秋万岁 Long Live the Future Generations	吉祥如意 Long Live the Future Generations	日利 Lucky Day	大吉 Highly Auspicious
肖形印 Portrait Seal	马车 Carriage	虎 Tiger	兔 Rabbit	狗 Dog
花押印 Signature Seal	花瓶 Vase	琵琶 Pipa	鱼 Fish	京 Capital City
成语印 Idiom Seal	从善如流 Cong Shan Ru Liu (Readily to Accept Good Advice)	返璞归真 Fan Pu Gui Zhen (Return to One's Original Nature)	云中白鹤 Yun Zhong Bai He (White Crane in the Clouds)	血性男子 Xue Xing Nan Zi (Passionate Men)

姓名字号印刻人的姓名、表字或号。斋馆印刻古人的居室、书斋的名字。收藏鉴赏印多用于钤盖书画文物之用。吉语印指印文刻吉祥的语言。成语印刻以成语、诗词，或牢骚、风月、佛道等语，一般钤盖在书画上。肖形印一般以古代吉祥瑞兽、花鸟虫鱼及人物为印文内容。花押印到元代才开始流行起来。花押印是一种信物，为了让他人不易模仿，类似于现在的防伪标记一样。

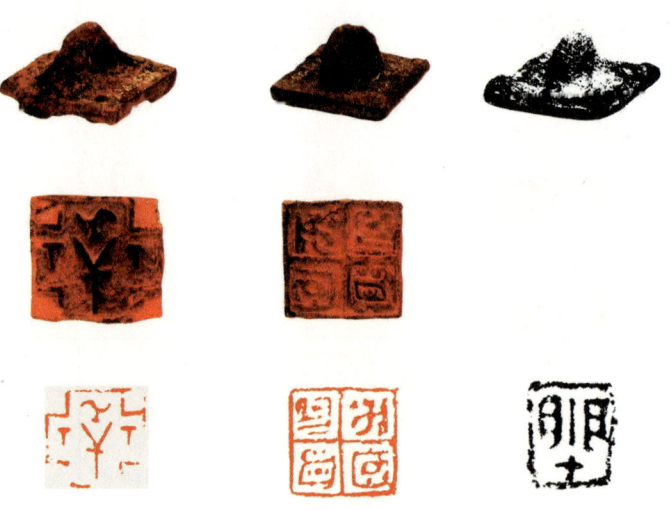

商代铜印
Bronze Seals of the Shang Dynasty

"Personal name, style name, and alias seals" imprint the personal name, style name, and alias of a person. "Studio or study seals" imprint the names of the ancient people's living room and study. "Storage and appreciation seals" are used for imprinting cultural relics. "Lucky sayings seals" are engraved with sayings regarding luck. "Idiom seals" engraved with idioms, poems, or grievances, romantic songs, Buddhist words, and Taoist words, and so on are typically used to imprint calligraphy and paintings. "Portrait seals" generally take the forms of ancient auspicious animals, flowers, birds, insects, and figures. "Signature seals" were not popular until the Yuan Dynasty, and these seals serve as a kind of token similar to the current false proof seal that makes it difficult for others to imitate.

三、汉字画

汉字画是以中国汉字为元素的一种独特的绘画表现形式。它是用一种独到的方式来诠释汉字的新概念，在剖析汉字字形、字义、字源等因素的基础上，通过变形、夸张、整合后的图形平面的"白"或"黑"，把汉字和绘画巧妙地结合起来。

汉字画综合版画、篆刻、剪纸等多种艺术的技法与技巧，将构图、章法和黑白灰的机理处理得浑然天成，以绘画语言形式诠释汉字的意义，既有可读性，又有可看性，赋予了汉字一种新的艺术形式，以绘画语言形式挖掘汉字的丰富内涵，形成了自然、灵活、素朴端庄而不失大气的风格。

| 美丽的家乡 | 美丽的姑娘 | 天竺少女 |
| Beautiful Hometown | Beautiful Girl | Young Girl of India |

爱心　　　　　　奔驰　　　　　　雄鹰翱翔
Loving Heart　　Gallop　　　　　Eagle Soaring

斑马　　　　　　蝴蝶　　　　　　舞
Zebra　　　　　Butterfly　　　　Dance

Ⅲ. Chinese Character Painting

Chinese character painting is a unique form of painting that incorporates Chinese characters as an element of the work. In consideration of the shape, meaning, and origin of Chinese characters, Chinese character painting is a skillful combination of the Chinese characters with paintings through the "white" and "black" of the graphic plane after applying deformation, exaggeration and integration.

Chinese character painting combines various artistic techniques and skills such as the woodcut, seal-cut, and paper-cut, and it also engages with the art of composition through black, white, and gray. This genre interprets the meaning of Chinese characters in the form of painting language, which is both readable and visible, and gives Chinese characters a new artistic form. It also excavates and exhibits the rich connotations of Chinese characters in the form of painting language and developing a style which is natural, flexible, simple, and dignified, yet always elegant.

熊猫
Panda

蟹
Crab

给力
Gelivable

快乐王子
Happy Prince

鸳鸯
Mandarin Duck

恭贺新春
Congratulations to the Spring

第五章

汉字的交融

Chapter V

The Blending of Chinese Characters

第五章 汉字的交融

　　文字是文化传播的重要载体。汉字产生后，随着汉文化向周边地区的传播而逐渐走进了许多民族和国家的生活，对这些民族和国家的发展产生了重要的影响，从而形成了地域广大的汉字文化圈，这个文化圈在汉字的熏染下，形成了独特的、性格鲜明的东方文化。

　　汉字也在交流的过程中不断学习，从外来文字中吸取营养来丰富自己，长久地焕发出新的活力与生机，这也使得汉字拥有了更强的生命力和包容性。

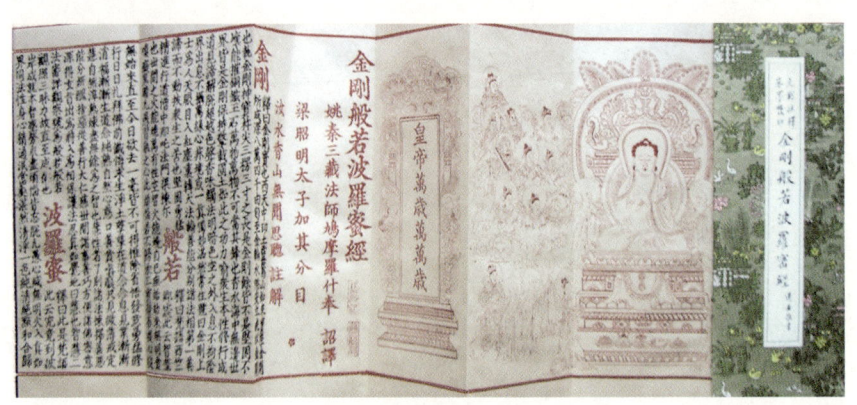

《套印金刚经注》
Two-colored Annotations to the Diamond Sutra

Characters are an important means of cultural transmission. With the spread of Chinese culture to neighbouring regions, Chinese characters gradually entered the lives of people from other nationalities and countries and have subsequently had an important impact on their development. Consequently, an expansive cultural circle of Chinese characters appeared. The cultural circle, influenced by Chinese characters, evolved into a more inclusive, unique, and distinctive Oriental culture.

Chinese language is continually incorporating foreign words to enrich itself and renew its vitality. This makes Chinese characters more adaptive and inclusive.

钱币上的西夏字
Characters of Western Xia State

一、传播

汉字向周边民族和国家传播的路线主要有三条：一条向南和西南，传播到广西壮族和越南京族，后又传播到四川、贵州、云南等省的少数民族，如苗族、瑶族、布依族、侗族、白族等；一条向北和西北，传播到宋代的契丹、女真和西夏；一条向东，传播到朝鲜和日本。

随着汉字的传播，非汉语的民族地区和国家慢慢地产生了各种汉字式文字。这些文字的发展大约经过了四个阶段：学习阶段、借用阶段、仿造阶段和创造阶段。

不同的民族和国家先是学习相同的古代汉语书面语，在熟悉了汉字书面语后，他们开始借用汉字书写自己的语言。借用汉字一段时间后，又开始进一步仿照汉字创制本民族的新文字，他们利用汉字、汉字的笔画以及汉字的造字方法，最终创造了适合本民族和国家的汉字型新文字。

1. 壮字

壮字也叫方块壮字，是壮族历史上曾经使用的文字。壮族是中国人口最多的少数民族，主要分布在南方，中国专门设立了广西壮族自治区，为中国五大民族自治区之一。

標音	be	rau	fv	ho:i	jik	mo:k	kvn	sang	ro:k	ro:ng
漢译	展开	头	荒凉	雇工	懒	猪食	上面	擤	外面	光亮

壮字
The Ancient Zhuang Characters

I. Dissemination

The most notable disseminations of Chinese characters and language to neighboring places and peoples include the Guangxi Zhuang Autonomous Region; the Vietnam Jing ethnic minorities; the ethnic minorities such as Miao, Yao, Buyi, Dong and Bai located in parts of Sichuan, Guizhou, Yunnan and other southern and western Chinese provinces; Qidan, Jurchen, and Xixia of the Song Dynasty; North Korea and Japan.

As Chinese characters spread, various Chinese-style characters emerged in non-Chinese ethnic regions and countries. These characters went through approximately four stages of development: learning, borrowing, imitating and creating.

First, different nationalities and countries learned the same ancient written Chinese language. Then they began to use Chinese characters to write their own language. Gradually, they began to further imitate Chinese characters to create new characters of their own nation. Ultimately, they created new Chinese-style characters suitable for their own nationalities and countries by borrowing Chinese characters, strokes of Chinese characters and methods of creating Chinese characters.

1. The Ancient Zhuang Character

The ancient Zhuang characters, also called sawndip, were used by the Zhuang ethnic minority. The Zhuang people have been the most populous ethnic minority in China and scattered across southern China. To unify the nation, China established the Guangxi Zhuang Autonomous Region, which was one of the five major ethnic autonomous regions in China.

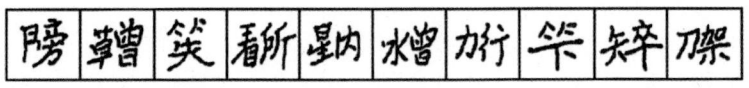

标音：ba:ng　jang　rat　qjo　dai　rang　reng　rong　rvt　ka
汉译：部分　荒草　蘑菇　看　星星　肚胀　力量　鸟笼　萎缩　杀

壮字
The Ancient Zhuang Characters

壮字是一种孳乳仿造的汉字型文字,有的全部借用现成的汉字,有的夹用部分自造壮字。自造壮字以汉字或汉字偏旁为材料,大多使用形声法造字。

2. 喃字

越南历史上长期使用汉字,历时约1000年。后来,越南人开始利用汉字书写本民族的语言,创造了喃字。越南有几个短暂时期以喃字为正式文字,跟汉字并行,多数时期只用于民间。19世纪后期,越南开始推行拉丁化拼音文字,并于1945年以后成为全国通用的法定文字。

喃字的形制和壮字相同,都是利用现成汉字或汉字部件组成新的本民族文字,可以说喃字和壮字开创了孳乳仿造汉字型文字的先例,影响着后来中国西南许多少数民族也创造此类文字,如苗字、瑶字、布依字、侗字、白文、哈尼字等,形成了汉字文化圈的重要组成部分。

喃字
The Nan Characters

The ancient Zhuang characters were produced in a Chinese-style derivative character. Some ancient Zhuang characters were borrowed entirely from Chinese characters while others were self-created. Self-created Zhuang characters were modelled on Chinese characters or used the radical side of Chinese characters, and were produced with pictophonetic characters.

2. The Nan Character

The popular use of Chinese characters in Vietnam lasted approximately 1,000 years. The Vietnamese first used Chinese characters to transcribe their own language and then gradually developed the Nan characters. Although several short-lived periods witnessed Nan characters' official status as equal to Chinese characters in Vietnam, the Nan characters was typically used only by the general public. In the late 19th century, Vietnam began to promote Latinized alphabetic writing of their Nan characters, but it was not until 1945 that this new alphabet became the new standard.

The word-formation method of Nan characters was identical with that of Zhuang characters. They set a precedent for Chinese-style derivative characters and influenced many ethnic minorities in southwest China, such as the Miao, Yao, Buyi, Dong, Bai, Hani. Derivative characters formed an important part of the cultural circle of Chinese characters.

契丹小字
The Khitan Small Script

3. 契丹字

公元907年，契丹族在中国北部建立辽国，后在全国推行契丹字。契丹字分为契丹大字和契丹小字，这两种文字曾一同作为辽国的通行文字。

契丹大字看上去有点像汉字，有的字符是直接从汉字照搬过来的，有的只选取汉字的一半，有的是参照汉字笔画重新设计的。契丹小字是一种表音文字，字符比大字简单些。《宣懿皇后哀册》刻于公元1101年，册盖正面刻契丹小字4行16个，组成7字，意为"宣懿皇后哀册文"。

4. 西夏字

西夏是11至13世纪由党项族在中国西北部建立的一个政权。西夏字是西夏王朝的官方文字，记录的是党项语。西夏字的基本笔画仿照汉字，也有"点、横、竖、撇、捺、拐、提"等笔画，但是决不借用一个汉字，全部形体都要从头新造。

3. The Khitan Script

In 907 AD, the Khitan established the Liao Kingdom in northern China and promoted the Khitan script throughout their kingdom. It was divided into the Khitan large script and the Khitan small script. These scripts were commom and popular in the Liao Kingdom The Khitan large script resembled Chinese characters. Some were directly copied from Chinese characters, some used half of Chinese characters, and others were created by combining the strokes of Chinese characters. The Khitan small script is a kind of phonography, and its characters are simpler than Khitan large script. Engraved in 1101 AD, "XuanYi Queen's Lamentation" included 4 lines and 16 Khitan small scripts (7 characters) on its front cover.

4. The Xixia Script

Xixia was a political power established by the Tangut in the northwest of China between the 11th and the 13th century. The Xixia script is a record of the Tangut language. Its basic strokes were modeled on those of Chinese characters, including strokes such as dots, horizontal lines, vertical lines, left diagonal lines, right diagonal lines, turns, and lifts. However, it never copied a single Chinese

西夏字

The Xixia Script

西夏字总数约6000字,造字方式以会意为主。由于有出土字典《番汉合时掌中珠》的帮助,当前能够准确认识的西夏字约有2000个,解读一般的西夏文献并不太困难。西夏字寿陵残碑碑文为阴刻楷书,字体刚劲、挺拔、美观。

5. 女书

文字是中性的,男人写的女人能看懂,女人写的男人能看懂,这似乎是亘古不变的真理。然而,这一真理却被中国境内的一种文字给打破了,那就是湖南省江永县的女书。

女书在湖南省江永县潇水流域已经有几百年的历史了,是当地妇女专用的文字符号,由妇女创造,妇女使用。这种文字传女不传男,男人不学也不用。女书外形是右高左低的长菱形,从文字类型来看,女书是变异仿造的汉字型汉语方言音节文字。每逢节日,女人聚在一起,共同读唱女书。女书内容为人们展示了农村妇女从少女到出嫁,从婚后到晚年的一幅幅生活画面。

女书
Nǚshu

character. All Xixia script was unique to the Tangut language.

The Xixia script consists of approximately 6000 characters in total, and its formation method is mainly ideographic.By consulting the unearthed Xixia-Chinese script dictionary, *Pearl in the Palm*, students today can accurately recognize about 2000 Xixia characters and as such, it is possible for them to interpret the vast majority of general Xixia literature.What is more,Xixia tablet inscriptions are usually in regular script carved in intaglio with bold,square and vigorous strokes, and the above tablet inscription on Xixia Shouling's broken tombstone serves as a good example.

5. Nüshu

Generally speaking, characters do not indicate the gender of the author. Accordingly, females can typically understand characters written by males, and vice versa. However, the Nüshu of Jiangyong County, Hunan Province, developed a system of characters that was used exclusively among women in their reading and writing.

The Nüshu had a history of hundreds of years in Xiaoshui River Basin in Jiangyong County, Hunan Province. The characters of the Nüshu and its writing were only passed on to women. The shape of Nüshu was rhomboid with high right and low left strokes. From the perspective of the type of character, Nüshu was a Chinese dialect syllable character based on variation. On holidays, women gathered to read and sing Nüshu. The contents of Nüshu were about the lives of rural women from childhood to matrimony and old age .

6. 日文

日本民族有着古老的文化，但文字的创制相对较晚。晋朝时期，汉字传入日本。长期以来，日本人借用汉字，称汉字为"真名"。后来，日本开始借用汉字作为音符来书写日语，形成日语音节字母。《万叶集》是最早用汉字作为字母写成的古代歌集，这种借用现成汉字的日语字母，称为"万叶假名"。"假"是假借的意思，"假名"就是借用的汉字。

假名不是有计划地设计的，因此产生了两套系统。一套叫"片假名"，主要是根据汉字楷体偏旁创造；一套叫"平假名"，主要采用汉字草体创造。假名起初是汉字的注音符号，正式文字中间没有它的地位。日语有词尾变化，有助词和其他虚词，用汉字书写极不方便。自然地产生一种混合写法，就是用汉字书写实词和词根，用假名补充虚词和词尾。于是假名伴随着汉字进入了正式文字的体系，这就形成汉字假名混合体。时至今日，正式日文仍旧是汉字和假名的混合体。

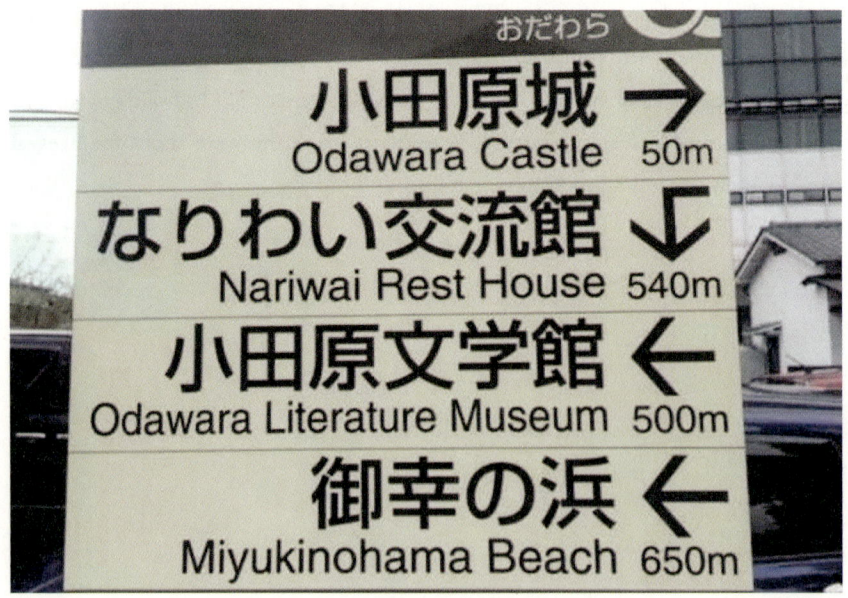

日本路标

Japanese Road Signs

6. Japanese

The Japanese had an ancient culture, but the creation of their characters was relatively late. During the Jin Dynasty, Chinese characters were introduced to Japan. For a long time, the Japanese borrowed Chinese characters and called them "眞名"(まな). Later, Japan began to use Chinese characters as syllables to form Japanese syllables. まんようしゅう was the earliest ancient song collection written with Chinese characters as syllables. These Japanese syllables, borrowed from ready-made Chinese characters, were called "まんようかな". "假" meant phonetic loan. "仮名"(かな) meant borrowed Chinese characters.

The kana scripts were not designed according to a master plan, thus it resulted in two systems of scripts. One script, "Katakana," was developed using the radicals of Chinese characters' regular script. The other script, "Hiragana," was developed as an adaptation of Chinese characters in cursive script. The kana scripts were originally the phonetic approximations of Chinese characters, and claimed no official status. Japanese language suffixes, auxiliaries, and other function words made it inconvenient to write in Chinese characters. Consequently, a mixed writing method appeared, that is, writing notional words and roots in Chinese characters and supplementing function words and suffix in kana. Thus, kana scripts entered the system of official characters along with Chinese characters and formed a mixture of Chinese characters and kana. Today, official Japanese is still a mixture of Chinese characters and kana.

7. 朝鲜谚文

在汉末和三国时期，汉字传入朝鲜。在朝鲜谚文创制以前，朝鲜人读汉字文言文的四书、五经。朝鲜的人名、地名都是用汉字书写的。为了发展民族文化，朝鲜创制了朝鲜语的表音字母，并于1446年刊印于《训民正音》一书中，公布施行，称为"正音字"，又称"谚文"，就是通俗文字的意思。

谚文共有28个音素字母，其中辅音17个，元音11个。谚文字母不是从汉字直接变来的，但谚文字母叠成汉字方块形式，明显是受了汉字笔画元素的影响。

韩国路标
Korean Road Signs

7. Korean Han-krur

During the late Han Dynasty and Three Kingdoms Period, Chinese characters were introduced to Korea. Before the creation of Korean Han-krur, the Koreans read the Four Books and the Five Classics written in classical Chinese characters. Korean names and place names were written in Chinese characters. In order to develop a national culture, Korea created a phonetic alphabet of Korean language and published this system in the book, *Hangul* in 1446. This book is also known as *Standard Sound Words* and *Han-krur*.

There are 28 phonetic letters in the Han-krur, including 17 consonants and 11 vowels. Han-krur characters were not directly derived from Chinese characters, but they were stacked and organized in the block form of Chinese characters.

二、注音

中国古代没有标准的汉语拼音，人们用汉字为汉字注音，主要有读若法、直音法、反切法等方式，后来才出现拉丁字母注音法。

1. 直音法

直音法是指用一个汉字为另一个汉字注音的方法，前提是这两个字是同音字，如"蛊，音古"。这种方法简捷明了，但也有较大的局限性，在无同音字或同音字较冷僻的情况下，就往往无法注音或者注音不准。

有的字找不到同音字，这种方法就不能使用，例如"蹭"字；有的字虽然有同音字，但都比较生僻，注音效果就不理想。例如，"然"的同音字只有"燃、蚺、髯"三个字，它们都比"然"字生僻，用其中的任何一个为"然"字注音，都难以帮助认读。

2. 反切法

反切法是指用两个字来为另一个字注音的方法。用作反切的两个字，前一个叫反切上字，后一个叫反切下字。被注音的字叫被切字。反切的基本原则是反切上字与被切字的声母相同，反切下字与被切字的韵母和声调相同，上下拼合就是被切字的读音。如，"红，胡笼切"，就是取"胡"字的声母"h"，取"笼"字的韵母和声调"óng"，拼成"红"字的音"hóng"。

反切的产生，是为了补救读若法、直音法的不足，是汉字注音方法的一个巨大进步，标志着汉语语音学的开始，人们从此懂得了对汉语音

Ⅱ. Phonetic Notation

There was no standard Chinese pinyin in ancient China. People used Chinese characters as a way of phonetic notation through Duruo, Zhiyin, and Resection. Later, the Latin alphabet phonetic notation was brought into Chinese pronunciation.

1. Zhiyin Method

Zhiyin method refers to the method of indicating the pronunciation of a Chinese character by citing another character with the same pronunciation. For example, 古 (gǔ) for 蛊 (gǔ). This method is simple and clear, but it also has a limitation. If there is no homonym or a homonym is rare, it is often impossible or inaccurate to make that phonetic notation.

In cases where there were no homophones for a character such as蹭, this method could not be used. Although some characters have homophones, their uncommon use leads to imperfect phonetic effects. For example, the homonyms of 然(rán) are 燃, 蚺, and 髯. However, these homonyms are all more obscure than the character 然 and thus it remains difficult to use these homonyms to help speakers pronounce the word correctly.

2. Resection

Resection is a method of using two characters to phoneticize another character. The former of the two characters used for resection is called the top word, and the latter is called the down word. The word being phoneticized is called the sliced word. The initial consonant of the top word should be shared by the sliced word and it is referred to as the upper stitch. The final sound and tone of the down word should resemble that of the sliced word and this is referred to as the lower stitch. In combination, the upper and lower stitches produce the resection. For example, "hóng" borrows the initial consonant "h" of the character of "Hú" and the final sound and tone "óng" in the character of "lóng" which results in the resection for "hóng".

Resection was used to remedy the deficiencies of the Duruo and Zhiyin methods, and it was an impactful development in the phonetic transcription of Chinese characters. The introduction of resection marks the early beginnings of Chinese phonetics. Even today, people continue to phoneticize characters by

节做音理上的分析，把一个音节分成声、韵两个部分。

3. 威妥玛拼音

明清时期，来到中国的西方传教士及外交家为了学习汉语、传教和翻译的需要，开始尝试用拉丁字母为汉字注音，并由此形成多套汉语拼音方案，影响最大的是威妥玛式拼音方案。

威妥玛是英国人，长期在中国担任外交官。他成功发展了用拉丁字母拼写汉字的方法，即威妥玛式拼音方案。自清末开始，威妥玛式拼音方案一直是国际流行的中文拼音方案，影响虽然不小，但并未成为官方标准。

1958年现代汉语拼音方案推行之后，威妥玛拼音方案在中国基本不再使用，但在西方学术界仍然较为流行。为保证历史的延续性，少量享誉海内外的中国商标至今仍旧使用威妥玛拼音法，例如，茅台、中华等。有些使用威妥玛拼音的专有名词已被吸纳为英文的外来词，例如，功夫、太极、易经等。

名称	数量	注音符号
声母	27	p、'p、m、f、v、t、't、n、l、ts、ts '、s、tz、tz '、ss、ch、ch '、sh、j、ch、ch '、hs、k、k '、ng、h、y、w
韵母	40	a、o、ê、êrh、ǔ、ih、ai、êi/ei、ao、ou、an、ên、ang、êng、i、ia、io、ieh、iai、iao、iu、ien、in、iang、ing、iung、u、ua、uo、uai、uei/ui、uan、uên/un、uang、ung、ü、üo、üen/üan、üen、ün
声调	4	1 上平（高平调）、2 下平（低平调）、3 上声（升调）、4 去声（降调）

威妥玛拼音方案
The Wade-Giles System Program

dividing syllables into vowels and consonants.

3. The Wade-Giles System

During the Ming and Qing Dynasties, Western missionaries and diplomats coming to China began developing methods for using the Latin alphabet to indicate the pronunciation of Chinese characters for the purpose of Chinese learning, missionary work, and translation. They created different latin alphabet approximation of Chinese characters and pronunciation of which the Wade-Giles system was the most influential.

Wade, after whom the Wade-Giles system was named, was British and had long served as a diplomat in China. Since the late Qing Dynasty, the Wade-Giles system has been the most popular pinyin system internationally. In spite of its great international influence,it is not adopted as the official one by China.

After the implementation of the Pinyin system in 1958, the Wade-Giles system program ceased in China. However, the system is still widely used in Western academic circles. In order to avoid discontinuity, some Chinese trademarks such as Moutai and Chunghwa, which are renowned at home and abroad, still use the Wade-Giles system. Some proper nouns using the Wade-Giles system have become the loan words of the English vocabulary, such as Kungfu, Taichi, and I Ching.

4. 现代汉语拼音方案

现代汉语拼音方案是中国官方于1958年公布使用的汉字注音方案，采用国际通用的拉丁字母系统来拼写和标注汉字读音。现代汉语拼音方案使用26个拉丁字母和四个声调符号标注汉字的读音，使汉字发音可以通过一种具有国际通用意义的符号、以书面的形式定义、记录和传播。

现代汉语拼音方案的施行，大大有利于帮助认字，统一读音，推广普通话，同时有利于国际交流。在国际汉字教学中，汉语拼音的注音功能发挥着汉语和其他语言之间语音沟通的桥梁作用。

汉字输入法可分为形码和音码两种基本类型，其中音码输入法就是以汉语拼音方案为基础，直接运用西文键盘的字母键输入汉字。目前，拼音输入法是应用最广泛的汉字输入法。

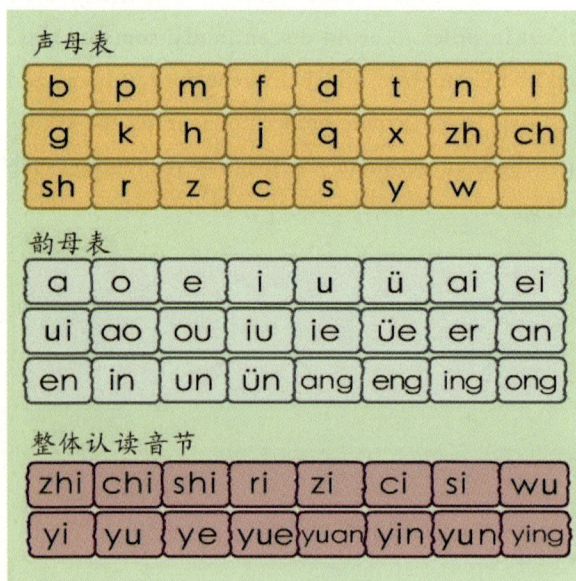

汉语拼音字母表
Pinyin Alphabet

4. The Pinyin System

Pinyin is a Chinese phonetic annotation system issued by the Chinese government in 1958. It uses the international Latin alphabet system to spell and describe the pronunciation of Chinese characters. It includes 26 Latin letters and four tone symbols to describe the pronunciation of Chinese characters so that Chinese pronunciation can be defined, recorded, and transmitted in written form by the international standard.

The implementation of the Pinyin system has been conducive to recognizing characters, unifying pronunciation, promoting Mandarin, and facilitating international cultural exchanges. When teaching Chinese characters to new learners, the phonetic notation of Pinyin builds a bridge between Chinese and other languages.

The Chinese character input method for typing can be divided into two basic types: sound code and shape code. The sound code is based on Pinyin and directly inputs the Chinese characters by using the letter keys of the Western keyboard. At present, it is widely used throughout the Chinese world.

三、外文汉译

追溯中国历史,每当中外文化交往密切的时候,新的汉字和词汇就会大量产生,一些汉字的义项也会大量增加,这都使得汉字更加丰富多彩,具有更大的包容性和更强的自我更新能力。

外来文字要进入汉字系统,必须接受汉字多方面的改造,以符合汉语的发音习惯和语法规则,通过音译、意译、音意兼译、直译等方式进入汉字词汇。

1. 丝绸之路的开辟

丝绸之路是古代东西方之间最重要的贸易往来和文化交流通道,包括陆地丝绸之路和海上丝绸之路两大干线。两千多年来,丝绸之路宛如一座桥梁,把中国与世界紧紧联系在一起,繁荣着沿途国家和地区的经济和文化。

西汉时期,丝绸之路促进了汉朝与西域的交流,大量新的汉字词汇随着新物种的引进而不断产生,主要包括动物、植物、食品、乐器等名词。

中国原来没有狮子,狮子被引进后,汉朝人一开始假借"师"字来表示狮子,称狮子为"师子",后来加"犭"旁另造"狮"字表示狮子。

"葡萄"被引进后,曾有"蒲陶""蒲萄""蒲桃"等多种叫法,但读音都是一样的。古代汉字基本都是单音节词,"葡萄"这样的双音节词显然是某种外来词汇音译过来的,可能是把葡萄当作草本植物而加了"艹"字部首。"葡"和"萄"不单独使用,类似的还有玻璃、苜蓿

III. Loanwords of the Chinese Vocabulary

In Chinese history, whenever there were frequent cultural exchanges between China and foreign countries, new Chinese characters and expressions would proliferate, and some Chinese characters took on additional meanings. These cross-cultural exchanges made Chinese characters more colorful, inclusive and strong in self-renewal.

When foreign words enter the Chinese character system, they are often reformed to conform with the common pronunciations and grammatical rules of Chinese. These foreign words become part of the Chinese vocabulary through transliteration, free translation, transliteration and semantic translation or literal translation.

1. The Silk Road

The Silk Road was the most important channel for trade and cultural exchange between the East and the West in ancient times. It included two major routes: the Land Silk Road and the Maritime Silk Road. For more than two thousand years, the Silk Road was like a bridge linking China to the world while influencing the economies and cultures of different countries and regions along the way.

During the Western Han Dynasty, the Silk Road promoted exchanges between the Han Dynasty and the western regions(a Han Dynasty term for the area west of Yumenguan Pass). A large number of new Chinese words were created along with the introduction of new species of animals and plants, cuisines, and musical instruments.

Following the introduction of the lion to China, people in the Han Dynasty began using the character 师 (shī) to represent the lion, and called the lion 师子 (shī zi). Then the Chinese character component 犬 was added to the character 师 to denote 狮.

After 葡萄(grape) was introduced, there were many names such as 蒲陶, 蒲萄 and 蒲桃, but the pronunciation was the same. The ancient Chinese characters are mostly monosyllabic words. The two-syllable words such as 葡萄, are typically transliterations from a foreign vocabulary. It may be that 葡萄 was used as an herb and thus the radical 艹 was added to the character. Furthermore, 葡 and 萄 are

等词汇。

秦汉时，汉族人称中国北方以及西方的民族为胡人，所以也在他们的事物之前加入了一个"胡"字，从西域引进的物种就有了胡琴、胡椒、胡麻等名称。

2. 佛教的传入

西汉末年，佛教传入中国，这是世界文化交流史上的大事，佛教又经中国传入日本、朝鲜、越南等地。佛教对中国文化产生了深远的影响，一些从佛经中翻译过来的词汇已经融入了中国百姓的日常生活，有的和汉字结合得天衣无缝，普通人已经分辨不出它们曾经是外来词汇。

佛教词汇"般若"是梵语Prajna的音译，由"般"和"若"两个字组成，除了保留了汉字的形体，读音和意义已和原来的汉字有了天壤之别，"般若"读bō rě，而不能读作bān ruò，意思为"终极智慧"，而不能按照"般"和"若"原来的字面意思来理解。"南无"是梵语namas音译，读作nā mó。别的佛教字、词还有很多，如佛、禅、刹、塔、僧、尼、兰若、伽蓝、菩萨、罗汉、阎罗、世界、因果、庄严、圆满、魔鬼、法宝、阿弥陀佛等，大量出现在书籍和口语中。

3. 西方文化的影响

明清及以后，西方大批传教士和商人来到中国，同时带来了西方的科学技术和思想文化，使得汉语词汇又一次大量增加。这些词汇多是关于物质、文化和科技等方面的。比如鸦片、铁路、银馆、温带、热带、地球、雷达、飞机、香波、啤酒、咖啡、蓝牙、乌托邦、巧克力、迷你裙、马拉松、维他命、蒙太奇、盘尼西林等。

not used alone, and this phenomenon is also present in words such as 玻璃(glass) and 苜蓿(alfalfa).

In the Qin and Han Dynasties, the Han Chinese referred to ethnic peoples in northern and western China as Hu. Subsequently, the Han also added the character of Hu before words related to these people. For example, the Han incorporated words such as huqin (musical instrument), hujiao (pepper), and huma (flax).

2. The Introduction of Buddhism

In the late Western Han Dynasty, the introduction of Buddhism to China was a major event in the history of world cultural exchanges. Buddhism was introduced to Japan, Korea, Vietnam and other countries through China. Buddhism has had a profound influence on Chinese culture. Many words translated from the Buddhist scriptures had been integrated into the daily life of Chinese people. Some words were so seamlessly integrated with Chinese characters that ordinary people could not tell that they came from a foreign culture.

The Buddhist word 般若 is the transliteration of Sanskrit Prajna. It consists of the characters 般 and 若. Despite using Chinese characters, the pronunciation and meaning differ vastly from the original Chinese characters. 般若 reads as bō rě, not bān ruò, which means ultimate wisdom, and cannot be understood according to the original literal meanings of 般and 若. 南无 is a transliteration of Sanskrit namas which reads nā mó. There are many other Buddhist characters and expressions , such as Buddha, Zen, Brah, Taji, Sui, Ni, Lan Ruo, Jia Lan, Bodhisattva, Arhat, Yama, World, Causality, Solemn, Consummation, Devil, Treasure, and Amitabha. They appear throughout texts and spoken language.

3. The Influence of Western Culture

In the Ming and Qing Dynasties, and beyond, a large number of Western missionaries and businessmen came to China and brought with them Western science and technology, ideologies, and culture. As a result, Chinese characters and expressions of materials, culture, and science and technology proliferated, such as opium, railway, night club, temperate zone, tropical zone, earth, radar, aircraft, shampoo, beer, coffee, bluetooth, utopia, chocolate, miniskirt, marathon, vitamins,

在这些词汇中，值得特别一提的是化学元素名。现已发现的化学元素有106种，而表示化学元素名的汉字大都是后造的，并且造得非常成功，有很强的规律性。这些字基本上都是形声字，如果是金属元素，左边金为形旁，右边为声旁，如"钠、锰、镭"等。如果是非金属元素，常态为气体，则上边气为形旁，下边为声旁，如"氧、氢、氖、氮、氩、氯"等；常态为液体则以左边水为形旁，如"溴"；常态为固态则以左边石为形旁，如"硫、砷、碘"等。这样，人们看到一个化学元素名，就知道它属于哪一类和哪一种形态。

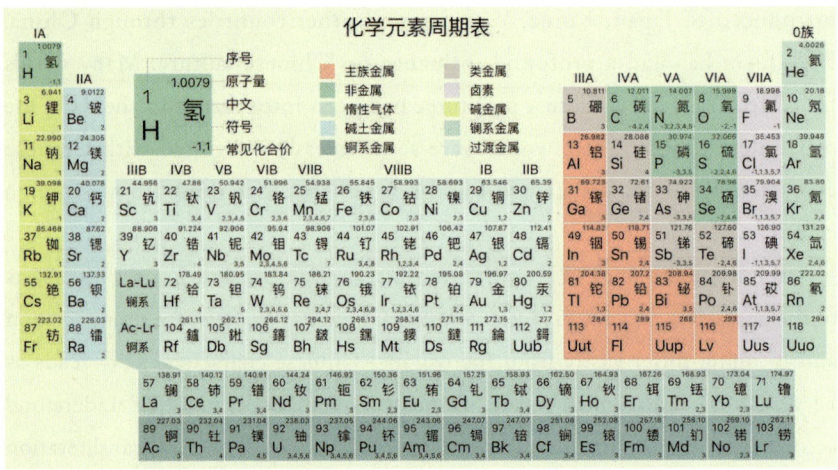

元素周期表
Periodic Table of Chemical Elements

montage, and penicillin, etc.

Among the new vocabulary, the names of chemical elements also emerged. 106 chemical elements have been discovered, and the Chinese characters representing the names of chemical elements are mostly created with success and strong regularity. These words are mostly pictophonetic compounds. Metallic elements are represented by 金 and an accompanying character as in 钠(sodium), 锰(manganese), 镭 (radium). Non-metallic elements, particularly gasses, are represented by 气 and an accompanying character as in 氧(oxygen), 氢(hydrogen), 氦(helium), 氮 (nitrogen), 氩(argon), or 氯(chlorine). Liquid-state elements are represented by 水, such as 溴, and solid-state elements are represented by 石, such as 硫(sulfur), 砷 (arsenic), and 碘(iodine). In this way, Chinese characters can indicate the category of the chemical element as well as its state of existence.

四、交流平台

为进一步传承和弘扬汉字文化，中国国内和世界各地搭建了许多汉字交流的平台，这些平台为爱好汉字的人们提供了许多的服务项目，促进了人们对汉字文化的了解和学习。

1. 孔子学院

孔子学院是中国和其他国家共同设立的学习汉语、汉字和中国文化的非营利性机构，宗旨是增进世界人民对中国语言和文化的了解，发展中国与其他国家的友好关系，促进世界多元文化的发展。

自2004年首家孔子学院在韩国首尔设立起，全球已有140多个国家和地区建立了500多所孔子学院。孔子学院的主要职能包括：面向社会各界人士开展汉语教学，培训汉语教师，开展汉语考试和汉语教师资格认证业务，提供中国教育、文化、经济、社会等信息咨询，开展当代中国研究等。各地的孔子学院充分利用自身优势，开展丰富多彩的活动，逐步成为当地学习汉字文化、了解中国的重要场所。

英国班戈大学孔子学院举办新春庆典活动

The Spring Festival Celebration Held in the Confucius Institute at Bangor University, UK

Ⅳ. Communication Platform

In order to inherit and promote the Chinese character culture, many platforms for the exchange of Chinese characters have been established in China and around the world. These platforms have provided many service projects for people who love Chinese characters, and have promoted the understanding and learning of Chinese character culture.

1. The Confucius Institute

The Confucius Institute is a non-profit organization jointly established by China and other countries for learning Chinese language and culture. It aims to enhance mutual understanding between the Chinese and other peoples, extend the hand of friendship towards other countries and reinforce the development of multi-culturalism in the world.

Since the establishment of the first Confucius Institute in Seoul, South Korea in 2004, more than 500 Confucius Institutes have been established in over 140 countries and regions around the world. The main functions of the Confucius Institute include: teaching Chinese to people from all walks of life, training Chinese teachers, conducting Chinese language examinations, certifying Chinese language teachers, providing information consultation on China's education, culture, economy, and society, and carrying out research on contemporary Chinese. The Confucius Institutes around the world have made full use of their own advantages to carry out rich and colorful activities, and have become important places for learning and understanding Chinese culture.

河南省大力支持孔子学院的建设与发展，郑州大学、河南大学等省内学校积极与印度、美国、坦桑尼亚等国的学校展开合作，建立孔子学院（课堂）。截至2017年底，河南省高校和中学与国外高校和中学共建有3所孔子学院和4所孔子课堂。这些孔子学院（课堂）运行正常，始终把汉语教学当作核心工作来抓，不断促进汉语教学健康发展，同时开展丰富多彩的文化活动，影响力逐步扩大。

2. 殷墟

殷墟位于河南省安阳市，由于出土大量的甲骨文而享誉全球。2006年，殷墟被联合国科教文组织列入《世界文化遗产名录》。2017年,甲骨文成功入选联合国教科文组织的《世界记忆名录》。除了甲骨文，殷墟还出土了大量精美的青铜器、玉器等器物，发现了商代都城、宫殿、王陵遗址，这些都证明了3000多年前的中国就已经有了高度发达的文明。而甲骨文也将中国有文字记载的历史提前到了商代，同时也产生了一门新的世界性学科——甲骨学。每年都有无数来自世界各地的文字爱好者来到殷墟，深入探讨汉字的源头。

殷墟——世界文化遗产
Yinxu (Ruins of the Yin Dynasty) — World Cultural Heritage

Henan Province strongly supports the construction and development of Confucius Institutes. Zhengzhou University, Henan University and some high schools have been in active cooperation with India, the United States, Tanzania and other countries to establish Confucius Institutes or Classes. By the end of 2017, there have been 3 jointly built Confucius Institutes and 4 Classes, which pay great attention to cultural communication as well as to language teaching, steadily achieving a good reputation across the world.

2. Yinxu (Ruins of the Yin Dynasty)

Located in Anyang City, Henan Province, Yinxu is known worldwide for the large number of oracle bones excavated there. In 2006, Yinxu was listed on the *World Cultural Heritage List* by UNESCO. In 2017, oracle bone inscriptions were selected successfully in the UNESCO's *Memory of the World Register*. In addition to the oracle bone inscriptions, a large number of exquisite bronze wares, jade wares and other artifacts were also unearthed in Yinxu, and the capital, palaces and royal tomb sites of the Shang Dynasty were discovered, too. These discoveries prove that China had a highly developed civilization more than 3,000 years ago, and the oracle bone inscriptions also see the recorded history of China existing as early as in the Shang Dynasty, and henceforth a new world discipline —oracle bone studies, has come into being. Every year, many Chinese enthusiasts from all over the world come to Yinxu to further explorations of the source of Chinese characters.

3. 中国文字博物馆

中国文字博物馆位于河南省安阳市，是以文字为主题的国家级专题博物馆。中国文字博物馆的基本陈列是"中国文字发展史"，展示中华民族一脉相承的文字、灿烂的文化和辉煌的文明。

研究汉字，就离不开甲骨文，就必须到河南省安阳市。安阳也当之无愧地成为了文字圣地，吸引着世界各地的文字专家、学者、爱好者来这里考察学习。致力于成为汉字文化的科研和科普中心、对外展示中华优秀传统文化的窗口、国际性的文字文化交流平台也成为了中国文字博物馆的奋斗目标。

为更好地传播汉字文化，中国文字博物馆精心打造了面向国内外的"汉字"巡展。展览通过系统全面地展示汉字的起源、发展、演变历程以及数千年积淀下来的书写艺术与妙趣精华，再现了汉字对推动中华文明乃至世界文明的贡献。"汉字"国际巡展已在加拿大、尼泊尔、德国、法国、泰国、日本、韩国、斯里兰卡、马来西亚、新加坡、南非、毛里求斯、俄罗斯、印度、英国、秘鲁等国家成功举办。

中国文字博物馆
The National Museum of Chinese Writing

3. The National Museum of Chinese Writing

The National Museum of Chinese Writing is located in Anyang City, Henan Province. It is a national-level museum dedicated to writing. It mainly exhibits "History of the Development of Chinese Characters," showing the Chinese nation's consistent characters, splendid culture and brilliant civilization.

The study of Chinese characters is impossible without seeing the oracle bone scripts. As such, the museum has also deservedly become a sacred place for writing, attracting character experts, scholars and enthusiasts from all over the world to have a study tour there. The museum is committed to becoming a scientific research and popular science center of Chinese character culture by showcasing China's excellent traditional culture, and it strives to serve as an international character and cultural exchange platform.

In order to better spread the Chinese character culture, the National Museum of Chinese Writing has elaborately organized the "Chinese Character" tour exhibition for both domestic and overseas visitors. By systematically and comprehensively displaying the origin, development and evolution of Chinese characters, as well as the writing art and essence accumulated over thousands of years, the exhibition displays the contribution of Chinese characters to the promotion of Chinese, and even world civilization. The International Tour Exhibition of "Chinese Characters" has been successfuly held in Canada, Nepal, Germany, France, Thailand, Japan, South Korea, Sri Lanka, Malaysia, Singapore, South Africa, Mauritius, Russia, India, Britain, Peru and other countries.

德国展览现场
German Exhibition Site

毛里求斯展览现场
Mauritius Exhibition Site

"汉字"国际巡展为其他国家提供了一个了解中国文化的独特视角,吸引了更多的外国朋友开始喜欢和学习汉字,增进了汉字在文化交流中的纽带作用,加深了中国与其他国家民众之间的相互了解与认识。

4. 国际汉字大会

汉字是中国的,也是世界的。2015年以来,河南省安阳市每两年举办一届中国(安阳)国际汉字大会,以汉字的历史、传播、美学、文化等为主线,通过学术交流、社会考察、审美体验等活动,搭建起中国与世界各国进行汉字文化交流的桥梁,使汉字成为中外文明互鉴的基础性平台和人文交流的持久性纽带,使世界各国的朋友通过汉字共同开发和享用人类社会所积累的伟大文明宝藏。

2019年中国(安阳)国际汉字大会开幕式
Opening Ceremony of 2019 China (Anyang) International Conference of Chinese Characters

The International Tour Exhibition of "Chinese Characters" provides a unique perspective on Chinese culture for other countries and it attracts more foreign friends to enjoy and learn Chinese characters. It allows Chinese characters to play a greater role in cultural exchanges while deepening mutual understanding between China and other countries.

4. International Conference of Chinese Characters

Chinese characters belong to China as well as the world. Since 2015, Anyang City, home to the oracle bone inscriptions, has held the China (Anyang) International Conference of Chinese Characters biennially. By offering an opportunity for participants to learn about the history, dissemination, aesthetics and culture of Chinese characters, the conference facilitates international cultural exchanges through academic communication, social investigation and aesthetic experience. In these ways, Chinese characters have become a basic platform for mutual learning between Chinese and foreign civilizations, and serve as a lasting link for cultural exchanges. It enables friends from all over the world to jointly develop and enjoy the great treasures of civilization via Chinese characters.

2019甲骨文杯国际学生"我与汉字"演讲大赛
2019 Oracle Bone Inscriptions Cup "Chinese Characters and Me" Speech Contest for International Students

附录
Appendix

A Brief Chronology of Chinese History
中国历史年代简表

五帝时代 Period of the Five Legendary Rulers c. 2600 BC-c. 2070 BC	黄帝 Huangdi (Yellow Emperor)	
	颛顼 Zhuanxu	
	帝喾 Diku (Emperor Ku)	
	（唐）尧 Yao	
	（虞）舜 Shun	
夏 Xia Dynasty	c. 2070 BC— c. 1600 BC	
商 Shang Dynasty	c. 1600 BC— c. 1046 BC	
西周 Western Zhou Dynasty	c. 1046 BC— c. 771 BC	
东周 Eastern Zhou Dynasty 770 BC-256 BC	春秋 Spring and Autumn Period	770 BC—476BC
	战国 Warring States Period	475 BC—221 BC
秦 Qin Dynasty	221 BC—206 BC	
汉 Han Dynasty 206 BC-220 AD	西汉 Western Han	206 BC—25 AD
	东汉 Eastern Han	25—220
三国 Three Kingdoms 220-280	魏 Wei	220—265
	蜀汉 Shu Han	221—263
	吴 Wu	222—280
晋 Jin Dynasty 265-420	西晋 Western Jin	265—317
	东晋 Eastern Jin	317—420

续表 Continued Table

南北朝 Southern and Northern Dynasties 420—589	南朝 Southern Dynasties	宋 Song	420—479
		齐 Qi	479—502
		梁 Liang	502—557
		陈 Chen	557—589
	北朝 Northern Dynasties	北魏 Northern Wei	386—534
		东魏 Eastern Wei	534—550
		北齐 Northern Qi	550—577
		西魏 Western Wei	535—556
		北周 Northern Zhou	557—581
隋 Sui Dynasty		581-618	
唐 Tang Dynasty		618- 907	
五代十国 Five Dynasties and Ten States	五代 Five Dynasties 907-960	后梁 Later Liang	907—923
		后唐 Later Tang	923—936
		后晋 Later Jin	936—947
		后汉 Later Han	947—950
		后周 Later Zhou	951—960
	十国 Ten States 902-979	北汉 Northern Han	951—979
		吴 Wu	902—937
		吴越 Wuyue	907—978
		闽 Min	909—945
		南汉 Southern Han	917—971
		荆南 (又称"南平") Jingnan (Nanping)	924—963
		楚 Chu	927—951
		南唐 Southern Tang	937—975
		前蜀 Former Shu	907—925
		后蜀 Later Shu	934—965

续表 Continued Table

宋 Song Dynasty 960-1279	北宋 Northern Song	960—1127
	南宋 Southern Song	1127—1279
辽 Liao（契丹 Qidan/Khitan）	907—1125	
金 Jin	1115—1234	
西夏 Xixia (Tangut)	1038— 1227	
元 Yuan Dynasty	1206—1368	
明 Ming Dynasty	1368—1644	
清 Qing Dynasty	1616—1911	
中华民国 Republic of China	1912—1949	
中华人民共和国 People's Republic of China	1949—